D0064928

Regional Cultures, Managerial Behavior, and Entrepreneurship

Recent Titles from Quorum Books

Productivity and Quality through Science and Technology
Y. K. Shetty and Vernon M. Buehler, editors

Interactive Corporate Compliance: An Alternative to Regulatory Compulsion
Jay A. Sigler and Joseph Murphy

Voluntary Corporate Liquidations
Ronald J. Kudla

Business-Government Relations and Interdependence: A Managerial and
Analytic Perspective
John M. Stevens, Steven L. Wartick, and John W. Bagby

Career Growth and Human Resource Strategies: The Role of the Human
Resource Professional in Employee Development
Manuel London and Edward M. Mone, editors

Guide to International Real Estate Investment
M. A. Hines

Occupational Job Evaluation: A Research-Based Approach to Job
Classification
Wilfredo R. Manese

The Professionals' Guide to Fund Raising, Corporate Giving, and
Philanthropy: People Give to People
Lynda Lee Adams-Chau

Financial Forecasting and Planning: A Guide for Accounting, Marketing, and
Planning Managers
Sharon Hatten Garrison, Wallace N. Davidson, Jr., and Michael A. Garrison

Professional Accounting Practice Management
Joseph T. Kastantin

The New Oil Crisis and Fuel Economy Technologies: Preparing the Light
Transportation Industry for the 1990's
Deborah Lynn Bleviss

Press and Media Access to the Criminal Courtroom
Warren Freedman

Regional Cultures, Managerial Behavior, and Entrepreneurship

An International Perspective

Edited by Joseph W. Weiss

Quorum Books

NEW YORK • WESTPORT, CONNECTICUT • LONDON

Library of Congress Cataloging-in-Publication Data

Regional cultures, managerial behavior, and entrepreneurship : an
     international perspective / edited by Joseph W. Weiss.
          p.   cm.
     Bibliography: p.
     Includes index.
     ISBN 0–89930–327–7 (lib. bdg. : alk. paper)
     1. Organizational behavior.   2. High technology industries—
Management.   3. Entrepreneurship.   4. Culture.   I. Weiss, Joseph W.
HD58.7.R437 1988
302.3′5—dc19   87–32278

British Library Cataloguing in Publication Data is available.

Library of Congress Catalog Card Number: 87–32278
ISBN: 0–89930–327–7

First published in 1988 by Quorum Books

Greenwood Press, Inc.
88 Post Road West, Westport, Connecticut 06881

Printed in the United States of America

∞

The paper used in this book complies with the
Permanent Paper Standard issued by the National
Information Standards Organization (Z39.48–1984).

10   9   8   7   6   5   4   3   2   1

Contents

Tables

Preface

This book was started three years ago when I began interviewing computer company founders and executives around Massachusetts Routes 128 and 495 on the topic, "Does the New England cultural environment affect the ways executives manage and do business in this industry?" The executives seemed interested in the topic and especially in comparing their work experiences around the country. André Delbecq, dean of the Santa Clara Graduate Business School in the heart of Silicon Valley, joined me by interviewing computer executives in and around San Jose, California. After extensive interviewing, we discovered that regional cultures played a major role in the way computer executives reportedly managed their operations, dealt with customers, obtained venture capital, marketed their products, managed product development and life cycles, communicated in their workplaces, and managed entrepreneurship. The results of this study prompted my investigation into the relationship of regional cultures and business behavior internationally.

In the summer of 1986 I went to an international management conference in Manchester, England, under the auspices of Bentley College. It was there with Dean David Fedo, also from Bentley, that the actual beginning of this book took shape. At the conference several of the authors and scholars who later contributed to this book presented overviews of their countries' management, educational, and industrial systems. As I listened closely I discovered that they were emphasizing many regional differences in their countries without explicitly stating so. After discussing the idea of my project with several of the presenters at the conference, including Geert Hofstede, I decided to "internationalize" the research topic on comparing regional cultures and management practices. The response from the scholars, international management consultants, and professors was decidedly affirmative.

The basic message of this book is that regional cultures within individual nations play an influential role in shaping, and are in turn shaped by, industrial and management practices, whether it is in Silicon Valley, Route 128, Bangalore, Geneva, the French Riviera, or Bonn. Entrepreneurship, in particular, is an interesting and, in today's internationally competitive business environment, a necessary subject to study with regard to regional cultures. One can observe the extent to which a region's values, infrastructure, financial and educational institutions, and industrial traditions support or obstruct risk-taking and innovative ventures. Contributors to this book undertook the challenge of observing and examining the ways in which regional resources and cultures in their respective countries are or are not evolving to support entrepreneurial activities and enterprises. This book also focuses on how regional cultures interact with national cultures to influence managers, industrial development, and entrepreneurial projects. Regional cultures are part of larger mosaics of national, international, corporate, and occupational cultural grouping.

This undertaking is admittedly exploratory and somewhat novel. Most of the readings are qualitatively researched, based on experience as well as observation, and were written for practitioners as well as for scholars. But this is part of the attractiveness of their works: they bridge academic and practitioner interests. It is hoped that the reader will find that this goal has been achieved.

Acknowledgments

Special thanks are given to the authors who contributed to this book: Dr. Max Daetwyler, Drs. Pedro Nueño and Nieves Martinez, Dr. Jean-Paul Larçon, Dr. Horst Albach and Mr. Hermann Tengler, Dr. Henri J. Vartiainen, Dr. Raghu Nath, Dr. Sam Hai, Dr. André Delbecq, and Dr. Lynn Kahle. They gave their time and energy in interviewing professionals in the field, visiting industrial sites, researching historical documents, and then writing and helping in the continuous editing process. They took an original idea, a set of themes that had little if any literature or bibliographic precedent, and shaped creative essays that are well documented, readable, and interesting to a variety of audiences.

I would also like to thank those colleagues at Bentley College who offered constructive support, and Vice President Tony Bonapart and Dean O'Connell at Bentley College who helped me shape and obtain funding to launch the first project on this topic.

Thanks are in order to Diane Viveiros, our word processing specialist at Bentley College, without whose support this manuscript would never have been submitted.

I also wish to thank Tom Gannon at Greenwood Press. Tom's support and helpful comments have made it possible for this manuscript to become a book.

Final thanks to Hayat and Taya, my wife and daughter. They continue to offer solid support throughout my projects.

This book is dedicated to a friend and scholar, Adib Gharzouzi.

Regional Cultures,
Managerial
Behavior,
and
Entrepreneurship

Introduction

Joseph W. Weiss

The influence of regional cultures on management behavior is an important but neglected area in organizational science. This neglect is surprising inasmuch as so many other dimensions of cultural influences on management have been studied: national culture, corporate culture, occupational culture, even global culture. Why have regional cultures within nations been overlooked in management literature? Several explanations may be offered. First, it is easier to locate, justify, and measure national and country than regional cultures. Second, the assumption that regional and local cultures "melt" into predominant national cultures has prevailed. Finally, the notion that regional cultures are insignificant when compared to national and international business environments has been accepted as fact.

The importance of regional cultures regarding business practices is finally gaining recognition among scholars, forecasters, and practitioners. Alvin Toffler (1983, 2) stated,

Today, when we look at Kyushu in southern Japan, or Scotland, or Quebec, or Texas, we find regional economies that have become as large and complex as national economies were only a few decades ago. Because of cultural and technological trends, it is now possible to produce certain goods for regional or even local markets that until now could only be supported by national markets. . . . More and more, these regional economies will break out of national economic frameworks and demand to go their own way. And they are growing more divergent. This helps account for rising regionalism in culture, from poetry to cuisine, and, of course, in politics.

Similarly, John Naisbitt (1984, 116–34) observed what he termed a "new regionalism" emerging in the United States. He stated, "The regional differences we enjoy stressing are not imaginary. The people within a region have similar values, attitudes, a sort of geographic state of mind." Joel Garreau argued in his book *The Nine Nations of North America* (1981, 1) that North America is culturally divided into nine nations or regions:

Each has its capital and its distinctive web or power and influence. A few are allies but many are adversaries. ... Some are close to being raw frontiers; others have four centuries of history. Each has a peculiar economy ... each nation has a distinct prism through which it views the world.

These observations are not startling when one considers that California, for example, negotiates with other countries over economic exchange, and that southern states in the United States are increasing their share of foreign direct investment. In an article in *The Wall Street Journal* (October 7, 1986, p. 35), Eugene Carlson stated:

There's a shift under way in the regional pattern of U.S. foreign investment. Measured by the number of workers on payrolls of foreign-affiliated corporations, the Southeast and the Southwest are the major growth areas for overseas investment, while the Great Lakes and the mid-Atlantic states are falling behind.

It is already an established trend among several industries to use regions as bases to market and sell products. Campbell Soup Company, for example, carved the United States into twenty-two regions. As reported by Christine Dugas and Mark Vamos in *Business Week* (January 26, 1987, pp. 68, 69), "There is a combined sales and marketing force in each one [region], which no longer operates merely as an extension of the corporate office. Every regional staff studies marketing strategies and media buying and gets an ad and trade-promotion budget." The article goes on to state that "Regionalization may also give consumer-goods companies a way to get on a more nearly equal footing with increasingly powerful supermarket and grocery chains."

These observations are by no means intended to promote a parochial view of culture or to suggest that global and international cultural and management strategies are unimportant. We argue here that industrial and management behaviors are multicultural and that the dimension of regional culture, in particular, both as determined by and as determiner of business behavior, has until recently been neglected.

FOCUS AND SCOPE

This book presents a selected and a largely solicited set of original essays and studies that explore and focus on the importance of regional culture as influencing and being influenced by industrial and management practices. The book covers eight countries: India, Spain, the United States, Finland, France, Belize, Switzerland, and West Germany.

The underlying theme in these studies is that nations are composed of regions whose economies, cultures, value systems, and histories have influenced and continue to affect industrial and, in several cases, entrepreneurial development or lack of development. An implicit theme in these essays is that, in order to be nationally and internationally competitive, national governments should support and enhance regional resources in those areas that can attract and sustain entrepreneurial enterprises and activities.

Regional Culture

What is meant by regional culture, entrepreneurship, and management practices? Regional culture is defined as both (1) environmental influences (Farmer and Richman 1966) that have particular historical, political, economic, and social characteristics; and (2) patterns of shared beliefs, observations, expectations, and traditions whose participants have similar ways of viewing space, time, things, and people (Schein 1985). Regions vary in their sharing of national cultural characteristics; this is a research question.

Entrepreneurship

Entrepreneurship emerged as a dominant theme in this book. Those authors from whom chapters were solicited viewed competitiveness and industrial development among regions in their country as a dominant economic and national concern. Thus, regions in these countries were profiled and studied from the perspective of initiating, importing, and/or supporting entrepreneurial values, resources, and industrial infrastructures that facilitated innovative thinking, recruitment and retention of entrepreneurs, and opportunities for venturing into new business activities. Because entrepreneurship can be viewed in a range of ways from a regional perspective, no one definition was forged or adopted to guide these essays. As a result, this book demonstrates that entrepreneurship is a process and profession that is influenced by historic, cultural, economic, and social forces in the environment.

Management Behavior

Although management behavior and practices were not defined *a priori* for the authors who participated in this project, the first chapter in the book, by Joseph W. Weiss and André Delbecq, was distributed.

In that essay, the authors present a model that includes the following suggested "organizational and management manifestations" that can be influenced by regional cultures: policies and procedures, rituals and folklore, strategic planning, organizational structure, management style and orientation, communication and networking, and compensation systems. These dimensions are derived from classic studies in organizational science and from Everett M. Rogers's and Judith K. Larsen's study (1984).

Finally, no prescriptive causal directions or imposed paradigm for studying the relationships between regional culture and industrial and management practices were required from the authors. As a result, as this book demonstrates, an eclectic, macrohistorical, economic, and sociological approach was taken to describe the evolution and reciprocal effects of regional cultures on industrial and management experiences and styles. It can also be noted that, in some instances, regional cultural characteristics are overwhelmed by national culture, as is the case with Switzerland. This observation reinforces what was said earlier: organizations and industries operate in multicultural environments with multicultural peoples. Managers and those who are managed gain from an awareness of these multicultural dimensions operating within their environments. This book emphasizes the regional dimension of culture as an influencer and determinant of management and entrepreneurial practices.

MAJOR ASSUMPTIONS

This book is based on the following major assumptions:

1. Nations are not monolithic cultural entities. Regions differ historically, culturally, politically, economically, and linguistically. These differences can and often do affect industrial and organizational behavior.
2. Regional culture is one important but neglected dimension of the multicultural environments of industries and organizations.
3. Entrepreneurship is a function of regional resources, networks, values, economic opportunitues, cultures, and institutions.
4. There is no one best or right way to study the reciprocal relationships between regional cultures, management and industrial behavior, and entrepreneurship. An eclectic approach that includes macro and micro levels of analysis from historical, economic, sociological, and strategic planning approaches can more accurately describe the dynamics of such relationships.

OVERVIEW

Chapter 2 by Joseph W. Weiss and André Delbecq deals with regional cultures and the high-technology computer industry in the United

States. The essay poses the following two questions: Do regional cultures and environments affect high-technology management practices? and, if so, are there differences between Silicon Valley and Route 128? The importance of this chapter lies in its presentation of a general, heuristic model for examining relationships between regional culture and organizational behavior.

Chapter 3, also written by Delbecq and Weiss, bears the title "The Business Culture of Silicon Valley: Is It a Model for the Future?" Less theoretical, it quotes several computer executives from Silicon Valley regarding the uniqueness of the region's culture and high-technology management styles. Reminiscent of the work of Everett Rogers and Judith Larsen on Silicon Valley (1984), this essay reflects many of their findings but does so from the point of view of CEOs and vice-presidents of several outstanding firms in the Valley. The topic of entrepreneurship is dealt with vividly and interestingly.

Chapter 4, written by Lynn R. Kahle, presents a quantitative approach to measuring regional cultures. This essay, entitled "The Nine Nations of North America and the Value Basis of Geographic Segmentation," succinctly summarizes Joel Garreau's conclusions in *The Nine Nations of North America* (1981). Garreau's pioneering work presents a framework for viewing regional cultural differences and divisions in North America. In addition, Kahle statistically compares and tests whether Garreau's regional cultural boundaries more accurately differentiate national value differences than the Bureau of Census's political regional boundaries. The chapter is, therefore, an interesting application for understanding how regional cultural boundaries can be defined and distinguished. Finally, Kahle's work stands in sharp methodological contrast to some of the other essays in this book which are exploratory in nature and consequently use qualitative means for examining the relationships between regional cultures and management practices.

Chapter 5 is Nieves Martinez and Pedro Nueño's original essay on "Catalan Regional Business Culture, Entrepreneurship, and Management Behavior: An Exploratory Study." The authors trace the evolution of major industrial activities in Catalonia and then update the historical profile by presenting their interview results with major industrialists in the region. Of particular interest are the authors' findings on the region's infrastructure and changing values which serve as resources and hindrances for entrepreneurs in Catalan. The identification and linking of Catalan values to entrepreneurship serves as a model for discussion for both researchers and practitioners.

Chapter 6, Jean-Paul Larçon's creative essay on "Regional Industrial Cultures and Entrepreneurship in a Centralized Country: The Case of France," argues that France's centralizing traditions, rooted in Paris as the cultural and geographic center, have not overwhelmed the importance of other regions as evolving high-technology and science centers. Larçon divides France into traditional economic and entrepreneurial-oriented regions. His detailed discussion of the success factors in the regions of Lyon and the Riviera indicates the innovative directions which these areas are pursuing with regard to developing entrepreneurial industries.

In chapter 7, "Entrepreneurship and Local Government Strategies in Finland: A Regional Perspective," Henri J. Vartiainen explains the Finnish government's recognition of the importance of local and regional cultures and economies in promoting entrepreneurial strategies to enhance personnel policies and planning. Vartiainen discusses Nordic values and historic trends that have influenced recent personnel planning in favor of the resurgence of local initiatives. The author's identification and discussion of specific strategies which local governments are using to initiate entrepreneurial projects should prove especially valuable to economists and policy makers.

Max Daetwyler's exploratory essay in chapter 8 is entitled "Local Cultures and Management: The Case of Switzerland and Its Societal Management Model." Following an informative overview of the historical and cultural milieu of Switzerland, Daetwyler introduces a novel concept regarding this small country's contribution to management: a unique, decentralized model that combines different managerial know-how from national and international experiences. The ideas presented in this chapter form an interesting contrast to the management models of Japan, Silicon Valley, and Route 128.

Chapter 9, Raghu Nath's "Regional Culture, Entrepreneurship, and High-Technology Development in India," presents a detailed profile of the industrial regions and cultures in India. Nath also examines the problems of fitting entrepreneurial high-technology ventures with Indian regional cultures and applies the models in the Weiss and Delbecq article to Bangalore. The essay innovatively integrates high-technology planning information with India's regional cultural characteristics and potential for such industrial development.

Horst Albach and Hermann Tengler present an economic study in chapter 10, "Industrial Competitive Development in Three Regions in the Federal Republic of Germany: The Case of Kassel, Bonn, and Duisburg." This essay reports the results of a study designed to show whether West Germany has regional differences in terms of economic and industrial development? Of particular interest are the sections on the competitive advantages between West Germany's more traditional, rural regions and the more urbanized, industrial regions. As Albach and Tengler's data show, regional stereotypes do not hold. Traditional regions have much to offer in terms of industrial development. The essay presents rich details on the area's industrial and entrepreneurial development, industry profiles, and regional resources.

In chapter 11, "The Entrepreneurial Enterprise of Changing Capitals across Regional Cultures: The Case of Belize," Sam Hai reports the results from the intended and the actual move of Belize's capital across culturally distinct and clashing regional groups and cultures. Hai intentionally entitled his chapter, " ... across Regional Cultures." His data graphically illustrate how this kind of entrepreneurial undertaking can fail if government planners do not consider the effects of regional cultural group acceptance of such an undertaking. The managerial implications of moving capitals within countries are also discussed.

All of these essays share the premise that regional cultures influence management and entrepreneurial values and industrial practices. Because culture in general is a "hidden" reality, these essays help make visible the specific dimensions of regional culture which intereact with national cultural characteristics. In particular, a region's physical, technological, social, historical, and cultural resources affect industrial and entrepreneurial location and development. Managerial value systems, communication patterns, networking, and other functional modes of operating are reciprocally related to regional as well as to national and international cultures. These essays attempt to identify these relationships.

Regional Cultures and High-Technology Management: Route 128 and Silicon Valley

Joseph W. Weiss and André Delbecq

INTRODUCTION

This essay extends the concept of corporate culture to the level of industry culture and examines regional influences on management practices in Silicon Valley and Route 128. In-depth interviews with CEOs and executives in mature electronics firms were conducted. Results from the data indicate that these high-technology cultures and related management practices differ significantly and are influenced by particular regional characteristics. Conceptual and consulting implications are discussed.

Do national regional characteristics influence high-technology industrial cultures and management practices? If so, how and what conceptual and practitioner-oriented lessons can be learned from evidence indicating that this is the case? These are the questions which guided our research into an examination of the influences of regional differences on management practices in selected mature computer firms around Route 128 and in Silicon Valley.

Arguments and evidence which connect national culture to management practices across nations have been established (Gallie 1978; Haire, Ghiselli, and Porter 1966; Hofstede 1980). Lacking in the literature on this subject, however, has been the examination of the effects of within-nation regional differences on management practices in and across industries. There are several reasons why research in this area has been

Joseph W. Weiss and André Delbecq, "High-Technology Cultures and Management: Silicon Valley and Route 128," *Group and Organization Studies* 12, no. 1 (1987): 39–54. Copyright © 1987 by Sage Publications, Inc. Reprinted by permission of Sage Publications, Inc.

neglected. First, the myth persists that the United States, for example, is a melting pot in which few if any significant regional differences exist. Second, conducting within-nation research between organizations from a regional perspective has been considered either ethnocentric or polycentric but not truly comparative (Adler 1982). Third, organizational theory and methodologies which have been used to compare management behavior between nations have been too deterministic to explicitly address the effects of regions on business cultures and practices (Nath 1985).

In this chapter, we argue that industrial cultures exist between firms in the computer electronics industry, that these cultures are influenced and conditioned by regional characteristics in which the firms are located and operate, and that these cultures affect management practices in and across companies. By identifying and comparing different regional industrial cultures and management practices, more can be learned about relationships between local environments and group behavior in industries. Consequently, managers and consultants may gain insight into interventions appropriate for corporate policies and procedures in different national settings. These arguments are presented by first clarifying the conceptual perspective used; secondly, the research strategy and methodology are explained; third, the results are summarized; finally, implications from the findings are reviewed.

Conceptual Perspective

While the concept of individual corporate culture has been widely addressed (Deal and Kennedy 1982; Schein 1984; Smircich 1983), the topic of general industrial cultures that include elements of but transcend single-company cultures has not been sufficiently examined or integrated into the literature on this subject. For example, Smircich's recent review (1983) of major concepts of culture did not mention business cultures or a regional level of analysis for examining this concept. Rogers's and Larsen's study (1984) of Silicon Valley described elements of the dominant high-technology industrial culture there, but unfortunately offered no explicit definition of that culture or of the regional context they examined. Deal and Kennedy (1982, 107) recognized the influences of the "social and business environment" on corporate culture. However, they limited their identification of the environment to two factors derived from the marketplace: "the degree of a company's activities, and the speed at which companies—and their employees—get feedback on whether decisions or strategies are successful." These authors did argue that differences between organizational cultures exist primarily across industries rather than between organizations in the same industry; however, their categorization of all businesses into four generic corporate culture types did not take regional differences and their effects on different industries into consideration.

For the purpose of this study, industrial culture was defined as shared beliefs, observations, and expectations held by organizational members which define their organization, its ways of adapting externally and integrating internally within the regional environment of the firm. This definition is partly derived and extended from definitions of Schein (1985), Schwartz and Davis (1981) and Triandis et al. (1972). With Schein (1985, 9), our adapted definition of culture turns the researcher's attention to "cultural predispositions (the assumptions, perceptions, thoughts, and feelings that are patterned) . . . by the situational contingencies that arise from the external environment." However, unlike Schein's focus, we did not exclude observations and experiences from organizational members' descriptions of culture. Critical incidents and experiences often tell a lot about the culture of organizations. Also, we were specifically interested in discovering whether or not and, if so, to what extent an industrial culture was evident in the local environment across firms in the same industry. Therefore, we did not limit our definition of culture or our methods of inquiry to the internal organizational context, although this context was explored as part of a larger industrial culture.

While our definition of culture is generic—as are most definitions on this topic (Schein 1985, 6–9; Smircich 1983)—the elements offered here can be operationalized through the types of questions asked to respondents. For example, and as discussed in the next section, respondents were asked questions regarding workplace communication, networking, norms, entrepreneurial activities, as well as questions relating to environmental effects on their organization. Table 2.1 depicts the broader conceptual framework of this study and exemplifies elements of the definitions of culture offered here.

The reasoning underlying this table and the chapter is that influences in regional environments (Farmer and Richman 1966; Harbison and Myers, 1959) affect the formation and activities of cultures among firms of the same industry which, in turn, affect organizational and management practices inside companies. Regional characteristics need not be limited to some of the classical categories listed here. These influences may vary by industry. For example, Dorfman (1982) and Miller and Cote (1985) discuss several such characteristics relative to the high-tech industry which are not listed in this table (e.g., supply of professional skill, agglomeration of economics—i.e., a concentration of firms in related industries—availability of venture capital, presence of re-

Table 2.1

Influences of Regional Characteristics on Business Cultures and Practices

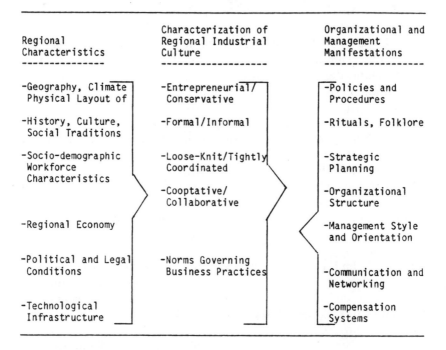

Regional Characteristics	Characterization of Regional Industrial Culture	Organizational and Management Manifestations
-Geography, Climate Physical Layout of	-Entrepreneurial/ Conservative	-Policies and Procedures
-History, Culture, Social Traditions	-Formal/Informal	-Rituals, Folklore
-Socio-demographic Workforce Characteristics	-Loose-Knit/Tightly Coordinated	-Strategic Planning
	-Cooptative/ Collaborative	-Organizational Structure
-Regional Economy		-Management Style and Orientation
-Political and Legal Conditions	-Norms Governing Business Practices	-Communication and Networking
-Technological Infrastructure		-Compensation Systems

search universities). Identifying particular regional characteristics and their influences on the creation and shaping of industrial cultures is part of the research task.

Regional industrial cultures in industries can take various forms. Deal and Kennedy (1982, 107, 108) list several creative classifications. Based on a review of general management literature, the broad descriptors of business cultures suggested in table 2.1 are by no means complete or definitive. These depictions are examples, viewed here as continuums. Moreover, the arrows placed between "Regional Characteristics," "Industrial Culture," and "Organizational Manifestations" should not be interpreted as causal relations, but as associational influences. The relationship between these described categories is dynamic and interactive.

Finally, we note that industrial cultures can influence firms' management behavior and practices through individual corporate cultures. Again, the extent to which corporate cultures reflect, share, or reject elements from an industry's dominant regional business culture is a research question. Relative to this study, Rogers and Larsen (1984) have argued that the "high-technology culture" in Silicon Valley affected several of the categories included here: e.g., communication, rewards, beliefs, attitudes, and professional working styles. Whether or not this is the case in the high-technology culture of Massachusetts has not, until this inquiry, been examined.

Table 2.1 is, then, presented as a heuristic device, not as a mechanical, causal model. Moreover, our study does not pretend to address all the nuances in the illustration; rather, this essay explores major themes of the reasoning discussed above with the intent of encouraging additional research on these topics.

Methodology

Because of the exploratory, novel approach taken here, we used qualitative methods aimed more at generating information than testing *a priori* statements (Van Maanen, Dabbs, and Faulkner, 1982). Examples of interview studies on the high-technology industry can be found in Maidique and Hayes (1984), Rogers and Larsen (1984), and Gregory (1983).

The design of the study is cross sectional. Interviews were conducted with executives in firms within the same general industry in two geographically separate areas. Because of our use of open-ended questionnaire items, the data are perceptual and can only provide associational, not causal relations.

Mature, high-technology computer firms which were well established in each region and whose CEOs were familiar with indigenous regional influences were selected at random from comprehensive lists provided by the Massachusetts Council on High-Technology and the American Electronics Association. The informants in both the Silicon Valley and Route 128 samples were not "young entrepreneurs." Rather, we sought seasoned executives. The question which concerned us in doing the study was how the dominant regional cultures of Silicon Valley and around Route 128 influenced management practices in mature and maturing organizations. By selecting executives in maturing companies, we hoped to identify the attributes of the business cultures of the regions well after the start-up phase.

Interviewees in the Silicon Valley sample included John Sculley at Apple Computer, Robert Lorenzini and Brad Wait at Siltec Corporation, Irwin Federman at Monolithic Memories, Kenneth Oshman and Gibson Anderson at Rolm, William Terry and John Flaherty at Hewlett-Packard, and Robert Fuhrman at Lockheed. Paul Wythes, the general manager of Sutter Hills, a venture capital firm, was also part of the sample. These executives were in their 40s. Their average tenure with their companies was 18 years. Four of the executives had either lived or worked on the East Coast. Three had attended college in the East. All had traveled between the coasts carrying out their professional duties.

The interviewers were Dr. Joseph Weiss, Assistant Professor of Management at Bentley College in Waltham, Massachusetts, and Dr. André Delbecq, Dean at the Leavey Graduate Business School, Santa Clara University in Santa Clara, California.

The size of the companies in this part of the sample, as measured by fiscal year 1984 dollars, ranged from $40 million (Siltec) to $4.71 billion (Hewlett-Packard). The age of the companies (measured by date founded) ranged from 18 years (Apple) to 38 years (Hewlett-Packard), with the exception of Lockheed which was founded in 1932.

The technology of the companies consisted mainly of the manufacturing of electronic components, including silicon products, semiconductors, and integrated circuits. Software development was also a major product developed.

The New England sample included Ken Olsen at Digital, John Poduska of Apollo, Joe Henson at Prime, Jim Berrett at Computervision, Mike Anderson with Nixdorf, Richard Spann from Adage, Ross Belson at Lexidata, Bob Miller at Data General, Ben Holmes with Hewlett-Packard, and Ash Dahod from Applitek. Andrew Taylor, a partner at Testa, Hurwitz & Thibeault (one of the oldest established legal firms in Boston which has a history of dealing with venture capital deals), was also included.

These executives were also in their 40s. Their average tenure with the East Coast companies was 8 years. Four executives had lived and/ or worked in California. Three are originally from New England.

The size of the companies in this sample, also measured by 1984 fiscal sales dollars, ranged from $26 million (Lexidata) to $4.17 billion (Hewlett-Packard). The age of the companies ranged from 18 years (Digital) to 3 years (Applitek).

Products represented by these companies include the manufacturing of electronic equipment and computers, development of computer-aided design and manufacturing systems (CAD/CAM), computer graphics, and a wide range of software products.

Interview Questions and Analysis

Open-ended questions were used beginning with the query: "Describe the way high-tech business operates around Route 128 as compared to Silicon Valley. Use your experiences and observations to explain any differences and why they exist, if they do." Neither environment nor culture was defined for the executives beforehand; rather, our intent was to permit the interviewees to describe external influences and the effects of these on their management cultures and practices (Gregory 1983).

A series of unstructured followup questions were then asked which required the executives to compare differences between the following general management practices. These questions included probes regarding workplace policies and procedures, communication patterns, risk-taking, entrepreneurship, networking workplace communication, workforce norms, strategic planning focus of the company, and compensation systems. These particular probes were chosen because they cover a wide range of well-known management practices and because several of these were used in a prior study on Silicon Valley (Rogers and Larsen 1984).

The interviews lasted between one and a half to two hours. All were tape recorded in the executives' workplaces and later transcribed verbatim. Repetitive themes were identified from the transcriptions by four judges. They analyzed each questionnaire item and themes which emerged spontaneously during the interviews (see Carney 1972).

RESULTS

Our findings support the contention that different types of high-technology cultures exist in Silicon Valley and around Route 128 and that these business cultures are affected by region-specific characteristics. Only three executives in the total sample offered little or alternative evidence regarding this proposition.

An overview of the results also showed considerable consensus of types of regional influences which affect these high-technology cultures and particular management practices. In both samples, the following regional factors, which are described below, were repeatedly given as significant influences on the business cultures: (1) historical and social traditions (or lack of these); (2) previous industrial experience and precedents in the region; (3) geography, climate and physical setting of plants; (4) sociodemographic characteristics of the professional workforce; and (5) economic conditions in the region.

Characteristics of these high-technology cultures and their described effects on management processes are summarized by regional sample.

Silicon Valley Profile

A summary of the findings from this sample is presented in table 2.2.

Taken together, the underlying thrust of these interviews suggests that Silicon Valley's lack of long-standing historical and social traditions provided an opportunity for the computer industry at the start-up stage to form a new and distinct professional culture in this region based on values of individualistic competition, informality, and experimentation. Even though many mature and successful computer firms operate in Silicon Valley, we found that elements of a start-up,

Table 2.2
Silicon Valley Profile

Regional Characteristics	High-Technology Regional Industrial Culture	Organizational and Management Manifestations
Historical and Cultural Traditions: Pioneers; lack of social traditions; future oriented	-Entrepreneurial, Experimental -Informal, Intense	-Short term R&D orientation; strategic planning, venture capital, beliefs on company tenure
Industrial Legacy: start-up high-technology computer partnerships and companies; Japanese competitive presence	-Dynamic Cooptative	-Horizontal structure: "less is best"
Socio-demographic Workforce Characteristics: Professional workforce young, competitive, entrepreneurial; values adventure, risk-taking, heterogeneous national origins	-Materialistic, Individualistic	-Decentralized, results-oriented management styles and decision making
Geography, Climate, Physical Setting of Plants; Plants Closely clustered in commercial park settings in northern California; mild annual climate	-Tightly knit network between employees across firms	-Informality in workplace procedures, dress, working styles
Economy; Industry downturn; regional economy less diversified than Massachusetts; cost of living high	-Belief systems center on self-fulfillment, wealth, professions	-Mobility rewarded, job-hopping not a liability -Stock options integral to reward system

high-technology computer culture still drive attitudes and management practices here. John Sculley's comment represents a recurring theme on this topic by other executives in this sample: "Eventually companies return to their roots and the roots in Silicon Valley are in start-up garages and their association with the universities."

Moreover, executives in this sample stated that it is this type of culture that attracts a sociodemographic mix of professionals who thrive on the organizational characteristics which are largely derived from this general business culture: namely, accepted individual mobility ("job-hopping"), a "free form" type of organizational structure; emphasis on short-term planning and product innovation turnaround time; stock options; professional independence; and the ability to have fun while being productive in the working place.

Descriptions of Silicon Valley's dominant high-technology regional culture are summarized in table 2.2. Many of these descriptions have been observed in other studies (e.g., Rogers and Larsen 1984). Of interest to this study was the particular observation by executives regarding the open, fluid internal organizational environment in firms compared with their descriptions of a tight-knit, highly competitive, sometimes cooperative professional network across firms, which John Sculley said, "You're either in or you're out of it." Because of the intense competition over technical professionals and the close proximity between firms, the regional high-technology culture reflected the "intense," "frantic," "exciting," but "cooptative" nature of these regional cultural characteristics.

Relevant to this study, the following conclusions from this sample are emphasized: (1) mature, successful computer firms reflect elements of Silicon Valley's dominant high-technology regional culture, which resembles a start-up, adolescent culture that is highly entrepreneurial, mobile, informal, tightly knit, and competitive; (2) executives in mature firms tend to reinforce and condone this business culture in many of their management practices listed in table 2.2. The notable exception in our sample was Hewlett-Packard. These executives believed that their company culture overwhelmed many elements in the general business environment. For example, Hewlett-Packard's practice of long-term employee tenure stands in sharp contrast to Silicon Valley's high turnover rate in the industry (Rozen 1985). Still, the interview results from the Hewlett-Packard executives affirmed the notion that a strong and observable regional high-technology culture exists here. The extent to which regional business cultures penetrate individual corporate cultures, like that of Hewlett-Packard, requires further examination.

Route 128 Profile

Evidence from our Massachusetts sample showed a distinctly different regional high-technology culture which is influenced by different environmental characteristics. Table 2.3 summarizes the interviews from this sample.

The independently repeated themes which executives used to describe this region's high-technology culture were: "formal, conservative, stodgy, structured, controlled." All executives in the sample believed that, compared to Silicon Valley, the Massachusetts business

Table 2.3
Route 128 Profile

Regional Characteristics	High-Technology Regional Industrial Culture	Organizational and Management Manifestations
Historial and Cultural Traditions: Puritanism, strong family, community and regional identity	-Formal Conservative	-Long-term orientation; strategic plan-ning, venture capitalists, beliefs about company tenure
Industrial Legacy: Mature, smokestack manufacturing environmental; European market presence	-Calculated Innovation	-Vertically structured, and top-down
Socio-demographic Workforce Charac-teristics: Pro-fessional workforce older, more conserv-ative, formal family oriented; values stability, loyalty, hard work; homogeneous regional backgrounds	-Loosely knit relations between firms -Analytic, control oriented -Group oriented -Belief systems center on loyalty, commitment, diligence	-Formality in workplace procedures, dress, work-ing styles -Individual mobility and job-hopping a liability -Reward system favors long-term incentives
Geography, Climate Physical Setting of Plants; Plants widely dispersed in several towns; greater cultural homogeneity among regional states where companies ex-panded; harsh winter climate		-Centralized decision-making and management styles
Economy, Industry downturn; regional economy growing; cost of living increasing		

culture in general is less entrepreneurial, less "trend oriented, but as intense and productive."

The "inhibited, controlled" regional high-technology culture was also believed to be reflected in the ways organizational and management practices were played out. For example, it was observed that high-technology management styles here tended to be more conservative and top-down oriented, even though several computer firms are going through a decentralization process. Moreover, firms here tended to rely on a more formal, vertical structure, even though teams are evident in several companies. There is also a long-term orientation in the strategic planning, in management's and employees' beliefs about their tenure with a company, and even in the way venture capitalists were observed to offer support to new ventures here.

Formality in the workplace, dress, communication patterns, and attitudes toward authority were also consistent themes repeated in the interviews to characterize the effects of regional characteristics on business behavior. One executive noted that "There is a less 'go-for-it' attitude here than in Silicon Valley, where I travel frequently. We also have more difficulty in getting people to brainstorm here. People seem to be afraid to be bizarre, to let themselves go."

"Job-hopping" is also considered unacceptable here compared to Silicon Valley. Executives in our sample expressed a preference for professionals who were "in it for the long-term," or as one person said, "We're not interested in people who just want to get rich fast." All executives in the sample noted that company loyalty and commitment here are values most employees adhered to, unlike in Silicon Valley.

The major regional characteristics which influence the high-technology culture and management practices here are listed in table 2.3. The most outstanding and repeated theme was the strong, conservative, formal traditions which are rooted in communities, neighborhoods, and families. Ken Olsen, in particular, continually referred to the Puritan traditions which, he believed, influence the attitudes of employees and managers in this region: e.g., self-reliance, ability to self-reflect, and willingness to admit error.

Relevant to this study, our findings from this sample indicate that (1) these CEOs and executives acknowledge the wider influence of the region's social, historical, and physical characteristics on a dominant high-technology culture and on specific management practices. These influences are characterized as more conservative, stable, and formal—a sharp contrast to Silicon Valley; (2) the influence of these seemingly unprogressive characteristics on the high-technology culture and business behavior does not impede but rather contributes to the innovation, productivity, and competitiveness of these firms with others nationally and internationally. Several executives attribute the presence of professional expertise, universities, the region's healthy and diversified economy, and the stable character of professionals' values and lifestyles to the success of the computer industry here.

We also noted that the dominant high-technology culture which exists between firms here is less cohesive, less tightly networked, and, therefore, seems to exert less influence over interfirm competition for professional resources, for example, as compared to Silicon Valley. The scattered physical setting of the firms, the climate, and the strong family and community orientation of professionals were offered as reasons why the communication network across firms is less defined and influential here than in Silicon Valley.

DISCUSSION

This study has extended the concept of corporate culture to the level of "industry regional culture," which includes both subjective and objective influences of external characteristics on organizational members. In this case, dominant regional high-technology cultures in Silicon Valley and Massachusetts were compared. Conceptually, this perspective offers a contribution to existing literature on corporate culture (e.g., Rogers and Larsen 1984; Deal and Kennedy 1982; Schein 1984) by explicitly taking regional contexts of industries as well as individual organizations into account when diagnosing the role of culture in management. This study, for example, showed that not all high-technology cultures are alike. Nor are the effects of regional environments on business practices necessarily the same. The findings also indicate that variables presented here, in addition to those most frequently used, such as presence of research universities, agglomeration of economies, technology and the like (Dorfman 1982; Miller and Cote 1985) may also be important determinants of the high-technology management practices and ways of doing business.

On a more practical note, there are implications of these findings for managers. Personnel managers, in particular, who recruit, relocate, and train professionals across regions, could use this type of information to better understand different business cultures with which they are working. For example, socializing employees into an organizational culture may also mean preparing them to succeed in a particular regional industrial culture. This may especially be the case for sales and marketing professionals who interact with others in the external environment more frequently.

Also for executives who move workforces across regional boundaries, this type of study may be helpful. For example, in our sample, two high-technology executives along Route 128 stated they pursued a conscious strategy of sending selected East Coast professionals to their

California facilties in order to "stabilize" and train components of that workforce. Another executive from Massachusetts stated that he "imports" Silicon Valley professionals to assist his manufacturing engineers to brainstorm and create new solutions to problems. Several Silicon Valley executives in our sample stated that there is a need for the analytical, disciplined, cost-conscious approach employed by Eastern professionals in solving problems in the Silicon Valley environment. This may particularly be the case during industry downturns when cost strategies are an asset to management.

With regard to organizational consultants, studies such as this offer contributions in at least two types of situations in which interventions are often used. First, negative effects from company cultural clashes as a result of mergers and acquisitions have been documented (Buono, Bowditch, and Lewis 1985). Understanding regional industrial cultures and the effects of such cultural influences on management behavior can be informative to consultants hired to create or merge different corporate cultures across regional boundaries. Second, consultants from different industries and/or regions could also benefit from findings as those presented here. An executive relocated from a service industry in the South may not, for example, share similar business cultural assumptions and standards as does the management in the Eastern firm to which he or she is sent.

From a more general perspective, findings from studies in this area could be useful to executives and managers in examining different policies, procedures, and unwritten customs or standards in their firms. To what extent are the beliefs, customary ways of doing business, communication patterns, structuring methods of tasks and people, and procedures for relating to clients reflective of local and regional cultural business patterns? How are careers, developmental and mobility policies, appraisal and evaluation systems influenced by regionally conditioned standards and belief stystems? These types of questions require more comparative research on regional business cultures.

The questions this study raises exceed the methods and findings presented. As a qualitative field research project which attempted to be comparative, the limitations of the study are obvious. Additional research is needed which examines more detailed hypotheses. More structured methods and larger random samples in different, perhaps more regions, could better test the propositions stated here. Questions can be addressed which we did not include: e.g. What types and characteristics of corporate cultures reject and/or reflect dominant regional industrial influences? Do certain industries have stronger regional industry cultures than others? Also, studies showing how and why industry cultures change and how these changes affect firms would provide a contribution in this area.

3

The Business Culture of Silicon Valley: Is It a Model for the Future?

André Delbecq and Joseph W. Weiss

In 1979 the senior author moved from the Midwest to Silicon Valley. At the time both "high tech" as an industry and Silicon Valley as a geographical region had obtained mythical proportions in the business press. The success of Silicon Valley with many companies showing annual growth rates of 100 to 300 percent stood in stark contrast to the industrial Midwest suffering from a severe recession. "Smokestack" America looked with envy toward Silicon Valley. The question was frequently asked: What makes Silicon Valley dynamic? Are there lessons for the reindustrialization of older American industries? Should other regions seek to spawn "little Silicon gulches?"

The purpose of this chapter is to focus on Silicon Valley as a business culture; to try to capture those elements of the business culture which differentiate this region from other business regions. In our view, regional differences are worthy of examination when exploring the compatibility of certain types of enterprise of industrial niches with geographical locations.

As Toffler (1983, 22) stated: "Today as we look as Kyushu in Southern Japan, or Scotland, or Quebec, or Texas, we find regional economies that become as large and complex as national economies were only a few decades ago ... more and more these regional economies break out of national economic frameworks and demand to go their own way." This perspective that regions are critical influences is shared by Garreau (1981, 1) and Naisbitt (1984, 116–34), both of whom argue that North

Reprinted by permission of the publisher, from *The Future of Organizations*, edited by Jerald Hage (Lexington, Mass.: Lexington Books, D. C. Heath and Company, copyright 1988, D. C. Heath and Company).

American regions have distinct cultural prisms through which the practice of business is viewed. Nor is this simply a recent perspective. Political and sociological writers (Vance 1952, 124–25 and Elazer 1966) had earlier argued the same point.

THE ÉLAN OF SILICON VALLEY

Two stories can illustrate the sense of contrast immediately felt by someone moving from a conservative Midwestern region to Silicon Valley. The first story concerns a young entrepreneur, and the second story concerns the action of a Board of Directors.

When the senior author first arrived in Silicon Valley to accept the position of Dean of the School of Business at Santa Clara University, within two weeks a young man arrived in his office carrying a business plan. The would-be entrepreneur was 21 years old, had not yet graduated with his baccalaureate engineering degree, but intended to start an electronics business. He asked: "Would you help me meet the appropriate individuals so that I can raise half a million dollars to begin my company?"

In truth, in light of my Midwestern ethics the request seemed bizarre. However, being new to the region, I took the business plan to a member of the business school's advisory board who had spent the last decade in Silicon Valley, and asked for his advice. He read the business plan quickly but thoughtfully, and suggested he would set up a luncheon with a venture capitalist, a real estate developer, a senior entrepreneur who had established a similar company six years before, and a representative from a local accounting firm. The result of the luncheon meeting was that the young engineer was subsequently partially funded through a venture capitalist and partially funded through a bank loan, guided through the rental of appropriate industrial property by the local bank developer, and provided counsel by two outside board members (one of whom was present at the first luncheon.) This past year the business initiated at the luncheon was sold for $15 million.

I recall telling this story to ex-Speaker of the House Tip O'Neill at a meeting on the Georgetown University campus and seeing the Speaker's face grow reflective. I remember his comment: "It couldn't happen in Massachusetts!" The fact that it did happen and happened swiftly and smoothly illustrated one of the first cultural lessons I learned in Silicon Valley. Entrepreneurship and all business plans are taken seriously. Age, whether the would-be entrepreneur is 21 or 61, is not a critical variable. The Jobs and Wozniak Apple Computer's "shoestring" initiation formula continued then, and continues now, as a regular part of life in the Valley. Clearly, Silicon Valley is a business community that sees one of its major tasks as enabling entrepreneurship.

The second story is a Board of Directors meeting dealing with developing a critical market strategy. There were eight directors at the meeting. The discussion originally proceeded with vigor, and varied points of view were expressed. The strategic direction originally recommended by the CEO was subject to many suggestions for modification. Upon leaving the meeting there appeared to me, as an outside observer, to be no consensus. I felt a sense of compassion for the Chief Executive Officer subject to such varied pressures. Three weeks later when I met with the CEO, I asked him how was he going to reexamine the issue of the market strategy at a subsequent board meeting. He replied: "What do you mean? We dealt with the marketing strategy at the last Board meeting!" I was stunned. "But there was no consensus, there was no agreement, there was no mandate given!" He looked at me with a perplexed frown. "There's never consensus. The risk is mine. The Board gave me their advice. Everyone understands that having listened to their advice I will have to make my own synthesis and get on with it. If we waited until we had consensus, we would be out of the market!"

These two stories indicate a business culture that clearly operates at a different pace. Businesses are established in a matter of weeks. Businesses rise and fall monthly. Entrepreneurial decisions internal to more mature firms seemed equally rapid. In one single year, one-half of the members of my Advisory Board of the School of Business changed positions. Three were initiating new businesses. Critical decisions were made without consensus. Product life cycles averaged two years, while product development cycles averaged four years. What is the business culture, "the rules of the game" as perceived by these business elites, that allows Silicon Valley to move at such a rapid and unique pace?

AN INTERVIEW STUDY

What follows is a descriptive report. It seeks to capture the spirit of the Valley. However, it makes no pretense that it provides a definitive answer. It is based on interviews during 1984 with a small number of electronic firm executives in Silicon Valley.[1] The executives and background data are presented in table 3.1.

Deliberately, the informants selected were not "young entrepreneurs." Rather, we sought seasoned regional executives. The question which concerned us in doing the pilot interviews was how the culture of the Valley influenced the mature and maturing organizations. By selecting mature executives in maturing companies, we hoped to identify the attributes of the business culture of the region well after the start-up phase. While there have been changes in the companies since our study, the bases of our observations remain intact.[2]

Table 3.1
Demographic Profile of Executives and Firms: Silicon Valley

Name	Company	Inc[1]	Sales[2]	Title	Yrs W/Co	Age	Degree	School
Ken Oshman	Rolm Corporation	1969	$ 300	President & CEO	16 yrs.	40s	PH.D	Stanford
Robert Lorenzini	Siltec Corporation	1969	40	President & CEO	16 yrs.	40s	MSME	Stanford
Irwin Federman	Monolithic Memories	1969	185	President	13 yrs.	40s	BS	Brooklyn College
Robert Fuhrman	Lockheed Missiles	1932	6490	Group President	27 yrs.	50s	MS	Michigan
William Terry	Hewlett-Packard	1947	4710	Exec. Vice Pres.	27 yrs.	50s	BSEE	Santa Clara
John Flaherty	Hewlett-Packard	1947	4710	Manager Corporate Personnel	29 yrs.	50s	BSBA	Northeastern University
Gibson Anderson	Rolm Corporation	1969	300	Director Human Res.	14 yrs.	40s	MSEE	Stanford
Brad Wait	Siltec Corporation	1969	40	Vice Pres. Finance	1/2 yrs.	40s	BSBA	Berkeley
John Sculley	Apple Computer, Inc.	1977	335	Chairman, CEO	3 yrs	40s	MBA	University of Pennsylvania
Payl Wythes	Sutter Hills Ventures	1962	---	General Partner	22 yrs	50s	MBA BS	Stanford Princeton

Executive's average age: 40s
Average time with company: 18 years
Number who live and/or worked on the East Coast: 3
Number of doctorates: 1

Number of master's degrees: 5
Number of bachelor's degrees: 4
[1]Data incorporated
[2]Fiscal 1983–84 sales in millions of dollars

It is important to note before reporting on the cultural attributes that we are reporting only on themes which were consistent across the interviews, and which we feel have the value to management and organizational scholars. In summary, this report is presented modestly as the shared interpretations by four analysts of interviews with experienced executives. (For a discussion of study methodology and types of questions asked in interviews, see chapter 2.)

ENTREPRENEURSHIP AND RISK-TAKING

Any reader sifting through the pages of transcripts or listening to the tape recordings would have no problem identifying the number one cultural theme which all informants agreed upon as the central driving force of Silicon Valley: risk-taking entrepreneurship.

It is important to remember we were interviewing senior executives in established, maturing firms. Yet, over and over when asked to describe the central cultural drive of the business setting in Silicon Valley, risk-taking and entrepreneurship were emphasized. Listen to some of the expressions of this cultural value:

OSHMAN (Rolm): The genesis of Silicon Valley lies in a business style which is entrepreneurial. Companies in Silicon Valley and their managements are characterized by an open-mindedness regarding the future, a welcoming of change, a belief in trying things to see if they work, experimentation. This is achieved by relying on delegating to people in a decentralized management style, a reluctance to depend on consultants or staffs for important business decisions, and a positive value toward innovative approaches.

TERRY (Hewlett-Packard): When I think of the West, I think of individuals who are dynamic! Willing to take risks! That's the critical characteristics of Silicon Valley.

WAIT (Siltec): You immediately sense the focus in this Valley is on entrepreneurship. The companies here are the most entrepreneurial I have ever worked with, very different than those in other parts of the Bay area. The style of top executives in the Valley is clearly entrepreneurial and unless you can meld into the entrepeneurial style you can't succeed.

LORENZINI (Siltec): I see Silicon Valley as being filled with experimental people. Being experimental is the prerequisite.

FEDERMAN (Monolithic Memories): People actually talk about being entrepreneurial, about the value of intuition. The central characteristic is that managers in Silicon Valley are willing to take more risks. They are more intrepid and eclectic. They are less respectful of constituted authority. I think that all of these characteristics reflect the one word *entrepreneurship* which is the essence of Silicon Valley.

SCULLEY (Apple): I just sense that Silicon Valley tilts more toward zany ideas. I think it is a place that values change for its own sake. I think the regional culture values energy and excitement associated with originating new things; it attracts people who look for radical change.

Pages of interviews are littered with quotations reflecting this spirit. All the informants agree that trying something new, taking risks, being entrepreneurial is at the heart of the business culture of Silicon Valley. The myth stories are not simply associated with start-up founders beginning in garages (Jobs and Wozniak of Apple). They include executives who leave one company and move on to found another. This sense of entrepreneurship penetrates even the area defense firms. Listen to Bob Fuhrman at Lockheed:

FUHRMAN (Lockheed): The sense of experimentation we have incorporated into our program management in Sunnyvale couldn't have occurred if we had kept our operations in Burbank. There was a spirit of experimentation, a willingness to engage in new decentralized programs here. That was counter-culture to the conservative defense industry in Los Angeles but was natural here in Sunnyvale.

We asked the interviewees to speculate on how this particular entrepreneurial cultural emphasis emerged.

The informants stressed three themes in explaining why entrepreneurship was so dominant and why risk-taking was such a highly valued element of the local business culture: (1) the West as populated by "frontiersmen," (2) experimentation for its own sake, and (3) technological push. Exemplary quotations reflective of the first theme generally followed the logic expressed by Federman:

FEDERMAN (Monolithic Memories): To a large extent many of our employees are transplants. I am too. I came from the Last. We have all made breaks in our lives. It's not surprising, along Route 128, to find that one is involved primarily with people who have been brought up in New England, perhaps right in Boston. The percentage of native Californians one would find in California meeting in Silicon Valley is radically different. Our companies are comprised primarily of people who have abandoned familiar surroundings, left their friends, and struck out for new adventures. They have already taken great risks, and are unabashed at further risk-taking.

A second theme was the pride of the Westerner in experimentation for its own sake. An exemplary quote can be taken from John Sculley:

SCULLEY (Apple): Silicon Valley offers a free form approach. I'd be really surprised if the next great industry emerged from the East Coast. I think it's more likely to come from a place that has no traditions. There aren't any traditions that I can see in California. There are no villages. There are just shopping centers. One day a company is written about in the business news and acclaimed as phenomenal. Six months later it's gone. It doesn't exist. It's not the people who disappeared. It's just that particular new idea has disappeared. Another new idea will be emerging in another company.

The third theme was "technological push." Given housing and labor costs, both of which disadvantage firms in the area as "low cost procedures," and a desire for "big wins" (which we will return to under our discussion of rewards), the big win or success was seen as associated with a breakthrough at the early phase of the product life cycle, when profit margins are high. The hope for the big win pushes the cultural emphasis on entrepreneurship as a path to fame and wealth.

Which of these themes is the more dominant? Most frequently mentioned was the belief that those who shake off their past and come West demand and value both independence and change, a refrain that will continue throughout the interviews. The "technological push" and early product life cycle niche does not, by itself, appear as frequently or as redundantly in the interviews.

STRUCTURAL IMPLICATIONS

If this theme of entrepreneurship and risk-taking is a core value in the culture of the Valley, one would expect that it would have an impact on structure, an impact on process, and an impact on reward structures in area companies. The interviews are clear that, indeed, such impacts are present. The most dominant and frequently quoted impacts related to patterns of decision making, communication, decentralization, mobility, and reward structures.

Decision Making

All of the informants agreed that they perceived decision making in their companies to be more intuitive and less formal than in the companies they had worked for or presently work with in the East. Again some exemplary quotes:

SCULLEY (Apple): I'd say that decision making in the West reflects the entrepreneurial tradition. The discipline of formal analysis and data evidence is prescribed in the East. Also, the process and channels in the organization are carefully defined. The work starts at a lower level and moves through various levels of management. In this process decisions tend to get sanitized as they move through levels of management. In the East, management has the right to say no (but really say yes) so as the project moves up people at each level want to add their little comments. It tends to be a longer process and a somewhat less innovative process, although it is certainly a more thorough process. By contrast, I see decision making in Silicon Valley as more creative, more insightful, more eclectic. The focus is on new markets, new products, new ideas. It tends to be based on less thorough analysis. Nowhere in Silicon Valley do I find the intense market and internal performance analyses characteristic of the East Coast companies I am familiar with.

FEDERMAN (Monolithic Memories): Decision making in the East was always more deliberate, more analytical and more quantitative. More classical in its analysis. In Silicon Valley, great value is placed upon the intuitive process. While one can be skeptical and posit that as an excuse for not doing homework, there is no question that we have come to value the net sum of experience as it expresses itself in intuition. We're more willing to take action based upon modest quantitative data.

LORENZINI (Siltec): Decision making in Silicon Valley is clearly more experimental. I think we're more willing to try things that may or may not work. Sometimes it will work very well and sometimes it doesn't work at all, but there is a spirit of trying something new that is different here on the West Coast.

One of the more charming anecdotes told to illustrate the style of communication was told by Flaherty of Hewlett-Packard. Earlier in his career he had worked for a firm (which he saw as typical of East Coast firms) which was subsequently purchased by Hewlett-Packard. He talked about the first major presentation that he made with the new West Coast managers. He had been asked to prepare an analysis in support of a proposal. He had only been able to obtain some very preliminary data, which was not decisive. He had presented the results hesitantly.

FLAHERTY (Hewlett-Packard): And then the free-wheeling open-shirt, short-sleeved managers said: "What do you think might work?" I hesistantly indicated that I was in favor of a change, although I couldn't prove the case. I was told to "do and see what happens." That just never would have happened in the culture of the firm under Eastern management.

If there is a tendency to be more intuitive, to be more spontaneous, to make decisions based on less analysis, what drives the culture? The informants returned to earlier themes. The first rationalization was the press of technology. The emphasis on entrepreneurship required the decision making to focus on the cutting edge of technology. In itself, this early technological emphasis implies that there is less certainty. In the absence of certainty, one reaches towards intuition. It's also true that if one wishes to capture the early phase of the product life cycle, the window of opportunity is minuscule. Given the rapid pace of technology associated with these firms, all the participants agreed on a heightened sense of time pressure and accelerated pace associated with decision making. It was clearly felt that it was better to take a chance and experiment than to wait and be more certain but miss the window of competitive opportunity. In the words of John Sculley:

SCULLEY (Apple): The essential observation I would make about our technology driven companies in Silicon Valley is time compression. Things happen more rapidly. There are fundamental changes made in a short period of time. A major product can have a half life of just a few years. You can establish a new product in a matter of months. All of this heightens the pressure to act quickly on the basis of limited evidence. The essential stake for the firm in Silicon Valley is being at the cutting edge of technology. This is entirely different from the focus on market share in established industries. In this industry (high tech) no one has any idea what share of the market is. There is no accurate way of measuring the market. Much of the time we are *creating* the market, not *sharing* the market. We can't even forecast correctly several months out because there is no way that you can use history to give you trend line.

A second aspect of a willingness to accept nonconsensual intuitions was the need for independence of engineering and technical "champions." Since no one could be sure, one had to allow a champion freedom to "make the future happen" as a result of the champion's and the team's sheer energy. If the champion was not given support for the dream, there was always the possibility the champion would join another competitor or form a start-up. Thus intuitive, nonconsensual support was reinforced by the champion's need for independence and wish to be an entrepreneur.

Communication

Another concomitant of an intuitive style of decision making was the presence of communication structures that are eclectic and decentralized.

FLAHERTY (Hewlett-Packard): The West Coast is simply more casual in its communication style. It's easier to communicate with all significant others. It's less pretentious and there are fewer status barriers. Once you're given a mandate in a project group on the West Coast, you can talk to anyone in the company at any level that might be useful in carrying out your project.

There was a wonderful story told by one manager who talked about his experiences in an East Coast company where he had worked on a project team and had wanted to discuss an idea with the vice-president. He indicated that it took him three weeks to make the appointment, two weeks before he was ushered into the office, that he made sure that he wore a pin-striped suit the day that he had the appointment, that no decision was arrived at as the result of the meeting since his revised project report had to be reviewed by several other officers in the organization, and that as a result timely action was never taken. He contrasted that with a recent circumstance in Silicon Valley, where an idea had occurred to him while jogging. He turned around, and in his sweat-suit rushed into the CEO's office during the lunch hour, shared his idea, and was given permission on the spot to go forward with the adaptation.

One should not assume, however, that the informality of communication implies a form of decentralization that "deals out" key executives. Quite by contrast, the intuitions of the key executives are seen as critical to a firm's capacity to respond intuitively to market demands.

FLAHERTY (Hewlett-Packard): At Hewlett-Packard as well as other companies in the Valley, there are still key entrepreneurs who really control much of what goes on. It's because you have the entrepreneur to talk to that you can bypass an awful lot of structure. Once one moves beyond the period of time when these entrepreneurs turn their businesses to professional managers, I think decision making will change in Silicon Valley.

This emphasis on the critical role of the entrepreneur was echoed by many of the informants. Key executive–entrepreneurs were talked about as charismatic, as understanding what was happening in technology, as being very close to the developments in the marketplace. As a result (and we will return to this theme when we deal with networking), while communication was informal in the sense of access, and decision making appeared informal by often abdicating the need for traditional rules of evidence, key executives (often founding entrepreneurs) served as critical checkpoints in the testing of ideas for rapid decision making.

OSHMAN (Rolm): I think it's very difficult in some of the large Eastern companies to know what's happening. Communication is formal. There is so much staffwork done before top managers see anything, so much report generation that you're not really involved intuitively in key decisions. This may be a function partly of size, but it's also a function of culture. It seems to go with the territory. There is an absolute desire to be highly informal on the West Coast. Individuals find it easy to communicate quickly. This informality allows us to share consensus and move rapidly.

WYTHES (Sutter Hills): The communication patterns are clearly different in Silicon Valley. There is far more openness and much less worrying about whether someone goes around you. There's not only a tendency not to follow channels, there is a deliberate attempt to stimulate a wide variety of ideas. Innovations bubble up in unexpected places. Champions receive support from unexpected sponsors. People have no sense of an organization chart in Silicon Valley. On the other hand, there are wise entrepreneurial sponsors who filter the intuitions and provide informal mandates and progress.

Decentralization

Decentralization was an elusive variable for the informants to describe accurately. Everyone agreed that the critical investment is an investment in the right people (meaning entrepreneurially oriented risk-takers). Everyone agreed that individuals (no one ever used the word *subordinates*) are granted relatively long leashes, and that loosely coupled task force groups, program groups, and design teams were a critical part of the structure of companies in the Valley. On the other hand, there was enormous energy associated with maintaining communication between the decentralized team and the executive entrepreneurial elites. There was a constant discussion of communication events, of meeting people by the pool, while jogging, in the hallways. It was clear that, while formal controls over decentralized units were relatively absent in comparison with traditional corporate America, informal communication was extraordinarily intense. The exact manner in which this was carried out is somewhat difficult to describe.

FEDERMAN (Monolothic Memories): It's possible for a Bob Noyce and a Gordon Moore to walk around Intel in open shirts. John Sculley can wear a plaid shirt to work and walk among the crazies. Having visited most of the companies in this Valley, I am always struck with the continuous interaction between senior executives and their people at all levels of the organization.

LORENZINI (Siltec): The most important communications that occur in our company are informal, the ad hoc meetings that occur when we walk around the plant. Structured meetings held between 2:30 and 3:30 p.m. on specific topics really are atypical.

WAIT (Siltec): Even as Rolm becomes a larger organization there is a pattern in communication and decentralization that is different. Top management actively deals with problems several levels below the vice-presidential level. We had a meeting this morning spontaneously associated with a major customer change. Our CEO wanted to get the story first hand. There is a willingness of top level executives to be involved.

SCULLEY (Apple): Today even in Apple where we have several thousand people at our Cupertino headquarters, people still expect that the leadership of the company should be out with them on a frequent basis. Consequently, I spend a great deal of time every day with engineers in their different groups just talking with them. Further, top management plays an important role in informal communication of events. There are things called communication meetings which I never heard of before I came to California. On occasion I have gone out in the parking lot with 600 or 700 people. Recently with our reorganization, I went over and spent an hour and talked to 2000 employees at the DeAnza College Center. You wouldn't find the Chief Executive Officer of an East Coast company engaging in that behavior.

Finally, again one should not assume that these are patterns only associated with newer firms. Listen to Bob Fuhrman at Lockheed.

FUHRMAN (Lockheed): I think in the West there's a very clear sense of team management. You can't be successful without teams. Despite all the formalities of government paperwork, there's a sense that top management must operate through teams, and we communicate freely with every member of the organization.

In summary, the critical unit of organization in Silicon Valley seems to be a loosely coupled engineering team. The team, however, is not an independent "skunkworks." It is a set of individuals with a strong sense of entrepreneurship, joined around a project mission associated with a technology-driven change, who remain in contact frequently and informally with multiple levels and functions within the company through intense informal communication.

None of the executives talked about organization charts, channels, or procedures as controlling mechanisms. Rather, they talked about allowing a spirited group of individuals focused on a developmental endeavor "to have a go" at their ideas. In turn, the team feels free and obligated to stay in touch with company leadership. Likewise, company leaders felt obligated to maintain frequent communication with the teams. In closing, it's worth reminding ourselves that this pattern was true in the largest organizations, as well as the newer and younger organizations. Bob Fuhrman, speaking for Lockheed Missiles and Space Company, commented:

FUHRMAN (Lockheed): Entrepreneurship is located in program groups at Lockheed. The program is the center of loyalty and the center of innovation. I think in the older firms in the aerospace tradition there is much stronger functional management. The overlying aircraft firms tend towards very strong functional management groupings. We feel this stifles entrepreneurship. Individuals are loyal to their function (engineering, marketing management) as opposed to creatively aggregating resources to get an innovative job done. I'm not sure we could have carried this off (decentralized programs) if we had remained in Burbank. Moving from Burbank helped us pick up the spirit of innovative program teams which have facilitated our success here in Sunnyvale.

Mobility

If this loosely coupled structure and emphasis in entrepreneurship has a cost, there seems to be agreement about this essential cost. It's not the cost of failure. In the culture of the Valley one can fail, rise, and begin again without embarrassment. Rather, the cost is employee turnover; indeed, the Valley is a frenzied place of labor mobility.

Deeply rooted in the Silicon Valley culture is the belief in small, flexible organizations. Fuhrman speaks about the fact that a contribution of the culture in Silicon Valley has been to create flexible program management by means of confederations of small organizational teams, with substantial autonomy during the life of their program. These smaller organizations provide the excitement and the basis for innovation. But there is another story associated with small flexible organizations: In the mythology of the Valley the team hopes to share in a big win and big dollars. If this opportunity is not available inside, it is seen as associated with leaving your present employer.

LORENZINI (Siltec). The stories that everyone has in the back of their minds is that people have made millions of dollars by starting their own successful companies. It's really difficult to match that increase in net worth internally in a normal organization. Inevitably you have employees moving to another organization and setting up separate projects with large equity stakes, or founding new businesses.

There's hardly anyone in the Valley who can't tell the stories of Jobs, Wozniak, Bushnell, Packard, Hewlett and other entrepreneurial heroes. Deep in the mind of each employee is an implicit belief that one can be an entrepreneur at 23, or an entrepreneur at 53. There is no age, social stratum or status that precludes the possibility of a new beginning. There are two types of new beginnings: one is the classic entrepreneurial start-up company. Another is the possibility of going with another organization where equity rewards will be more closely tied to the entrepreneurial adventure which your prior company couldn't fit into its strategic plan.

OSHMAN (Rolm): One of the realities of Silicon Valley is that you can walk right next door and get a new job. There are continuous job offers for anybody at any level who is any good from other companies in the area. There is the added competition from venture capital ready to finance new ventures. There is a great deal of money available at all times to finance any reasonable idea. As a result, if you don't recognize innovation in your own organization, a venture capitalist will.

Rates of turnover in the firms in Silicon Valley often seem scandalous compared with national data. Seventeen percent turnover rates among scientific and technical participants in organizations are not unusual. Managers as well as engineers move from company to company or from company to start-up.

Most of the informants felt that the role of universities (MIT scholars or Stanford engineering spinoffs) was overplayed. The general consensus was that the major spawning grounds for start-ups were other companies, as opposed to spinoffs from universities. The willingness of people to leave companies and to initiate start-ups, while giving Silicon Valley an edge in the development of entrepreneurial activity, has also demanded a unique pattern of rewards.

Reward Structures

OSHMAN (Rolm): There is a difference in the reward structures for our people. Key employees don't care about things like pensions. They don't have a concern about long-term appointments. They have great self-confidence. They are very independent people. Therefore, things like guaranteed pension programs and unusual medical programs are not very important. They really are not worried about paternalistic or egalitarian kinds of rewards and compensation. They are very *happy not* to get a reward if they fail, but if they *succeed* they want a very significant, tangible, and unusual reward. People here believe in entrepreneurial rewards and they want a shot at it.

SCULLEY (Apple): I admit when I first came from the East I saw mobility as a lack of loyalty. I've been here long enough to see that it really isn't lack of loyalty. It is simply the mores of the Valley. Here it is accepted that people aren't going to spend their entire career with you. We don't have a pension program and no one particularly cares, because nobody expects to be here until he/she is 65 years old. I think that's probably true of many companies in the Valley. The world in which Apple employees live is a world in which they come from little companies, move to a larger company, then move back to another little company. I think you can cope with this as long as you understand it. The ground rules are different. But it does create a labor pattern that is unique.

All of the informants talked about discussions with colleagues from lower organizational levels who came to visit concerning the possibility of either joining another firm or joining a start-up group. None of the informants attempt to penalize talented people who leave their own organization. They expect loyalty from people while they are part of the organization, but they understand that part of the culture of the Valley is a sense of freedom. If the executive perceives one of his or her people has a technical or scientific opportunity that cannot be realized in the priorities of their own company, the attitude is: "I think they should move. I moved and started this company (or this program).

They deserve the right to move and start their company (or new program in Company X)."

To be sure, as much as possible, the executives would like people to find opportunities for entrepreneurship inside their company. But a certain percentage of the time they realize it is not possible and they see part of their obligation to assist the continuous spinoff process that has created a unique and prolific genealogy in Silicon Valley.

SCULLEY (Apple): The mobility among people strikes me as radically different than the world I came from out East. There is far more mobility and there is far less real risk in people's careers. When someone is fired or leaves on the East coast, it's a real trauma in their lives. If they are fired or leave here, it doesn't mean very much. They just go off and do something else. There is no penalty or very little penalty associated with that. I think the impermanence that you see in the walls of offices, the mobility of the physical ecology is entirely different.

If I want to go back East to start a company the infrastructure that you have to tap into doesn't exist or is difficult to find. Where do you go to find accountants who understand start-ups? Where do you go to find law-yers? Where do you find people who can just move into an open space, create the office for you, set up your furniture and get you going? The whole attitude of facilitating start-ups here has a tremendous bearing on labor policy. Out here the way Silicon Valley companies are managed reflects the start-up mentality. For example, one of the things that struck me when I came to Silicon Valley was the impermanence of all the facilities. The walls are all temporary because everyone knows that the configurations will be changed six months later. And my experience at Apple has been that everything does change in six months increments. The idea of per-manent walls with windows and doors that was part of corporate America is not part of Silicon Valley.

Organizations respond in two ways to this challenge. The first is to do what's possible to keep the individual inside the organization to benefit the strategy of the firm. As a result, compensation programs reflect emphasis on stock options and the opportunity to share in sub-stantial earnings associated with major breakthroughs. By contrast, there is much less emphasis on job security and pension plans. Making money is important in the Valley. The chance to "win big" has to be built into the reward structure internally, or talent will seek to "win big" externally. Some companies have even gone so far as to share in the underwriting of entrepreneurial businesses started by their former employees. While the feeling is that the "jury is out" with respect to this practice, the pattern of exceptional labor mobility has become part of the culture of the area.

NETWORKING

There seem to be three facilities of networking as a critical variable in the Valley. The first is that the area is compact geographically. With mountains on one side and the tidal flat marshes of the San Francisco Bay on the other, individuals are accessible to each other geographically. The second facilitator is that key figures are still very much part of the communication hub. Third is implicit in the mobility, discussed above. People have many contacts with prior employees.

SCULLEY (Apple): The heritage of this Valley is that it's driven by a few individual gatekeepers. In this Valley there are probably a half-dozen or a dozen leaders who started their companies, are still associated with their companies or with the industry, and provide a network. You are either in the network or you aren't in the network. The network is a very small one. These individuals all talk to each other, see each other quite frequently, know what's going on, and provide guidance to many start-up enterprises in the area. I think this network represents a key aspect of the character of the Valley.

The network, however, is not simply associated with elites. It is also part of the scientific and technical culture which allows engineers to stay close to developments in technology and close to potential adaptions by clients.

LORENZINI (Siltec): There are people gathered together once or once every two months to discuss every area of common scientific interest in the Valley. Around every technological subject, or every engineering concern, you have meeting groups that tend to foster new ideas and innovate. People rub shoulders and share ideas.

This networking (while somewhat infamous in the literature of international espionage and the leaking of "secrets") is part of the stimulation for the constant and rapid-paced change. A company president in San Diego indicated that the thing he missed most in leaving Silicon Valley was this informal networking.

The institutional luncheon circuit made it possible for companies to serve as faculties to each other regarding technologies, customer developments, and market potentials. In San Diego we can't share any secrets. I miss the forum of communication that was characteristic of the Valley.

MARKET-DRIVEN TECHNOLOGY

There seems to be a consensus that a final driving force in the Valley is technology. The Valley in many ways has become one vast R & D park. Many firms have moved their manufacturing overseas, or to other parts of the country both because of land scarcity and the cost of labor. Nonetheless, they wish to keep a corporate foot in the Valley for two reasons: (1) It possesses a fluid talent pool close to the cutting edge of new technologies, and (2) it is a source of endless idea generation regarding new niches that meet new customer needs.

LORENZINI (Siltec): It's obvious that our only advantage is truly understanding customer needs as the primary driving force. This means that we must constantly force engineering and manufacturing to listen even if it means grabbing the manufacturing guys by the necktie and repeating again, "listen." It's critical to balance the marketing function which has to have enough power and ability to shape priorities along with the technological and manufacturing wizards.

Observers of the companies in the Valley who have perspectives on other parts of the nation express the market and technology link even more strongly.

WYTHES (Sutter Hills): With respect to parts of the organization that initiate priorities, Silicon Valley is much more market-driven. Apple created a market that didn't exist for personal computers. Firms are engaged in the design of technologies for which markets don't even exist. I think the rest of the country is far more concerned with market share, or far more concerned with decreasing costs through better management in order to penetrate or capture a particular product line. By contrast, Silicon Valley still emphasizes new products driven by new technologies and the creation of new markets for new technologies. The Valley obviously has less of a manufacturing advantage. This is clearly a weakness in the West. However, the Valley has an instinct for innovation and entrepreneurship around the initiation of new products and market innovations. This will have to be its comparative advantage. It will have to be more market- and technology-driven because it has no unique advantage with respect to decreasing costs or penetrating traditional markets.

THE FUTURE

We have tried to capture the business culture of Silicon Valley. There is no implication that this particular culture is the only fertile humus for technology. The business culture of Route 128 as a geographical region is entirely different. It is more formal, orderly, has greater employee stability, focuses on long-term market share, and achieves decisions through a more ordered analytical process.

It is not the intention of this essay to be normative. It is, rather, to examine the hypothesis that workplace behavior is influenced by regional and environmental variables that create a "business culture" specific to the region. We believe that the interviews attest to this reality.

Nor would we portray the culture or environment of the Valley as laudatory in all regards. For example, with respect to environment, everyone agrees that a dominant weakness is that the sheer physical ecology of the Valley is beginning to constrain its potential. The double-edged ecological sword poised to limit future growth is housing and transportation.

FEDERMAN (Monolithic Memories): Housing is a stumbling block, especially for people who grew up in the Midwest or the East. There is a quality of neighborhood and house to which they aspired that is not achievable here. It is rewarding to live on two acres surrounded by trees. Stable neighbor-hoods are attractive rewards. While we in Santa Clara can create exciting equity packages, even that enrichment often fails to deliver some of the basic wants and/or needs.

Increasing population density, an impacted transportation network, increased pollution, and a high cost of living are all taking their toll.

A more radical threat is the maturing of the electronic industry itself and increased international competition. Doomsayers say that "Silicon Valley" focused on electronics will see an aging and maturing cycle not unlike machine tools and automobiles. Optimists argue that while certain types of products may mature and take on attributes of a com-modities oligopoly, the electronic revolution is still in its infancy, and "user friendly" adaptations to meet new needs will be virtually endless. They argue the flexible, fluid, market-technology, driven, innovative culture of Silicon Valley will allow for future generations of entrepre-neurs to replicate the Silicon Valley success story independent of the fate of selective older companies.

However, regardless of one's prognostication of the future, or personal evaluation of the pros and cons of the culture of the present, there is no doubt that it would be difficult to replicate in other regions the unique business culture which exists in Silicon Valley in 1986.

Finally, is it a model for the future? Many authors argue that loosely coupled fluid organizations are prerequisites for organizations which wish to focus on innovation. Silicon Valley is a laboratory which con-veys both some of the advantages and disadvantages of such organi-zational models. It is clearly not a culture for all businesses or all individuals but deserves careful scrutiny as we look toward the future.

NOTES

1. This report is part of a larger study which included interviews with ten executives from Route 128 in Massachusetts (see chapter 2).

2. Among the changes that have taken place are the following. In the New England sample, the Adage and Lexidata companies have merged, and Bob Miller of Data General in Massachusetts moved to the Silicon Valley area. John Poduska left Apollo to start another company in Massachusetts, and Jim Berrett left Computervision. In the Silicon Valley sample, IBM has taken over Rolm.

4

The Nine Nations of North America and the Value Basis of Geographic Segmentation

Lynn R. Kahle

Geographic segmentation is a useful concept in consumer theory (Hawkins, Best, and Coney 1983). Different regions of the United States have different cultures, climates, histories, and resources. These differences and others influence such consumer activities as use of media, shopping areas, products, and services; therefore, any serious examination or utilization of consumer behavior knowledge ought minimally to consider the potential importance of geography. A number of marketing managers already realize this fact. For example, R. J. Reynolds promotes different brands of cigarettes in different geographic areas, and General Foods flavors Maxwell House coffee differently, based on region. People in the West prefer stronger coffee (Kotler 1983). At a most basic level the values of the regions differ, which provides the psychological basis of geographic variation in consumer behavior.

Except for several highly specialized approaches, such as unique purpose segmentation (e.g., soft drink marketing is different in jurisdictions *with* [versus *without*] "Bottle Bills") or postal zip code segmentation, probably the most attention has been given to the Bureau of Census (BOC) divisions of the country and to the revision of the South used by such places as the University of Michigan Survey Research Center. This essay tests whether values differ as a function of BOC geographic regions and as a function of another theory of regions by Joel Garreau.

Garreau (1981) proposed an alternative conceptualization of regions

Lynn R. Kahle, "The Nine Nations of North America and the Value Basis of Geographic Segmentation." Reprinted from *Journal of Marketing* 50, no. 2 (1986): 37–47, published by the American Marketing Association.

within the United States in his book, *The Nine Nations of North America*. He has traveled across North America, taking copious notes in the tradition of an anthropological participant observer. His divisions theoretically follow cultural rather than political boundaries, and the nations extend throughout North America and the Caribbean, rather than just through the United States. Indeed, of his nine nations, only Dixie lies entirely within the United States, and Quebec lies entirely outside of it. The nine nations, as conceived by Garreau and based on his anthropological research, are described in table 4.1; the BOC regions are summarized in table 4.2.

Most academic reviews of Garreau's book have been quite favorable (Baerwald 1983; Salter 1983; Williams 1982); however, Williams criticizes the book because "the lack of an undergirding epistemological exploration weakens the secondary structural theory" (174). Sometimes Garreau's logic lapses (Baerwald 1983, 215), as when he blames New England's problems on the "sad surplus of Harvard architects" (Garreau 1981, 30). But such assertions probably more represent unsuccessful humor through hyperbole than unsuccessful logic through syllogisms. More common descriptions of the Nine Nations theory by scholars include "effective" (Salter 1983), "imaginative" (Polsby 1981–1982), and "first-rate" and "basically sound" (Baerwald 1983). Although little new empirical work has to date resulted from the theory, clearly, the idea of Nine Nations by Garreau has generated theoretical interest in geographic division by such diverse disciplines as geography (Shelly, Archer, and White 1984), diplomacy (Feld and Brylski 1983), politics (Polsby 1981–1982), ekistics (Henrikson 1983), landscape planning (Young et al. 1983), business management (Bisesi 1985), and, of course, marketing (Major 1983).

What has not yet been independently established is whether Garreau's book is also empirically justifiable. Garreau claims, "Each nation has its own list of desires. . . . Most important, each nation has a distinct prism through which it views the world" (p. 2). Important research questions can be posed concerning Garreau's propositions. Are these desires and prisms more accurately described by the Nine Nations theory than the nine regions of the BOC? Do the Nine Nations encompass more homogeneous cultures and values than the other nine regions? More importantly, do the Nine Nations describe segments that differ in the consumption of goods and services?

The answers to these questions will help determine the utility of the Nine Nations theory for geographic segmentation, which is in large part based on the assumption that geographic differences reflect differences in values. The social science concept of *value* probably comes as close as any social science concept to an operationalization of Garreau's concepts of *desires* and *prisms* through which to view the world.

Table 4.1
Summary of Garreau's Nine Nations of North America

Nation	Capital City	Location	Values of Differential Importance
New England	Boston	Extends North from central Connecticut generally following traditional definition	not sense of accomplishment, self-fulfillment
Quebec	Quebec City	Province of Quebec	self-respect?
The Foundry	Detroit	Surrounds the Great Lakes (excluding Superior) and extends to the Atlantic	sense of accomplishment, being well-respected?
Dixie	Atlanta	Traditional South extended north to Indianapolis and St. Louis, cut off in the west at Dallas, and excluding south Florida	not self-fulfillment, self-respect?
The Islands	Miami	South Florida and the Latin American Rim	security
Empty Quarter	Denver	Rocky Mountains; excludes eastern Colorado but includes eastern Washington, Oregon, and California	sense of belonging, sense of accomplishment
Breadbasket	Kansas City	Well north of Winnipeg, west nearly to Denver, as far east as Indianapolis--it excludes Midwestern cities such as Milwaukee, Chicago, and Cincinnati but includes most of the farmland in Illinois, Wisconsin, the Dakotas, Nebraska and Oklahoma	not fun and enjoyment in life, warm relationships with others
MexAmerica	Los Angeles	Extends as far north as the San Joaquin Valley of California and Pueblo, Colorado, but not as far north as Las Vegas or Austin	sense of accomplishment, self-respect
Ecotopia	San Francisco	Follows the Pacific Ocean from south of San Francisco to Alaska	not sense of accomplishment, self-fulfillment

Table 4.2
Summary of Bureau of Census Regions

Region	Collapsed Region	States Included
New England	Northeast	ME, NH, VT, MA, RI, CT
Middle Atlantic	Northeast	NY, PA, NJ, DE
South Atlantic	South	WV, MD, DC, VA, NC, SC, GA, FL
East North Central	Midwest	WI, IL, MI, IN, OH
East South Central	South	KY, TN, MS, AL
West North Central	Midwest	ND, SD, MN, NE, KS, IA, MO
West South Central	South	TX, OK, AR, LA
Mountain	West	NV, ID, MT, WY, UT, AZ, CO, NM
Pacific	West	OR, WA, CA
Border South*	South	WV, MD, DC, OK, KY, TN
Solid South*	South	VA, NC, SC, GA, FL, AL, MS, LA, AR

*These two regions are sometimes used to replace East South Central, West South Central, and South Atlantic

Garreau makes numerous references to the assumption that social values underlie his conceptualization of nations. Even in the preface, he clarifies his distinction between political borders and nations by noting, "Our values are separable from our regimes" (p. xvi). He describes Quebec as "A place where people feel like a nation. In food, music, fashions, values" (p. 366). And he describes why Americans sometimes like to move to a different nation: "It allows us to try on different values" (p. 12).

Repeatedly, he characterizes the nations themselves by their values. Ecotopia has a "clash of values" (p. 265) with the Empty Quarter. People in the Breadbasket "genuflect in the direction of values they believe are taught by the family farm" (p. 350). Once it would have been "unthinkable to value leisure over the honest gains from hard labor" (p. 337) in the Breadbasket. Now it is thinkable but not often thought. "Laid back is still a regional idea. It doesn't necessarily play in Peoria" (p. 337). The Empty Quarter is a "repository of values" (p. 303). The concept of *California* fails to explain "anything terribly important"

(p. 5) because "San Francisco and Los Angeles are not just two cities. They represent two value structures" (p. 5). Later, he again describes California as a "monumental clash of values" (p. 264)—the values of Ecotopia versus MexAmerica. Chicago's importance derives from "directing trade in values and enterprise" (p. 5).

The present study examines value differences in regions as defined in the Nine Nations theory, the Census Bureau approach, the Survey Research Center approach, and the collapsed quadrants. Values, which have been shown to relate to consumer behavior (e.g., Beatty et al. 1985; Gutman 1982; Kahle 1984a, 1984b.; Pitts and Woodside 1984; Pollay 1984; Prakash 1984), were measured using a system recently shown to relate to a number of important social phenomena (Kahle 1983).

VALUES OF THE NINE NATIONS

Many specific values may be related to certain nations. The quotation we saw above illustrates why the Breadbasket should devalue a leisure orientation described as *fun and enjoyment in life* (cf. Pottick 1983). Rather, Breadbasket people should value *warm relationships with others*. "As people stumble toward an explanation of what they value in their friends and neighbors around here, the words are *always* " 'open,' 'friendly,' 'hardworking,' 'there when you need them' " (Garreau 1981, 350). Eisert and Kahle (1983) have shown that, among Americans, friendliness is most closely associated with valuing *warm relationships with others*. "Individuals who value warm relationships with others appear to be those people who have satisfying and intimate relationships with others" (p. 221).

In the Empty Quarter state of Utah, formal religious affiliation is not as crucial for acceptance as some outsiders think. "It's not being a Mormon; it's whether your values coincide" (p. 325). And what are the central Empty Quarter values? "It's a family oriented way of life" (p. 313). Eisert (1983) has shown that the strongest family-oriented value is *sense of belonging*. People who endorse this value belong to their families. They "report the most value fulfillment and satifaction from marriage, parenting, and housework" (p. 165).

The Empty Quarter and Ecotopia take opposite views toward economic development. "Development is a religion in the Empty Quarter" (Garreau 1981, 306), but Ecotopia takes "a jaundiced view of development" (p. 9). "There are some Ecotopian paths into the 21st century that are very different from the bigger-is-better, growth-is-inevitably-good, sons-of-the-pioneers philosophies that are especially well represented in the MexAmerican and Empty Quarter nations of the West" (p. 250). Development and business prowess have been associated with the value of *sense of accomplishment* (Pottick 1983; Timmer and Kahle 1983a).

Ecotopians share their antimaterialistic ideals with New England, not with the rest of the West, according to Garreau. "If Ecotopia feels kin to any of the Nine Nations, it is to New England, from which so many of the Pacific Northwest's original settlers came, and with which so many of its successful social patterns are traded" (p. 2). "The talk is about the quality of life in New England for the voluntarily poor" (p. 45). "In New England poverty has become rather chic" (p. 30). Thus, we may hypothesize kinship between Ecotopia and New England, on the one hand, and between accomplishment-oriented MexAmerica and the Empty Quarter, on the other.

Ecotopians do "value self-sufficiency" (Garreau 1981, 272). "A person can live simply, and relatively close to nature" (p. 275) in Ecotopia. "Even the middle class has moved on the idea that a person may have to lower his monetarily described standard of living in order to raise his overall quality of life" (p. 262). This dual emphasis on self-sufficiency and quality of life is manifested among people who endorse *self-fulfillment* as the primary value (Kahle and Pottick 1983; Piner 1983; Yankelovich 1981).

From Mexico, MexAmericans inherit "fundamental values" of "Harmony. Within oneself, among others, within nature" (Garreau 1981, 231). Such internally oriented harmony may be manifested in *self-respect*. Timmer and Kahle (1983b, 73) conclude that people who value self-respect "want satisfaction in their own minds about their lives." To value self-respect, it may be necessary to be satisfied with one-self and be in harmony with one's social and natural surroundings.

Garreau builds his concept of The Islands around drug traffic and its associated crime. He cites law enforcement officials who believe that drug crimes and homicide are out of control. Timmer and Kahle (1983a) note that when people value *security*, their choice "may be in part tapping the fear associated with living in a crime-ridden neighborhood" (p. 95). Thus, people in The Islands should be expected to value security.

Although Garreau does not unambiguously hypothesize any specific values related to Dixie, The Foundry, or Quebec, we may speculate about the possible links. These links are indicated with question marks in table 4.1.

HYPOTHESES

To state it more formally, the major hypothesis guiding this research is:

H1: Values vary as a function of regions within the coterminous United States, regardless of whether *region* is defined as the Bureau of Census defines it, as some have revised the BOC definition, or as Garreau defines it.

Within the context of Garreau's theory, we may state several more specific hypotheses about how nations should vary:

H2: Sense of accomplishment is less often endorsed as most important in New England than in other nations.

H3: Self-fulfillment is more often endorsed as most important in New England than in other nations.

H4: Security is more often endorsed as most important in The Islands than in other nations.

H5: Sense of belonging is more often endorsed as most important in the Empty Quarter than in other nations.

H6: Sense of accomplishment is more often endorsed as most important in the Empty Quarter than in other nations.

H7: The value of fun and enjoyment in life is less often endorsed as most important in the Breadbasket than in other nations.

H8: The value of warm relationships with others is more often endorsed as most important in the Breadbasket than in other nations.

H9: Sense of accomplishment is more often endorsed as most important in MexAmerica than in other nations.

H10: Self-respect is more often endorsed as most important in MexAmerica than in other nations.

H11: Sense of accomplishment is less often endorsed as most important in Ecotopia than in other nations.

H12: Self-fulfillment is more often endorsed as most important in Ecotopia than in other nations.

Several other hypotheses may be inferred from Garreau's work, although they are not as explicitly stated and are, therefore, less noteworthy as tests of his theory.

H13: Sense of accomplishment is more often endorsed as most important in The Foundry than in other nations.

H14: Being well-respected is more often endorsed as most important in The Foundry than in other nations.

H15: Self-fulfillment is less often endorsed as most important in Dixie than in other nations.

H16: Self-respect is more often endorsed as most important in Dixie than in other nations.

METHOD

The survey involved face-to-face interviews with 2,264 noninstitutionalized adults over twenty years of age who resided in the coterminous United States, of whom 2,235 supplied usable data for the analyses presented here. All sampling, interviews, and data cleaning were conducted by the professional staff at the University of Michigan's Survey Research Center (SRC). Kish and Hess (1965) have described the multistage probability area design utilized to draw the sample here. This procedure is designed to yield a national (but not necessarily regional) representative sample. The response rate for this study was 71 percent, which is lower than one would like but typical of contemporary, quality, face-to-face surveys. More details of the survey, which was presented to respondents as a "Study of Modern Living," are presented in several books that have described other aspects of the research (Iglehart 1979; Kahle 1983; Tamir 1982; Veroff, Douvan, and Kulka 1981), and in numerous articles.

The data for this sample have been compared to the census data obtained at the same time (Veroff, Kulka, and Douvan 1981) in 1976, as represented in the Bureau of the Census Current Population Survey. The percentages for sex, age, race, marital status, education, income, and region were quite comparable. The differences for region, for example, were as follows, with the census data given second: New England (6 percent versus 6 percent), Middle Atlantic (15 percent versus 18 percent), East North Central (18 percent versus 19 percent), West North Central (10 percent versus 8 percent), South Atlantic (15 percent versus 16 percent), East South Central (8 percent versus 6 percent), West South Central (11 percent versus 10 percent), Mountain (3 percent versus 4 percent), and Pacific (14 percent versus 13 percent).

The sampling areas (counties, cities, sections of counties, or sections of cities) were assigned Nine Nations coding categories by three separate judges working independently. Initial agreement on classification was 96 percent. Discrepancies among judges were resolved by the author through further examination of the maps and text of Garreau's book and through discussions with other scholars. Rather than eliminate data, Garreau's "aberrations" (Manhattan and Washington, D.C.) were classified within their geographic location, The Foundry. Garreau found some behavior to be unusual in New York City. But examples of unusual behavior can be found in all nations; therefore, New York and Washington were not excluded. Furthermore, one could argue that many of the extremes from New York City, at least, embody the dreams and spoils of The Foundry. And even Garreau himself seems to forget from time to time that New York and Washington have supposedly been excluded from The Foundry. For example, he says that most of the continental media are headquartered in The Foundry (p. 65)—an obvious reference to New York City and Washington, D.C. Also, the inferential consequences are not too great for including Washington and Manhattan, since only 15 people were selected for this sample. Alaska and Hawaii, two other aberrations, are not parts of the coterminous United States.

The measure of values asked respondents to select their most important value from the following list of nine values: sense of belonging, excitement, fun and enjoyment in life, warm relationships with others, self-fulfillment, being well respected, a sense of accomplishment, security, and self-respect. Because only 0.2 percent of the sample selected excitement, it was collapsed into fun and enjoyment in life. The rationale of the measure has been described in more detail in a book on the topic (Kahle 1983). It has been called the List of Values (LOV) by Beatty et al. (1985). Here, several demographics correlates of values were described, including age, sex, income, race, education, religion, birth order, and occupation—but not region.

RESULTS

Table 4.3 presents the pattern of values observed for the Nine Nations. Overall, values and the Nine Nations are not related as a statistically significant level of $p < 0.01$ (chosen because of the large sample size),[1] using a chi square with the Yates correction factor. In tests of hypotheses 2 through 16, only one of the hypothesized results emerged as a significant tendency—the Empty Quarter values sense of accomplishment *less* than other nations. This difference is in the *opposite* direction of hypothesis 6.[2]

Tables 4.4 and 4.5 present useful information about the value structure of the United States by dividing along political rather than cultural borders. Tables 4.3 and 4.4 more clearly divide along borders that meaningfully capture values, with the value divisions more distinctive. The quadrants in table 4.3, for example, manifest correlates of some of the Nine Nations hypotheses more clearly than did the data in table 4.2. For example, the Midwest (Breadbasket) selects warm relationships with others more often and fun-enjoyment-excitement less often than any other group. The South (The Islands, Dixie) selects security more often than any other region. Using the Border South and the Solid South in place of East South Central, West South Central, and South Atlantic in table 4.4 also shows differences in values as a function of region, $x^2(56) = 90.22$, $p = 0.0025$. Thus, only the Nine Nations system fails to manifest evidence consistent with hypothesis 1. The BOC has not articulated a value theory from which testable hypotheses can be drawn.

Table 4.3
Distribution of Values across the Nine Nations

Values	New England	The Foundry	Dixie	The Islands	Bread-basket	Mex-America	Empty Quarter	Eco-topia	N
Self-respect	22.5%	20.5%	22.5%	25.0%	17.9%	22.7%	35.3%	18.0%	471
Security	21.7	19.6	23.3	15.6	20.2	17.3	17.6	19.6	461
Warm relation-ships with others	14.2	16.7	13.8	9.4	20.5	18.0	5.9	18.5	362
Sense of accomplishment	14.2	11.7	10.0	9.4	12.4	11.3	8.8	12.2	254
Self-fulfillment	9.2	9.9	8.4	3.1	7.5	16.0	5.9	12.7	214
Being well-respected	8.3	8.7	11.0	15.6	10.1	2.7	2.9	4.2	196
Sense of belonging	5.0	8.4	7.5	12.5	7.8	6.7	17.6	7.9	177
Fun-enjoyment-excitement	5.0	4.5	3.5	9.4	3.6	5.3	5.9	6.9	100
Total	100.0	100.0	100.0	100.0	100.0	100.0	100.0	100.0	2235
N	120	750	653	32	307	150	34	189	

$a_X^2 (49) = 68.41$, n.s

Table 4.4
Distribution of Values across Quadrants of the United States

Values	East	Midwest	South	West	N
Self-respect	19.7%	19.1%	23.4%	21.6%	471
Security	18.9	21.6	22.0	18.4	461
Warm relationships with others	16.0	17.8	14.5	17.1	362
Sense of accomplishment	13.2	12.5	9.2	11.4	254
Self-fulfillment	9.5	9.0	8.1	13.5	214
Being well-respected	8.0	9.1	11.6	3.6	196
Sense of belonging	8.4	7.3	8.0	8.3	177
Fun-enjoyment-excitement	6.3	3.3	3.4	6.2	100
Total	100.0	100.0	100.0	100.0	2235
N	476	634	740	385	

$a_x^2(21) = 50.50$, p = 0.0003

DISCUSSION

The Nine Nations concept thus provides us with regions that are not more evident in values, in contrast to the traditional census regions. Certainly, Garreau has given us a more literate understanding of North America (e.g., the name *Breadbasket* is more literate than *West North Central*), but the empirical evidence on values does not seem to uphold the theory. Why does such a seemingly good theory predict values so poorly?

One difficulty with Garreau's systems is that many places deviate from their region. That Ecotopian hotbed, Santa Monica, lies in MexAmerica. The very name of Battle Creek, Michigan, makes one think of cereals, yet Battle Creek is a Foundry City, not a Breadbasket city. Parts of Texas have such oil reserves that they seem to belong in the resource-rich Empty Quarter, but the Empty Quarter does not extend as far south as Texas.

Another difficulty with the Nine Nations approach is the high diversity of culture within an area. The main Foundry city of Detroit, for example, celebrates its ethnic diversity each summer. In many regions

Table 4.5
Distribution of Values across Census Regions of the United States

Values	New England	Middle Atlantic	South Atlantic	East South Central	East North Central	West North Central	West South Central	Mountain	Pacific	N
Self-respect	22.6%	18.6%	23.1%	23.4%	20.2%	16.7%	23.8%	29.2%	19.8%	471
Security	21.2	18.0	18.3	26.9	22.1	20.6	23.8	18.1	18.5	461
Warm relationships with others	13.9	16.8	15.7	11.4	16.0	21.6	14.9	15.3	17.6	362
Sense of accomplishment	13.9	13.0	10.7	9.6	11.4	14.7	6.8	8.3	12.1	254
Self-fulfillment	8.0	10.0	10.1	7.8	9.3	8.3	5.5	6.9	15.0	214
Being well-respected	8.8	7.7	9.8	12.0	10.0	7.4	14.0	4.2	3.5	196
Sense of belonging	7.3	8.8	9.2	7.8	7.4	6.9	6.4	13.9	7.0	177
Fun-enjoyment-excitement	4.4	7.1	3.3	1.2	3.5	3.9	4.7	4.2	6.4	100
Total	100.0	100.0	100.0	100.0	100.0	100.0	100.0	100.0	100.0	2235
N	137	339	338	167	430	204	235	72	313	2235

$a_X^2(56) = 90.22$, $p = 0.0025$.

of the country, blacks and whites living in the same county speak with entirely different dialects and have entirely different experiences in life. Miami has many types of people, only some of whom have ties to The Islands. Powell and Valencia (1984), for example, found ethnic differences in values to be much more pronounced than differences attributable to cities from different regions.

Perhaps North America has more than nine regions. For example, Dixie may have tobacco, peach, cotton, mountain, and oil regions with entirely different values. Even Florida may have three regions rather than just two—The Islands and Dixie. Central Florida is rapidly becoming the tourist and retirement center for The Foundry. As another example, perhaps The Foundry should be viewed as several regions. Certainly, the Great Lakes Foundry differs from the Atlantic Foundry. Even the Empty Quarter concept may mistakenly link pious Salt Lake City with frolicsome Las Vegas.

All of these criticisms of Garreau could apply as well to the BOC regions, which did show variation in values. We must, therefore, turn to other accounts to explain the BOC variation.

Political boundaries, such as the BOC uses, regardless of their source, tend to develop significance apart from other influences. For example, politicians try to pull states together into coalitions. The ideal Indiana coalition may differ from the ideal Illinois coalition, but each must homogenize or transcend the different values that may come into conflict in those states. Politicians must seek to promote what is true of all regions within political borders and minimize differences within their constituencies. But, by their very nature, successful region-bridging skills tend to break down regionalism, often replacing it with pride toward political boundaries. This tendency, in turn, draws people within political boundaries toward one another.

Other forces also push political units toward homogeneity. Shared history and shared loyalties are two factors. In spite of three separate nations in Indiana (Dixie, Breadbasket, The Foundry), it's hard to imagine any area (except perhaps cities such as West Lafayette and South Bend, which have other universities) in the state that would not generally be pleased at the Indiana University basketball team winning a national championship. Consumers do not have intense regional pride (except perhaps in Dixie and New England) because regions are harder to identify. However, people and media do often identify with their states. Collections of states, then, may constitute more meaningful regions, even if there is no good historicocultural reason that they should.

Two other forces that push regions together are shared climates and resources. When the federal government rules on water projects or forest management projects, the impact is felt primarily in the West. The announcement of a grain embargo will predictably bring responses from senators representing all of the West North Central states and may initiate collective action from them because the Midwest suffers the most from grain embargoes.

A final flaw may be that Garreau has attended to what is salient or distinctive, rather than what is typical. Certainly, some people in Miami and Los Angeles speak Spanish, but both cities have prominent English-speaking populations as well. Some people in Ecotopia and New England oppose development, but many people there want jobs. Speaking Spanish or opposition to development may be salient and even distinctive in some regions, but they may nevertheless be minority positions.

It is unlikely but possible that this study might have found more compelling evidence for the Nine Nations if Canadian participants had been included. But marketers usually do observe national boundaries because regulations and monetary units differ across them. Including French-speaking Quebec may have improved predictions, but any other system of North American regions would also probably include Quebec and also comparably improve predictions by including it. Thus, the relative merit of Garreau's theory versus other theories would not improve by including Quebec, and Garreau otherwise argues that adding English-speaking Canada involves adding more of the same information, not entirely different information. Finally, the English-speaking parts of Canada constitute a relatively small percentage of North America's population. Thus, adding Canada probably would not alter the inference about the utility of Garreau's theory.

As with any empirical study, it is also possible that findings from this study resulted from Type I or Type II errors. Table 4.2 may actually display differences that would have shown up with a larger sample size. For example, the dramatic differences in the Empty Quarter may have failed to attain significance because of the sparse population of that region, not because of lack of true difference. Conversely, tables 4.3 and 4.4 may have detected differences that in fact do not exist. The most parsimonious response to these possibilities seems to acknowledge them but limits inferences about significance of the tables to statistical results.

IMPLICATIONS FOR MARKETING MANAGERS

Contemporary marketing managers must recognize that many consumers purchase various products and services in part based on the value fulfillment obtained from owning or using those products and services (Beatty et al. 1985). Values have been utilized for product development, segmentation, positioning, media selection, promotion, and environmental scanning (cf. Pitts and Woodside 1984). In media selection, for example, people who value sense of belonging watch "That's Incredible" and like *Reader's Digest*, people who value fun and enjoyment in life watch "Hill Street Blues" and read *Rolling Stone*, *Cosmopolitan*, and *Playboy*, and people who value self-fulfillment read *Time* and do not watch as much television as others (Beatty et al. 1985).

Likewise, managing employees depends in large part on the values of the employees and the corporate value culture (Deal and Kennedy 1982; Peters and Waterman 1982). These data show that those employee values can differ from region to region. Marketing managers should be aware of employee values in different regions.

The very meaning of a product can differ as a function of the values of a consumer. For example, a personal computer may be a necessity for a person who values a sense of accomplishment, a challenge (like a musical instrument) for a person who values self-fulfillment, a frivolous luxury for a person who values self-respect, a status symbol for a person who values being well respected, a toy for video games to a person who values fun and enjoyment in life, a "toy for the kids" to a person who values sense of belonging, a topic of conversation for a person who values warm relationships with others, and an unattainably expensive item for poor people who value security. Thus, the nature of the product attributes, the personal sales appeals, and the marketing communications will all vary as a function of the value group of primary importance in a certain context. The values linked to a product or service often provide the potential consumer with a basis for comparison shopping.

Contemporary marketing managers must also know that marketing activities often vary from one place to another. Because the underlying causes of success and failure in various places may not always be evident, understanding the values of various regions may provide an important clue in deciphering what sometimes seems like a regionally random pattern of successful experiences in marketing both new and established products (Sommers and Kernan 1968). For example, table 4.3 implies that an advertisement promoting the capacity for self-fulfillment (e.g., "Set yourself free with Stouffer's") of a product may be more successful in the West than in the South. Security, on the other hand, may be a more successful appeal in the South than in comparably urbanized areas of the West (e.g., "Protect your home from break-ins with Electron Touch Alarm"). To return to the personal computer example, an advertising campaign emphasizing how computers can help one accomplish his or her goals or emphasizing the computer attributes that facilitate accomplishment will probably be more effective in the East than in the South, and particularly than in the West South Central (table 4.4).

Value analysis may facilitate market expansion by aiding in the evaluation of the comparability of markets for future rollouts. If the product-relevant values of a region into which a firm wishes to expand are quite similar to the values of a region in which a firm's product or service is already successful, the rollout may proceed as soon as other concerns have been satisfied. If values differ, on the other hand, a firm may wish to develop new marketing communications, develop a product with more value-appropriate attributes, or even refrain from rolling out into the new region. For example, when Coors Beer was introduced in the South, it developed advertisements with appeal to regional values. This principle applies to international as well as intranational marketing.

The places in which value-based marketing strategies can optimally be implemented will vary, depending upon whether the Nine Nations or the BOC segmentation system is preferred. For example, if one accepted the Nine Nations concept, Los Angeles and El Paso would receive the same regional advertisement, since both are part of MexAmerica, but Oklahoma City and Minneapolis would receive a different advertisement, since both are part of the Breadbasket. Using the BOC regions, on the other hand, El Paso and Oklahoma City would both receive the advertisement for the West South Central, whereas Los Angeles would receive the Pacific advertisement and Minneapolis would receive the West North Central advertisement.

Consider the following cities with the BOC region in parentheses. Garreau classifies all of these cities as Dixie: Atlanta (South Atlantic), Bloomington, IN (East North Central), Nashville (East South Central), Springfield, MO (West North Central), and Little Rock (West South Central). If a marketer planned an advertising campaign at the most highly rated value in the region, using the data from table 4.2 (Nine Nations), all of the advertisements would appeal to security. Using the data from table 4.4 (BOC), on the other hand, we see that the most highly rated regional value in Atlanta is self-respect, in Springfield, warm relationships with others, and in Little Rock, either self-respect or security. Only Bloomington and Nashville would unambiguously receive the security advertisement. Conversely, all of Indiana is in the East North Central BOC region which values security most highly. But Garreau classifies Gary as Foundry (self-respect), Terre Haute as Breadbasket (warm relationships with others), and Columbus as Dixie (security).

This variation in value-based marketing strategy extends beyond the model value of the region. Consider two Empty Quarter cities, Spokane (Pacific) and Boise (Mountain). In Mountain states, sense of belonging is twice as frequently endorsed as self-fulfillment, whereas in Pacific States, the opposite is true. Or consider two Mountain cities, Phoenix in MexAmerica and Denver in the Empty Quarter. In MexAmerica, 18 percent of the people rate warm relationships with others as their most important value, whereas in the Empty Quarter, only 5.9 percent rate it as first. If one wanted to market a product linked to self-fulfillment (e.g., musical instruments) or warm relationships with others (e.g., gifts, personal grooming aids), the choice of division of regions would be quite important. The fact that the BOC regions do account for a significant amount of variance in values implies that a reasonable manager would select that division rather than the Nine Nations division. If no product-relevant value differences distinguished among regions, undifferentiated marketing or some other segmentation system would be preferable. But that is not what was observed in tables 4.3 and 4.4.

One advantage to the preference for the BOC regions is that it would be much more expensive to use the Nine Nations approach. Many reporting systems either use or follow the BOC system (e.g., Simmons), but Nine Nations segmentation would have to be developed anew for each data set. Although regional segmentation is more expensive than unsegmented national marketing, it is also usually more effective and considerably less expensive than developing a unique marketing approach for each subregion.

CONCLUSION

The values of a probability sample of Americans were measured in this study. Evidence was provided that these values ought to relate to several hypotheses proposed by Garreau (1981) in *The Nine Nations of North America*; however, the pattern predicted by Garreau's theory was not supported with these values. These values did, however, relate to BOC regions, implying that Garreau's division of North America is not optimal.

Other values, of course, may show different patterns. In an article that came to my attention after completing this research, Ogilvy and Mather (1983) purport to show a relationship between Values and Life Style (VALS) and the Nine Nations. Although their data were not assessable because they used population estimates from an undescribed sample, and although VALS has serious flaws (Kahle, Beatty, and Homer 1985), the possibility for future research on this relationship is intriguing. Likewise, the Rokeach Value Survey (cf. Beatty et al. 1985) and other value instruments (Levetin 1973) could provide evidence for other conclusions about the Nine Nations. The List of Values, however, does relate much more closely to consumer behavior than VALS (Kahle, Beatty, and Homer 1985) and somewhat more closely to everyday activities than the RVS (Beatty et al. 1985). Nevertheless, it would be interesting for future research to relate regions to these and other systems of value measurement and to monitor intraregional value trends and etiology. Experimental tests of regional variations in effectiveness of value-linked advertisements would be especially interesting and potentially important.

The advice to "Forget the bilge you were taught in sixth grade geography about East and West, North and South" (Garreau 1981, 1) seems premature. The admonition to "Forget the maze of state and provincial boundaries" (ibid.) is not valuable unless one plans to abandon geographic segmentation entirely. Of course, the best segmentation approach depends upon the particular goals and purposes of the segmentation, but when values are implicated in the goals and purposes, this study provides no evidence that we should abandon the Bureau of Census system.

NOTES

1. $p = 0.0348$.

2. If the alpha level had been 0.05, one would expect one difference to be significant by chance. In fact, two more differences were significant. People in the Breadbasket value warm relationships with others more than other factors, and people in the Empty Quarter value sense of belonging more than other factors. Such differences, however, should be interpreted with extreme caution, if at all, in the absence of overall significance.

5

Catalan Regional Business Culture, Entrepreneurship, and Management Behavior: An Exploratory Study

Nieves Martinez and Pedro Nueño

This essay examines the business behavior and regional values of the Catalan middle class and its impact on the economic environment of the region. Particular emphasis is given to the evolution of Catalan entrepreneurship. The decade of the 1980s is a starting point of a new historic period, especially since important political changes have taken place in Spain. To understand the Catalan entrepreneur of the 1980s, we must trace past regional industrial changes. This analysis combines an historic perspective with a qualitative analysis of recent business trends in Catalonia. Our aim is to explore the relationship between regional culture and business behavior in this Spanish context.

The study is divided into two parts. Part 1 is an overview of major historical factors that affected the characteristics and evolution of current Catalan business culture and behavior. Part 2 identifies the strengths and weaknesses of Catalan business values and behavior and is based on a review of relevant literature and on interviews with key personalities in the current Catalan business community.

PART 1: CATALONIA—A HISTORICAL OVERVIEW

Located in the northeast corner of Spain, separated by the Pyrenees Mountains from France and facing the Mediterranean, the region of Catalonia has more than 3,000 years of economic history. Its own culture is closely tied to the local Catalan language, a Roman language that is close to French. The population totals 6 million, half of whom are concentrated in the greater Barcelona area.

Catalonia has political autonomy as do other regions in Spain. The Catalan government is called the Generalitat. Catalonia is known as an "historical autonomy" because the independence of its government institutions date back to the thirteenth century. They were established in the form of a constitutional monarchy with a Parliament that controlled the Crown; this Parliament was made up of representatives from the church, the nobility, and the craft and trade middle class. With the marriage in 1469 of King Ferdinand of Catalonia and Queen Isabel of Castilla, Catalonia joined the Crown of Castilla but kept the local Parliament and related government institutions.

The discovery of America shifted attention from the Mediterranean to the Atlantic. In 1714 King Philip of Borbon decided to eliminate the autonomous government institutions of Catalonia and imposed the laws of Castille. In 1914 the local institutions were reestablished with the proclamation of an "Estatute of Autonomy," but in 1925 the dictatorship of General Primo de Rivera again abolished the local self-government. The advent of the Second Republic made possible the reappearance of the Generalitat, but the Dictatorship of General Francisco Franco put an end to it in 1939. The democratization of Spain, which began after General Franco's death in 1975, took into consideration the autonomy of Catalonia (as well as other regions of Spain), and the government of the Generalitat was reestablished in 1977 with a new Estatute of Autonomy.

The years 1977 through 1986 have witnessed a process of democratic institutional building in Catalonia along with devolution of powers from the central government to the Generalitat. The struggle for self-government has also promoted efforts to emphasize the language and local traditions. Political success has often been accompanied by a climate of optimism and the blossoming of institutions in general and business in particular.

The First Industrialization Stage: The Textile Saga

Catalonia always had a relevant role in the economic history of Mediterranean countries. Many ports on the Catalan coast were active outlets for exports of raw materials and food during the Roman Empire. Barcelona initiated the "commercial revolution" of the Middle Ages and in the twelfth century was an important European power in the Mediterranean. Barcelona's trade upsurge in the Middle Ages originated during the Crusades. In the sixteenth century, the Middle East economies declined and trade shifted to the Atlantic. Barcelona and Catalonia in general experienced an economic slowdown that lasted until the eighteenth century, when the entrepreneurial middle class of Catalonia manufactured products sent to the American colonies.

Catalonia joined other European countries in the nineteenth century in emphasizing the textile industry. The rest of Spain did not follow;

thus, demand remained stagnant in the entire country. As a result, Catalan manufacturers did not find the necessary market in Spain. Jordi Nadal Oller, an economic historian on the nineteenth century in Spain, said:

To have sound growth, the industry of the nineteenth century should have found a domestic market in a more advanced stage of development which required a certain degree of specialization and coordination. Each sector went its own way and, while wheat rotted in the barns of Castille, Catalonia had to import it from abroad; coal did not find a buyer in Northern Asturias, while in Castille they had to burn wheat straw.[1]

In addition to these conditions, the energy industry did not develop and agriculture remained at traditional levels. Financial institutions were practically nonexistent in Spain, and the central governments represented only the interests of the agricultural oligarchy.

In this context, Catalonia was able to industrialize in textile products and some light metallurgical activity. The business class of those years, although politically somewhat liberal, was economically conservative. It based its strategy on protectionist practices aimed at keeping the domestic Spanish market safe from European competitors.

Already in the last years of the nineteenth century, local and foreign interests started to exploit minerals from Catalonia. Coal was taken primarily to provide power for the textile industry as well as to eventually support the development of heavier industries. This exploitation added to the depletion of Catalonia's already poor resource base. But the region entered the twentieth century rather prosperous with its heavy protective duties for its industrial activity—still somewhat underdeveloped relative to Europe—and services industries, particularly in the areas of finance and insurance.

Many scholars have criticized the Catalan business community's lack of vision during those years, claiming that those professionals did not go one step further in developing a capital goods industry (one at least related to the textile industry). One explanation of why this development did not occur could be the fact of protectionism itself, since this policy made it possible for small companies to compete successfully in purchasing product and process equipment innovation from abroad. Antoni Jutglar suggests an additional reason for this lack of vision: namely, the lack of an adequate technical infrastructure—particularly in the educational system.[2] Vicens Vives argues that industrial leaders originated from rural areas and were therefore averse to investments in technological risks.[3] Pinilla de las Heras indicates that Catalan businesspeople have traditionally diverted resources from industry to nonindustrial activities, even when positive industrial results were observed.[4]

With the help of capital from the rest of Spain and from Europe, Catalonia began the deployment first of railroads and later of electric utilities. Catalan capital also financed the development of the cement and chemical industries. The first wave of important European companies came to Spain and located in Catalonia; so many came that, by the turn of the century, Catalonia was the leading industrial area in Spain. Key criteria for the decision to locate in Catalonia, in addition to the industrial infrastructure, were the local markets, the availability of educated employees and managers, a relatively important immediate market, and the port of Barcelona.

Heavy industries—steel and shipbuilding—did not prosper in Catalonia because of the lack of mineral resources and the competition from the northern Basque country where the resource endowment is more generous. The concentrated resource-based and basic industrial activities of the north gave rise to an accumulation of capital which, in turn, served as the origin of a solid banking sector that had a broad national perspective. The stock exchange was an alternative way of continuing to raise capital by those industrial groups. But Catalonia did not participate in this process, and the Catalan banks, whose capital was generated mainly by the trade profits of the nineteenth century and from the agriculture of the Tarragona province (south of Barcelona), were small, locally focused, heterogeneous, and disperse. In 1920 Catalan banking also suffered a severe crisis with the failure of one of the largest banks. Since that time Catalan banking continues to be weak and ineffective. The option of the Catalan industrial middle class was to manufacture consumer goods which required moderate financial support and which was consistent with the maintenance of family management and ownership.

The First World War represented an additional opportunity for Catalan industry. But, again, Catalan business professionals adopted a short-term view, and the markets gained were lost immediately after the war.

In conclusion, the first two decades of the century saw a prosperous Catalonia with a relatively strong textile industrial base and a wide diversification of light industry with effective technology in paper, cork, printing, electric motors, small appliances, light machines, and automobiles (Hispano Suiza, among others). Entrepreneurship, creativity, trade and hard-working capabilities presently contrast with the weak financial and strategic orientation of traditional businesses and the lack of networks with the political establishment.

Plight of the Catalan Entrepreneur

Joseph Pla has called the business perspective of the Catalan entrepreneur a "flight of the chicken."[5] The regional cultural traditions that have impeded the success of Catalan entrepreneurs reappear: namely, stubborn individualism, lack of trust to delegate responsibility to high caliber managers, overreliance on family members and unprofessional "trust-men"; the tendency to consistently underinvest; the diversion of a large percentage of revenue to unrelated core business activities; and inattention to resupplying equipment (keeping equipment beyond obsolescence). Pinilla de las Heras also suggests that the Catalan entrepreneur has tended to be pessimistic with regard to long-term business prospects.[6] Heras has portrayed the Catalan entrepreneur as a manufacturer-salesperson who set a premium on immediate profits. This in turn encouraged cut-throat competition leading to fragmented industries. Very seldom does the history of Catalan business portray people who hold a long-term perspective. The historian Vicens Vives, for example, argued that the individualism of Catalan businesspeople led them to avoid opportunities that required linking economic interests to industrial activity.[7] Hence, it can be strongly argued and evidenced that the businesspeople in this region experienced the end of Catalan banking. Also in the area of the procurement of raw materials, Catalan business professionals never approached the problem of getting joint control over the sources of supply. The result was lost opportunities in the sourcing of immediate resources.

The reluctance to make important industrial commitments also had a negative effect on commerical activity. Until the nineteenth century, business professionals engaged in trade with the rest of the Iberian Peninsula and abroad. Catalan businesspeople did maintain close relationships with the owners of sailing ships that transported the goods. However, with the advent of steamships, control over the trade logistics was lost since the Catalan business community was unwilling to make the investments associated with the new transport technology. As a result, trading slowed down substantially, and foreign shipping companies took most of the Catalan export commerce.

At the institutional level, however, the situation was more favorable. Industrial associations had existed in Catalonia since the sixteenth century. These associations started technical schools for the development of specialists in the trade. The institutions—many of which were involved in the textile activity—were financed by the private sector with partial help from the the Catalan government. An excellent study of the role of industrial engineers and engineering schools in the modernization of Catalonia has been published by Ramon Garrabou and covers the period 1850–1910.[8] Garrabou showed that the engineering schools limited their objectives to certain aspects of manufacturing and never emphasisized research and development.

The beginning of the century brought an interest in commerce studies. During those years, the School of Commerce of Barcelona was an important institution that provided training for accountants and administrative personnel employed by the most advanced companies. Several attempts were made to start a commercial University, but these activities never succeeded. The profitable but short-term light industries and the high standard of living reinforced the Catalan middle class's apathy with regard to political power and nontechnical education. However, the children of the entrepreneurs of that time continued to receive technical training. Still, few Catalans showed an interest in politics, and very few chose the military profession.

In the late 1920s, at the close of the first stage of Catalan industrialization, a deep social, political, and ideological crisis swept Spain. It was the Spanish version of the crisis that affected all of Europe. In Catalonia, the turbulence gave rise to a dormant nationalistic feeling. But this decade brought no new changes to the parochial traditions and individualistic customs that influenced the shortsightedness and introversion of Catalan industrialists.

The Second Industrialization Stage:
Metallurgy and Diversification

In 1939, after three years of Civil War and with General Franco in power, Catalonia began a new period of economic and social life. The postwar period was characterized by scarcity of raw materials, the development of a black market, and the rise of a new kind of speculative entrepreneur. Traditional industries did not grow significantly in that period, but the number of electric utilities, cement producers, and chemical companies increased. Spain was commercially isolated from the rest of the world owing to the general embargo of Franco's regime, and Catalan's industrial development emerged under autocratic conditions. Furthermore, the government did not help Catalonia since politicians gave priority to other less developed regions within Spain. So the decades of the 1930s and 1940s brought little change to the Catalan business orientation.

With the 1950s came change and a turnaround. In 1951 the gross national product (GNP) level of the pre–Civil War years was attained, and there was a renewed interest in promoting a Catalan banking system. While the rest of Spain followed a government-directed process of industrialization with the INI (an industrial organization of the government created in 1941) as a key instrument, Catalonia's business community undertook an entrepreneuring, industrialization process based on hard work, creativity, exhaustive use of equipment, and the stimulated pull of a large market. In a 1958 study on Catalan business professionals conducted by the authors, Professor Fabian Estape stated:

In an economic system like ours, the factor that limits progress is not the equipment, the capital or the markets; the really limiting factor is the entrepreneur. The most urgent problem of our industry is the scarcity of technically and economically well-trained entrepreneurs who have a broad perspective and consciousness of their mission.

In 1959 the government formulated the Estabilization Plan which was designed to effect a change from an autocratic and interventionist industrial policy to a more liberal free-market economy. The initial steps toward an international opening of the Spanish economy were also taken. This plan opened the door to a wave of foreign direct investment (mainly American and European) which, in most cases, chose Catalonia as the location for their plants. In many cases headquarters were established in Madrid because that city's administrative centralization was cultivated by the Franco regime. For this reason, among others, Catalonia lost the intellectual leadership to Madrid. It also lost the service industries which established themselves primarily in Madrid. Therefore, the majority of the financial service, consulting, and advertising companies—including business magazine publishers—are located in Madrid. In addition, the headquarters of all the major banks and most larger companies are in Madrid. As a result, there are more professional executives in Madrid than in Barcelona.

This wave of foreign and domestic investment and the related prosperity that followed during the 1960s affected Catalonia demographically. Immigration from other areas of Spain brought significant newcomers to the region. Parallel growth in the construction industry also produced significant economic changes. Agriculture became further industrialized. Products that were high-value added were created. Industrial dynamism shifted from textile to metal transformation and chemical industries and to a lesser extent to cement, ceramics, paper, and printing. The typical products of the metal transformation industry are light machine tools, automotive components, electric appliances, electric motors, instrumentation, and a variety of hardware. The chemical industry produced fertilizers, plastics, paint, pharmaceutical products, and, to a lesser extent, fine chemicals.

During this period, Catalan industry became largely dependent on either foreign multinationals or government-owned companies. In 1973, 40 percent of the large companies established in Catalonia were foreign-owned. Multinational companies representing chemicals, electric equipment, electronics, mechanic construction, automotive equipment, and food appeared. Government-owned companies were active in energy, petrochemicals, transportation, communications, and automotive. The typical Catalan entrepreneur continued to dominate the segment of medium-sized, family-owned companies in intermediate technology industries and in the subcontracting and supply of certain materials to the larger companies.

Francesc Cabana has studied the presence of multinational companies in Catalonia.[9] There is general agreement that multinational companies have been beneficial to Catalonia. The government of the Generalitat is currently making an effort to continue to attract foreign companies, particularly those active in high-technology fields.

The prosperity of the 1960s reawakened an interest in reequipping the Catalan society with basic institutions. Several banks, particularly the Banca Catalana group, took off aggressively and made industrial initiatives possible with important financial assets. Business schools appeared in Spain backed by Catalan entrepreneurs; Instituto de Estudios Superiores de la Empresa (IESE) launched executive development programs in 1958 in Barcelona and in 1964 started the first two-year MBA program in Europe. ESADE, also located in Barcelona, launched a five-year undergraduate program in business administration. These two schools have grown and today are considered among the finest in Europe in their respective fields. Both are private and enjoy the support of the local business community, which indicates that the Catalan business community was broadening its traditional planning horizon.

The Energy Crisis

The energy crisis reached Spain in 1975, practically stopping the active construction industry and slowing down the automotive sector. With these two industries in trouble, in addition to the general effect of the energy crisis, unemployment ballooned in Catalonia. The already weak banking sector almost collapsed. The autonomous government was reestablished in 1977, but because of its lack of resources it could do very little in terms of industrial policy. Catalonia went through a process of industrial rationalization that was implemented largely without any help from the government. (Most of the generous budgets of the late 1970s and early 1980s went to large government-owned companies and to companies located in other areas of Spain: steel, shipbuilding, mining.)

1975–1985: Reindustrialization

The Catalan entrepreneurial spirit again played a key role in the reindustrialization that took place from 1975 to 1985. The Catalan entrepreneurs understood the challenge of the technological revolution, and many Catalan companies were already active in high-technology fields. The entry of Spain into the European Economic Community

(EEC) posed another challenge to Spanish companies since the tariff walls protecting Spain from the European Community were progressively dismantled. To date, the Catalan business community has reacted with dynamism to this challenge, and after one year of membership in the EEC the Catalan economy seems to be coping well with the increasing liberalization.

By 1987 the Catalan economy was showing healthy growth. Some Catalan companies were success stories, having emerged strongly from the recession and being positioned for aggressive export activity. A new wave of foreign direct investment also favored Catalonia as a location site. An interesting case is that of Japanese investments which are more important in Catalonia than in any other European region. However, the transformation of light industries and medium- and small-sized companies continues to constitute the core of the Catalan economy. Still, practically all industrial activities are represented in the highly diversified economy of Catalonia: agriculture and fishing represent 2.7 percent of Catalan GNP, industry 40 percent and services 56.7 percent. Catalan companies became more export-oriented.

Moreover, the universities of Catalonia have improved in recent years. The number of Catalans with higher academic degrees from leading foreign universities has increased, and as a result interest in research has been stimulated. The Polytechnic University of Catalonia has developed into one of the most advanced institutions in Spain in terms of industry–university relationships.

Historical Traits of Catalan Entrepreneurial and Business Behavior

This study has shown that a common thread of behavioral characteristics differentiates the Catalan entrepreneur from other industrialists in that region. In summary, it can be said that the so-called typical Catalan businessperson is highly individualistic and tends to shape his or her company around personal capabilities. He or she tends to avoid or does not know how to approach building an organization with professional managers to whom authority and responsibility can be delegated. When the growth of the company becomes difficult to handle, the businessperson tends to look after so-called trust men—that is, individuals who will accept anything and will keep secrets, but, very often, will contribute little in terms of innovative ideas or cutting-edge activities.

The Catalan businessperson is also reluctant to seek help from other business professionals, and, therefore, joint ventures seldom occur. Neither do these professionals seek support from government. Whereas in other regions of Spain huge investments were made with soft government loans, Catalan businesspeople stayed as far away as possible from politicians, approaching them only to lobby for protectionism on a few occasions.

Catalan entrepreneurs also avoid large industrial commitments. Their approach is to sell and provide a certain industrial value-added. Investments that have to be evaluated over long periods of time are not considered. As the current president of the government of the Generalitat has said, this policy led to a "country with a lot of software but very little hardware."

For similar reasons, internationalization and multinationalization were limited. Catalan companies have always had an export orientation—Catalans speak more languages than the average Spaniard and relate well to foreigners—but they are reluctant to make investments in foreign markets, and, as a result, exports have shown some volatility.

Catalan entrepreneurs are austere in their business dealings, and they are also hard working. They seem to have a defensive position toward the central powers of a country that, in general, does not possess these values of austerity and industry. Vicens Vives has stated:[10]

The main characteristic of the Catalan psychology is not reason, like in the case of the French; nor metaphysics, as with the Germans; nor empiricism, as with the British; nor intelligence, as with the Italians; neither is it mysticism like the Spanish. In Catalonia, the main characteristic is the *will to be*. This willingness is persistent and unmoving. Do we have it as a result of early spiritual formations acquired in the first Marca? Or, is it the product of the fight that we had to maintain to go forward? It is a clear phenomenon that appears in every major event of Catalan life since 1680, both economically and spiritually. This is the program that we Catalans carry in our minds from centuries past.

PART 2—MAJOR VALUES AND PRACTICES OF THE CATALAN BUSINESS PROFESSIONAL

The following discussion of the dominant values and limitations of the Catalan business professional's management practices is based on the results of interviews with key persons from current Catalan businesses. The persons interviewed are identified in the chapter acknowledgments, along with a description of their titles.

Hard Work: A Business Virtue

All the interviewees, supported by results from a literature review, unanimously agree that hard work is a major characteristic of the Catalan businessperson. This value—or virtue—is an historical constant. Catalans are people of few words and specific results. A typical Spanish proverb states: "the Catalan from stones makes bread." In the recent reestablishment of democracy in Spain, one of the Catalan parties approached its propaganda with a typical Catalan question: "Democratization? To do what? The Catalan meets his commitments. Normally he is punctual."

Austerity: A Limitation on Marketing

There is also wide agreement about the high level of austerity among the Catalan people generally. According to many interviewees, this austerity limits marketing efforts. Catalan businesspersons prefer to keep a low profile; they hate to see their name or the company name in the press, even if a successful venture is reported. It is difficult for journalists to gather business news in Catalonia where no specialized business press is published. All the business magazines are published in Madrid, and they carry very limited business information from Catalonia.

Distrust and Individuality: A Constraint on Joint Venturing

It is universally agreed that the Catalans are distrustful of people whom they do not know well. Juan Plans[11] and his colleague Salvador Maluquer[12]—who know the Catalan textile businessperson—both assert that the origin of distrust and individualism is in an antagonistic feeling about superiority and inferiority vis à vis business counterparts or competitors. Catalan businesspeople fear they will be surpassed by others in the area they feel the need for control. They fear the group, and they feel insecure; as a result, they opt for individual action. This distrust has made joint venture efforts difficult for Catalan professionals and consequently for the region's economy. Such efforts could have led to the development of large industrial corporations and banks of Catalan origin.

In 1968 the economist Vicenc Oller, after conducting a survey sample of Catalan entrepreneurs, concluded that

The Catalan businessman behaves as if collaboration among enterprises made sense to prevent average profits from going below a certain level, never as a way to increase them.

Fiscal and financial incentives do not represent a meaningful stimulus for collaboration among Catalan businessmen.

Catalan businessmen who feel they could benefit from mergers are seldom willing to lead the process approaching potential partners for fear that this could be perceived as a symptom of weakness.[13]

Independence: The Will to Do but Not to Delegate or Lead

All the interviewees identified the "will to do" as intrinsic to the Catalan businessperson's character. Nevertheless, the Catalan's approach to making money individually, without partnerships, is not due to legal (fiscal or financial) incentives or disincentives, but to a characteristic of his or her personality. Distrust and individualism prevent the Catalan entrepreneur from being an effective leader, from building a good team, and from delegating. If things go very well, he or she might decide to acquire other businesses or to start them, even in the same activity, but will rarely consolidate units or concentrate growth to develop a large corporation. The Catalan entrepreneur is afraid of "bigness." He or she might sell the company if the economic size that will be needed to survive in the activity, in the long run, is big. Catalan business professionals do not like managing large companies because they want to take care of every detail personally. Catalonia is a country of successful small management enterprises.

The Catalan businessperson tends to fail in standing face to face with a group and so fails as a leader. But he or she does not easily accept another's leadership or imposition. This independence requires a qualification here. The Catalan society does not admire those who depart substantially from its traditional values. The admired individuals are those who achieve within the traditional parameters of this society.

Creativity: A Historical Regional Value and Virtue

Creativity is unquestionably a positive characteristic of the Catalan entrepreneur. Catalan entrepreneurs have made technological innovations throughout their industrial history. Very often, these innovations led to the simplification of processes and to increasing value added by manufacturing with little capital. Professor Gabriel Ferrate has said:

Catalan entrepreneurs believe in the profits of technological innovation but, until recently, have not relied enough on scientific knowledge. In recent years, however, the relationships between the businessmen and the scientific community have increased substantially and there are many joint projects going on involving business and university.[14]

Many of the interviewees indicated that they would also support the definition of the Catalan as a creative entrepreneur. The Catalan business professionals have engaged in innovations not only at the technological level but also at the institutional and cultural levels.

Ambition and Modesty: Obstacle and Opportunity

There is controversy on this point. Catalan entrepreneurs are reputedly modest in business undertakings as in other aspects of life, a characterization supported by the Catalans' failure to produce large enterprises, important banks, or multinationals. Also demonstrating their modesty is their propensity to diversify aimed at small empires of small businesses—which could pass unnoticed by counterparts—rather than important concentration of wealth in a single activity.

On the other hand, the same results supported the hypothesis that an excess of ambition leads entrepreneurs to participate in as many industrial or commercial activities as possible, and enables them to control and expand business.

Conservatism: Big Fish in Small Ponds

Catalan proverbs recommend not starting projects that will be difficult to control later: "Be the head of a mouse rather than the tail of a lion," "Do not put all your eggs in the same basket." Catalans have not taken large industrial risks; they have diversified risk. They have also tended to avoid political risks by counting exclusively with their own resources—instead of seeking government support—for their business projects.

Pragmatism/Realism: Personal Control without Large Risks

Catalan businesspersons are pragmatic and keep "their feet on the ground." They want to have a thorough understanding of what they manage. They tend to overemphasize technical issues. Traditionally, they managed their companies from the shop; their children were trained in the shop and, in some cases, in the technical institute. The commercial side of businesses was selling through direct relationship with the traditional customer. The excess of pragmatism sometimes has negative effects: critical business concepts such as marketing and strategy have not been applied extensively in Catalonia. Professional management is often perceived as having business under tight control with good accounting procedures, along with high productivity in the plant and a well-educated and -trained sales force. Taking risks is omitted from the list.

CONCLUSION

The traditional behavior of the Catalan entrepreneur is changing. For example, there are signs that indicate an unusual willingness to take business risks; some Catalan companies are aggressively penetrating international markets, in some cases by acquiring foreign companies and/or making foreign direct investments; an increasing number of companies are accepting the technological challenge by pioneering highly innovative fields such as biotechnology and new materials; Catalan business schools are extremely active providing well-trained executives who, undoubtedly, become part of managing teams of local companies. Whether this is just another wave of optimism resulting from any one or a combination of the following factors remains to be seen: (1) the gradual solution to many problems that Spain as a whole has had to solve, (2) Spain's economic recovery, (3) the after-effects of Spain's joining the European Economic Community, or (4) the reestablishment of Catalan institutions. In any case, the characteristics and personality traits of Catalan business professionals described here are likely to continue to have an influence on the way business will be conducted in Catalonia.

More rigorous research is needed to better understand the main sources of the strengths and weaknesses that have sustained this region's prosperity throughout history. "How would it be possible to further develop these strengths and what, if any, are the major effects that the important sociopolitical changes affecting Spain might have on the Catalan entrepreneur?" This question requires further inquiry.

NOTES

The original manuscript was revised and edited by Professor Joseph W. Weiss.

1. Jordi Nadal Oller, *El fracaso de la Revolucion Industrial en Espana, 1814–1913* (Barcelona: Editorial Ariel, 1975).
2. Antoni Jutglar, *El burguesos Catalans* (Barcelona: Editorial Nofreu, 1966).
3. Jaime Vicens Vives, *Historia economica de Espana* (Barcelona: Editorial Vicens Vives, 1959).
4. E. Pinilla de las Heras, *L'empresari catala* (Barcelona: Edicions 62, 1967).
5. Joseph Pla, *Obras completas* (Barcelona: Editorial Destino, 1983).
6. Pinilla de las Heras, *L'empresari catala.*
7. Jaime Vicens Vives, *Industrial i politics del S.XIX* (Barcelona: Editorial Teide, 1958).
8. Ramon Garrabou, *Enginyers Industrials, modernitzacio economica i burgesia a Catalunya* (Barcelona: L'Avenc, 1982).
9. Francesc Cabana, *Les Multinacionals a Catalunya* (Barcelona: Edicions La Magrana, 1986).
10. Vicens Vives, *Industrial i politics.* Marca was part of the Holy Roman Empire to which Catalonia belonged under Charles the Great (Charlemagne), year 800.
11. Juan Plans is the secretary general of the Sabadell (an important textile manufacturing city) Textile Manufacturer's Association.

12. Salvador Maluguer is the secretary general of the Association of Cotton Products Manufacturers.

13. Vicenc Oller, *El Asociacionismo en Cataluna* (Barcelona: Coleccion ESADE, 1969).

14. Professor Ferrate is the president of Polytechnic University of Barcelona.

ACKNOWLEDGMENTS

The authors wish to thank those who were interviewed in this study for the time they spent with the researchers, their interest in the topic, and the published materials they offered. The following list of persons interviewed is not complete; some preferred to remain anonymous. The authors take sole responsibility for any errors that may have resulted from consolidation of the views and opinions offered to them.

Antoni Serra-Ramoneda: Ph.D, economics; president, Caixa D'Estalvis de Catalunya (major Catalan savings bank).

Francesc Granell: Ph.D, economics; full professor, University of Barcelona (1980–1985, general director, Commercial Promotion, Catalan government).

Salvador Maluquer: secretary general, Cotton Products Manufacturers Association; member of the Board of AVUI (daily newspaper published in Catalan).

Juan Mas-Canti: textile engineer; businessman (textile and chemical); founder and promoter of industrial, financial, and sports ventures.

Gabriel Ferrate: Ph.D, engineering; president, Polytechnic University of Barcelona; president, BCD Foundation (Design Center); head, Technology Policy Committee.

Manuel Rucabado i Verdaguer: businessman, Food, Trading and Textile activities; promoter of numerous industrial associations in Catalonia.

Francesc Cabana Valcells: lawyer; former top manager, Banca Catalana (banking); historian of business and economic history of Catalonia.

Enrique Corominas: economist; businessman; chairman of several companies; president of the Circle of Economics (professional association).

Francesc Santacana: economist; director of Studies, CEAM (association of metal, electric, and electronics enterprises); president, association of Economists.

Ernest Lluch: Ph.D, economics; professor, history of economy; former minister of health (until 1986).

6

Regional Industrial Cultures and Entrepreneurship in a Centralized Country: The Case of France

Jean-Paul Larçon

France is a medium-sized country with traditions rooted in political centralization. In view of this background, can different regional industrial cultures exist there? If they do exist, it may also be questioned if, over the course of time, the dominant French culture identified with the values of Parisian intellectuals has overwhelmed the unique character of regional business identities. Answers to these questions are not easy, and we do not presume to address them completely. Rather, we intend first to describe the essential elements of France's centralizing cultural context, and then to examine selected regions as these influence business behavior through distinctive historical and cultural values and traditions.

The centralized traditions of the country acknowledge a wide diversity of regional cultures. This diversity of regional environments, in turn, remains interwoven in the economic behaviors, management styles, and values of specific firms. This chapter will explore the dialectic relationship between regional industrial cultures and France's centralized, dominant cultural context. Finally, we speculate on issues related to regional cultures, industrial behavior, and the country's mainstream culture. This essay is admittedly a pioneering one which seeks to initiate further research rather than prove or defend particular positions.

A CENTRALIZING CONTEXT

In comparison to its European counterparts, France has an extremely strong tradition of political, administrative, and social centralization. This tradition developed in part from France's political history and from certain aspects of the country's collective psychology. These subjects have been studied and explained in innumerable works.

From the establishment of the French royal house until the Revolution, the kingdom of France was built on conquest and the progressive assimilation of a series of provinces and cities in terms of language, culture, and administration. The cultural identities of these areas was so rich and strong that the central powers were compelled to subjugate them. The following examples show how France's centralizing physical, economic, and political culture was created and strengthened.

The network of French roads, which emanates from Paris like the spokes of a wheel, was constructed during the seventeenth and eighteenth centuries. The railroad network, undertaken in the 1870s, has the same characteristics. In the twentieth century, the airline network was also constructed to connect Paris with the major French cities and African nations. There is no question that Paris was designed to be the hub of France's centralizing material and immaterial culture.

On a political note, the term *Colbertism* was coined from the name of one of Louis XIV's ministers. The term is synonymous not only with the centralization of decision making in Paris, but also with state intervention in the economy. As minister of finance, Colbert spearheaded the establishment of the first public enterprises in France, the naval shipyards, armories, and factories of the Crown. *These undertakings not only tended to take precedence over local private enterprises, but they also restricted local initiatives.* The Revolution of 1789, followed by the rise of the French Empire and Napoleon, added to this movement, especially in terms of sectioning the country into administrative divisions, which were the basic units for locally implementing decisions made in Paris. In other countries, these decisions might have been delegated to the jurisdiction of provinces, territories, regions, or states. Political, economic, and other forms of centralization in France continued to be strengthened and refined until the years following the Second World War.

Concurrent with the development of political and administrative mechanisms of centralization, France experienced the gradual concentration of a large percentage of the population in Paris. Manufacturing, service industries, and financial markets were also located and concentrated in Paris. The immediate postwar nationalization fervor seemed to cap this centralized structure.

It was during this same period that an opposing national movement emerged. This movement envisaged the creation of a flexible planning system based on a relatively liberal conception of the state's relationship with its economic partners. This movement also foresaw a policy of regional development based on revitalizing regional centers.

In this favorable intellectual climate, General Charles De Gaulle became the first politician since the Revolution of 1789 to attempt true decentralization. He initiated the actual transfer of state functions to regionally and locally elected authorities. In 1969 a referendum was proposed which promoted both the creation of regional administrations and the decentralization of the Senate's focus. But De Gaulle did not succeed, 54 percent of the French voted against the referendum. This failure, combined with other conditions, marked the beginning of De Gaulle's departure from the public scene.

France did not finally achieve political decentralization until 1983. This time, under the presidency of François Mitterand, a new law finally laid the foundations for the gradual transfer of some of the central government's administrative and financial functions to regional deci-sion-making bodies. The French Left thus appeared to be more liberal on this particular point than the conservative governments that had preceded it. Within this dual tradition of centralizing state control and of an emerging entrepreneurial regional authority, how is it possible to explain the diversity of regional industrial cultures? Did these actually exist or were they more an ideological hope?

DECENTRALIZING TRENDS

It could be claimed that, even before Europe's Industrial Revolution, the cornerstone of local economic activity and autonomy existed in France, and that cultures, lifestyles, decision-making styles and indi-vidual regional identities were maintained in a low, dormant profile over decades. Dispersed communications reaching to the overseas ter-ritories and French colonies, including the maintenance of local com-merce and the harbor industry, all gradually contributed to regional development in France. The Industrial Revolution ultimately bolstered regions that were already developed but not officially recognized. These regional cultures were distinct and rich in human natural resources.

Apart from a few exceptional cases, the vitality of regional industrial cultures in France and the preservation of their unique characteristics over the course of time are more closely related to the setbacks and misfortunes of industrial life cycles in general and to the activities that generated them than to local sociological considerations. In the case of new industries, analysis of the most productive regions indicates that success depends on two factors: (1) a subtle balance between the values and skills of regional managers; and (2) the policy agreement and con-sensus between strategic regional interests and the objectives of the central government. Three examples are discussed in the following sections:

1. The case of the less dynamic traditional French economic regions.
2. The case of the Lyon region, a model diversified regional industrial capital.

3. The case of Sophia-Antipolis, one of France's progressive high-technology regional centers.

THE TRADITIONAL ECONOMIC REGIONS

A culture is identified as much by its taboos and restrictions as by its values and ideas. This discussion centers on both the taboos and values of the following more traditional French regions: Lille, to the north, which has a well-established textile tradition; Lorraine, to the east, which is the center of the French steel industry; Bordeaux, to the west, which is the great commercial port and capital of wine commerce; and Marseille, to the south, which is one of the major ports of the Mediterranean Basin. These four capital cities of these regions differ greatly among themselves. Some have been affected by a crisis affecting their traditional activity (the north and Lorraine), and in others, the economy is relatively stable or stagnant (Bordeaux and Marseille). These four regions and their respective capitals are representative of French industrial traditions built over the course of twenty centuries of commerce and banking.

Today, traditions remain a vital part of the business environment in these regions, as much among younger entrepreneurs as among established industrialists' heirs, merchants and bankers, chambers of commerce, and employers unions. The stated and observed values of these business leaders concur with those of locally elected politicians, mayors, city councilors, and the regional media professionals, as well as with those of the Parisian representatives in the area. When asked, these regional industrialists insist on the unique nature of their particular region's entrepreneurial culture and on its particular style of decision making, conflict resolution, and cooperation within an organization. When comparing their traditions to that of the central administration, they usually allude to Paris. The most frequent commentary is as follows: "Here, it's not like it is in Paris. We form a tight circle, it's a little bit like a club.... We don't air our difficulties in the public square." A discernible industrial culture does exist in these regions. It is relatively defensive with respect to practices and values outside the area, and probably even more so when viewed outside the French nation.

Regional values are more concerned with preserving the present and maintaining past traditions and practices than with taking industrial and financial risks for the future. Local firms and establishments remain fundamentally attached to the methods, markets, and technology that built the region's reputation in the past. It is probably outside the establishment, strictly speaking among the new entrepreneurs, that the greatest propensity for risk-taking can be found. One also finds a managerial outlook that is more national than global. However, the opposite is found among newer entrepreneurs who today are entering into partnerships with Japanese firms. Even though they are executives of very small firms, they also have had the greatest degree of success in the export trade.

Nevertheless, managerial culture in France's traditional regional capitals seems to have moved more toward a conservative than a future-oriented, global mode. Conversely, a high degree of innovation is taking place in the very old French cities such as Toulouse and Grenoble. It could be noted, for example, that the most dynamic, original, and self-styled regions are those where research centers, schools of management, and innovative engineering schools are flourishing, especially those that have developed their own originality and are more independent of Parisian traditions. This is the case of Toulouse and Grenoble.

The traditional regions have the resources with which they could experience an industrial renaissance like that of Detroit in the United States or that of Catalonia in Spain. Barcelona's selection as an Olympic site, for example, is testimony to the ability of the city's political and economic authorities to organize and mobilize a large-scale project.

Among the decisively negative factors of the traditional French regions are:

—High turnover in the traditional industries. With respect to management style, these industries are unable to sustain sufficient new activity.

—Lack of unity between the business community and the regional political establishment. This disunity ultimately encourages a past-oriented economic policy in the region based on an alliance between the most prominent conservatives in local industry with the most conservative political forces of either the left or the right.

—Regional perception of business being oriented to past practices and methods, and closed to the sociological, technological, and managerial changes necessary for innovation.

THE CASE OF LYON, MODEL REGIONAL CAPITAL

An industrial region of 5 million inhabitants, Lyon was one of the capitals of Gaul under the Roman Empire. It was the heart of the Roman Empire, strong in its own traditions. Over the course of its lengthy history, Lyon and its environs have experienced the highs and lows of the industrial activities that have been established there. Yet the leaders of these industries have always known how to find the resources for renewal and expansion.

Resisting the Parisian centralizing influence, Lyon is the only major French city that has managed to retain its own sociological identity and regional choices. More than any other city, it maintains unique industrial attitudes. The French consider Lyon the city of the *soyeux*, or silk industries, but it clearly exhibits well-developed industrial diversification and remains a significant financial center. The culture of Lyon's industrial executives does not encourage them to seek external models, but rather to draw on personal experience which seems appropriate to the situation.

In Lyon, industrial-academic cooperation works well and a commitment to cooperation unites industrial leaders, politicians, and citizens in the pursuit of regional industrial success.

How can the industrial culture of the Lyon region be described? In terms of regional industrial culture, the following elements stand out: favorable policies that reinforce the growth-oriented but autonomous strategic, economic and sociological strengths of the region. Contributing to this effort are the vibrant personalities and role models of the community's outstanding business leaders and those of political leaders whose attitudes favor business; the substance and quality of these leaders' interactions; the strength of regional economic policy, which is guided by regional institutions (economic development committees and public economic agencies); and quality policies formulated within each firm which are results-oriented.

Regional Success Factors of Lyon

The following four factors have helped make Lyon a leading regional business center in France. First, Lyon has a differentiated set of industries. The wide diversity of industries ranges from highly traditional to pace-setters; from huge conglomerates to very small firms; from internationally oriented companies to local businesses. Yet Lyon has also maintained a consistent industrial profile. That is, there are few radically different management practices and styles across industries. Lyon is unique in this regard. There are, for example, "economic zones" in France of which Marseille is the best example. In these zones there is an observable difference between the way newer, innovative firms like service or technology-run companies that are international in outlook are managed, and the way the majority of traditional local industries (which focus on production and the national or regional market) are operated. The newer companies resemble fast-track management styles, whereas the traditional are slower and more stodgy in style and outlook. Lyon does not reflect such a diversity of management styles.

Second, Lyon has a regional self-image that is based on the perceptions of its managers as vital, growth-oriented, and productive.

Third, Lyon's industrial executives perceive themselves as slow, attached to the land, prudent, conservative, clannish, stubborn, and rejecting showy advertising. Although the city's industrial executives accept these seemingly negative stereotypes, they also bring positive aspects to the perceptions of their business community. For them, the positive side is synonymous with sound, deliberate, but sometimes cautious management practices. The image of these managers has gradually taken root in business dealings based on the qualities and skills their competitors attribute to them.

Finally, Lyon's business leaders demonstrate a system of coherent and discernible collective behavior which creates a synergy among themselves. The result is mutually reinforcing community-based rituals and symbols that enhance creativity, belongingness, and growth.

Lyon's Regional Cultural Characteristics

In 1985 Lyon was linked to Paris by a high-speed train. This shuttle covered the 500-kilometer distance between Paris and Lyon in two hours and twenty minutes from city center to city center. Some observers predicted that important companies whose administrative offices and major facilities were located in Lyon would be tempted to transfer their headquarters to Paris. With their policy of collective communication, the Lyonnais immediately counterattacked through the regional and national press and television media. The campaign showed the benefits of transferring some commercial activity from Paris to Lyon. The transfer allowed businesses to take advantage of the new transportation facility and a business climate superior to that of Paris.

Lyon has a distinct regional business culture and identity that is vigorous, future-oriented, open to external competition, effective in its decisions, and motivating for the managers who participate in it. Inevitably, it could be argued that Lyon in comparison to rival regional capitals has been able to span twenty centuries of European history relatively unhindered. If it finds itself with the managerial resources enabling it to meet the challenges of the twenty-first century, this is due in particular to its sound regional industrial culture and historical identity.

THE CASE OF SOPHIA-ANTIPOLIS, SCIENCE COMPLEX OF THE FUTURE

Sophia-Antipolis is a science complex. One of its peculiarities is its location in the heart of the Riviera, a region almost exclusively devoted to tourism and leisure activities.

At present, Sophia-Antipolis is a growing composite of research centers, laboratories, corporate headquarters, and training centers assembled on a 6,000-acre park between Nice and Cannes. A few kilometers away are Nice International Airport and the highway that connects

France and Italy. In Sophia-Antipolis and its immediate vicinity, one finds firms such as Digital Equipment, IBM, Texas Instruments, Dow Chemical, or Searle, to name only the American interests that are in good company with the French and European multinationals as well as with smaller technology and service-oriented firms. A comment from Carl Hemingway of Digital Equipment illustrates the attractiveness of Sophia-Antipolis: "If you work in high technology engineering, then any place in the world would do. The importance of a site like Sophia-Antipolis is that you can attract and, above all, keep good engineers." However, fifteen years ago on the present site of Sophia-Antipolis, one would have found only a golf course and three sheep pens.

The creator of Sophia-Antipolis is a French scientist.[1] Pierre Lafitte is former director of the Mining School (L'Ecole des Mines) of Paris, one of the leading engineering schools of France. He is currently a member of the French Senate and a spokesperson on international matters of science.

For Pierre Lafitte, the challenge is two-sided: first, to persuade the business community and the Cote D'Azur of the viability of his high-technology science project, even though the community's experience and business culture were somewhat limited to industries like tourism, the hotel trade, conferences, transport, infrastructural projects, retail trade, and services; second, to convince the Parisian authorities, whose authorization and active assistance were both necessary, even though Nice is nearly 1,000 kilometers from Paris.

As Senator Lafitte put it in a personal interview with the author,

By virtue of its novelty the project had the advantage of not disturbing established interests. I was therefore able to arm myself with the modern France of the local entrepreneurs, particularly those who were active in the Chamber of Commerce and Industry. They were then able to persuade the rest of the business community. Nice was not foremost in the minds of most Parisian administrators as a potential high-technology center for France. However, several officials, as high as the Minister of Industry and the highest authorities for regional development, tipped the scales in favor of the decision. It is true that local politicans, bankers and officials had also prepared a portfolio and devoted much time and energy to convincing the Parisian authorities.

Sophia-Antipolis is therefore the exceptionally successful example of a project that seemed radically different from the traditional economic network destined to support it.

How was this science project experienced by regional business executives? Maurice Esteve, president of the Chamber of Commerce, stated his version of the story:

The majority of the entrepreneurs were not directly affected by the region's interest in diversifying itself into new sectors. Many thought it would be better to capitalize on and stabilize our heritage of tourism and traditional leisure activities. But Pierre Lafitte had a very clear vision. He had genius, charisma ... he is a native of the region. Personally, I was unable to evaluate all of the ramifications of the project, not even the high technology dimension. But by tradition, we are builders, entrepreneurs and risk-takers. Lastly, my predecessors in the Chamber of Commerce and I myself were used to large-scale infrastructural projects. We also had both the will and the means to increase the airport's capacity, the region's ports and the idea of developing our winter sports resorts. We were used to an international clientele. Sophia-Antipolis had many facets—some mysterious, some unknown—but we had to take the risk.

Nice is international. It is the sister city of Houston, Texas, and the city's main thoroughfare is called Avenue of the English (Promenade des Anglais) in memory of the first tourist to discover Angel's Bay. Jacques Medecin, Nice's mayor, sees himself as an international manager. Medecin, whose wife is American, styles himself after the Prince of Monaco, who was able to diversify the principality's economic activity and therefore increase its capacity to attract an international clientele.

The thrust of the successful launching of this science complex is based on innovation and leadership from Pierre Lafitte; policy agreement among Parisian officials, locally elected politicians from the business community; the region's innovative organizational image which values large-scale projects; and the international dimension of the region and the business community's risk-taking attitudes. It is not surprising that innovative, internationally oriented firms, both large and small, were the first to take root in Sophia-Antipolis. It remains to be seen to what extent the Cote D'Azur business community can continue to attract and grow venture capital.

CONCLUSION

For some, the preceding descriptions may constitute an oversimplification of complex and subtle realities. Nonetheless, they can serve as the beginning point for further research and examination by the business executive and researcher.

In all of these regional contexts, one must consider the role of the executive elites and their development in terms of innovation and risk-taking. One could also consider the role of business leaders, both native and foreign to the region. One could further examine and compare the richest or most traditional regions or those with the strongest culture and examine their difficulty in anticipating external change. According to each case, culture remains an important factor in examining adaptation and resistance to change from the regional business community. Education, in particular, plays a decisive role in a region's tendencies to grow or decline.

This exploratory essay touches on a number of perspectives for examining the relationship between regional and national culture in France, emphasizing the role of business in this relationship. First, it seems clear that, even in the case of a country with a strong centralizing tradition, regional industrial cultures endure as driving forces in the dynamics of regional economies. In view of the extensive variations in economic environments, culture is probably one of the most decisive variables used in determining the fate of a declining industry or an industry striving for renewal.

Second, regional cultures are multifaceted, but their essential components can be discerned through the history, traditions, economics, symbols, rituals, and behaviors of the inhabitants. The strengths and weaknesses of regional culture provide the impetus for action, particularly for business leaders who become aware of the traditions from which they originate or create.

Finally, culture is a consideration for any company that is locating or relocating in a region, including large firms that have potentially vast holdings of factories, research centers, and business connections at their disposal, as well as for small firms that often require a specific industrial and regional culture to survive and grow. In any relocation venture, culture will doubtless be one of the factors for investors and CEOs to consider.

NOTES

Translated initially by Elizabeth A. Usovicz, Department of English, Bentley College, and edited by Joseph Weiss, Management Department, Bentley College.

1. The name Sophia-Antipolis is derived from two sources: Antipolis is the name the ancient Greeks gave to the village of Antibes, upon which a part of the science complex is situated. Sophia is the given name of the creator's wife, which also calls to mind the goddess of wisdom.

7

Entrepreneurship and Local Government Strategies in Finland: A Regional Perspective

Henri J. Vartiainen

The Finnish economy, though buoyant by most Nordic standards, is undergoing a painful restructuring process which has been prompted by slack demand and turbulence. Companies in traditional export industries are experiencing marketing difficulties, and they are revising both their production and marketing strategies. Large companies are laying off employees in order to cope with competitive pressures, putting the onus of employment maintenance on small companies and new establishments. Many industrial localities, which have traditionally counted on only a few large employers, are awakening to these grim realities.

All of these experiences have led to a reassertion of the importance of local and regional economies. Their role is particularly relevant in the creation of employment—a challenge too great for conventional fiscal measures. Encouraging local and regional initiatives, entrepreneurship, and self-employment is thus an essential element of structural personnel policies in Finland.

The increased economic activity of local governments is the result of these developments. It can take the form of direct or indirect participation in local and regional initiatives. New ways of cooperation between the government and the business community have evolved. Limits set by legislation to participate in economic activities are also being explored.

Similarly, district administrations of the central government charged with employment issues pay more attention to local and regional conditions and projects. The relative weight of national policies and local strategies has shifted in favor of local initiatives. This activity has emphasized the growing importance of regions in Finland. Entrepreneurship and local government strategies are becoming more important means of handling employment issues and of stimulating economic activity. This is a marked change from past government policies and practices.

LABOR MARKETS AND LOCAL INITIATIVES

Until the end of the 1960s, labor market policies dealt mainly with unemployment and structural changes. The mobility and adaptability of the labor force through training were considered important for the economy to respond quickly to growth impulses. Incentives were developed to this effect. Internal migration of people and companies within the Nordic countries was lively between regions, between urban and rural communities, from primary to secondary industries and services. Urban population grew from one-third to two-thirds in the twenty-five years up to 1980.

The structural shift from agrarian to industrial and service occupations since World War II has occurred more rapidly in Finland than in any other country in Europe. (The percentage of those gainfully employed in agriculture and forestry fell from 36 to 11 percent between 1960 and 1980.) However, the share of those engaged in primary industries and of those living in rural districts is still substantial, which gives added emphasis to the rural districts.

Social cohesion still exists in the rural districts and in villages. This cohesiveness is an asset which both government and business leaders can exploit to revive, preserve, or raise initiative and resources to serve the ends of economic development.

Today, unlike the previous decades, the mobility of both companies and of the Finnish population generally has decreased. The emphasis is, therefore, on boosting entrepreneurship among each neighborhood's inhabitants, including prospective returning immigrants. Maintaining employment through large national public works programs is a less attractive alternative, particularly as claims are made for pruning public expenditures.

An understanding of the economic structure of the locality and the adjustment needs of local labor markets has become important for employment services and other policymakers who are seeking to achieve job creation initiatives that are most appropriate in different communities. Thus, the main thrust can be on:

—Permanent new job creation via imported new industries.

—Promotion of locally based employment initiatives.

—Creation of temporary employment.

—Tradeoffs between creating and maintaining employment opportunities.

—Creation of employment for special target groups.

These shifts will mean that the focus will be placed on increasing promising entrepreneurial economic activities, on indirect effects, and on preventative measures. But, above all, emphasizing experimentation at local and regional levels is necessary. The best results will be achieved when companies, local authorities and economic organizations are all committed to the same aims. These shifts will also mean focusing on preventive measures in anticipation of layoffs or on such long-term threats as depopulation.

Movement in these directions has already occurred. An action program on local employment initiatives ("Initiatives locales d'emploi" [ILE]) was started in the Organization for Economic Cooperation and Development (OECD) in 1982. Its purpose is to study the possibilities of job creation by forming small and medium-sized firms and promoting self-employment. The initiative can come from an individual, a company, government, local organization or community group. Typical examples include repairs, maintenance, and environmental care; operations include handicrafts, advisory and environmental services, tourism, children's day nurseries, and holiday relief pools. These initiatives are aimed at generating and responding to new local demand and at increased employment of underutilized local capacities. The OECD action program highlights the need to assist the development of innovative small enterprises.

The organizational range of ILEs can be large scale. They may be joint enterprises by groups or individuals, worker-controlled enterprises, establishments by voluntary organizations, or ILEs established in response to funds from government agencies to employ persons from specific target groups. The local authorities often play a role.

In most countries, special schemes have been set up to boost local initiatives: for example, "Jobskabelse" in Denmark, Community Business Ventures and Enterprise Agencies in the United Kingdom, "Boutiques de Gestion" in France, Landskrona Project in Sweden, "Canada works" in Canada, and CRESM in Italy.

INVOLVEMENT OF LOCAL AND REGIONAL GOVERNMENT

A recent Swedish report on the economic policies of local authorities described the present state as a transition from "industrial communal policies" (industriell kommunalpolitik) to "communal industrial policies" (kommunal industripolitik). Formerly, important local companies demonstrated their social responsibility by substantially supporting communal, social or recreational services (donating a track field, and so on). Today these companies are pruning both their work-force and expenses, while local authorities are active in planning new economic activities and encouraging new companies to be set up.

Concern for employment is a main reason for communal economic policies. An impending crisis may sometimes give rise to a search for new employment prospects. But forestalling a future crisis is also a likely reason, given the present-day sophisticated forecasting methods. It is not just the communities in crisis which plan their economic activities and policies. Another reason may be the need to diversify the local economy, both in technologies and labor markets. Local author-ities may be less than enthusiastic with the central government's sup-port measures, insofar as they are tailored to respond to the functional needs of sectors of companies, not to preserving or creating as many jobs as posssible.

The Nordic tradition vests municipalities with general powers, which is interpreted to mean that local authorities should not engage in spec-ulative activities and not give financial support to individual companies unless a general beneficial effect in the community is included. In most cases "favorable employment effect" is sufficient. Communities in Nor-way and Finland are less constrained in their economic policies than those in Sweden and Denmark.

The municipalities are normally responsible for general prerequisites and infrastructure. Today building factories are also included in this category. Because a housing shortage is often an obstacle to bringing in a new enterprise, many local authorities in Finland build houses for this purpose.

Loans and guarantees in the Nordic countries in general are not uni-formly employed. In Finland and in Norway, in particular, local loans and guarantees are widespread. It is sometimes said that the risks are greater for the less prosperous communities.

Also in Finland, the network of local authority trade and industry officials that grew up in the 1960s acts as a major link between company and local authority administrations. The officials' salaries are subsi-dized by the state. Some of the richer local authorities employ more than one official for different sectors.

Communities can participate indirectly through Development Com-panies in which legal questions are resolved by means other than by direct participation. These companies have proliferated in the last twenty years, but the evidence so far is inconclusive. A Swedish study suggests that companies set up purely for development purposes are less sensitive to losses than might be desirable from a business-making viewpoint.

The backbone of the Finnish economy is a modern, competitive, capital-intensive export industry that has a poor employment capacity.

With productive output slowing down in the recent phases of slack demand, it has been increasingly difficult to employ all the personnel which in the past was generated by agriculture and forestry, taken by service industries. Initiatives at the local level are of decisive importance. The question arises: "How to exploit regional and local entrepreneurial employment and industrial potential?"

STRATEGIES OF LOCAL GOVERNMENTS

Defensive strategies are often the first reaction: a desire to ward off or slow down an impending crisis. The logic of these strategies centers on the reasoning that jobs must be saved, and closure of plants averted. Financial support is necessary but it is not sufficient: for a sustained solution, further rescue operations and new strategies are needed. But if markets are stagnant, defensive measures will not be able to save production. Defensive strategies are a short-term, quick-fix solution if only to gain time for fact-finding and devising new strategies. But it is evident that devoting ingenuity and resources to finding new and expanding activities will be a better way out of difficulties in the long run.

Expansive strategies aim at facilitating the growth of existing industries, easing the formalities, improving cooperation and communications between firms, and promoting technological change. But these goals require expansive sectors; otherwise the prospects of the region will not be improved.

Pioneering strategies encourage innovations and the creation of new enterprises. These are long-term, supply-side strategies that promote entrepreneurship by identifying, encouraging, forecasting, and creating the prerequisites for potential entrepreneurs; by finding and activating market niches, local know-how and resources, and material bases; and by creating an atmosphere friendly and receptive to entrepreneurship. This strategy offers the best employment prospects in the long term. It also contains entrepreneurial risks and demands venture capital.

These strategies may also contain a mixture of *market-conforming* and *policy-oriented* elements. The market-conforming strategies assume that markets can best assess the prospects on the markets, product mixes, and technologies. If the governmental authorities take care of the general prerequisites and economic climate, few direct measures to support or subsidize local companies are needed. In policy-oriented strategies, the authorities decide what industries to promote with more direct economic participation.

The choice of local strategy also depends on a number of characteristics and on the economic and political structure of the locality or region. A commune with few large companies, another with a deep-rooted entrepreneurial tradition, or one endowed with primary industries, or neighboring on a growth center, are well advised to choose strategies appropriate to their initial conditions.

VARIANTS OF LOCAL STRATEGIES

With traditional (basic) strategies, the supply of allocational factors (i.e., industrial sites, infrastructure) is adapted to observed demand. This type of strategy is based on the traditional concept of the public sector providing general prerequisites and services. It can be passive as it used to be in localities, and it is well shielded by solid large companies as the main employers; or it may be an active strategy in attracting new, small, and medium-sized industries. Its best chances are in localities close to growth centers, which are a source of buoyant demand for allocational factors.

With surplus strategies, an excess supply of allocational factors is deliberately created (i.e., factory estates, industried premises, port facilities) in the hope that supply will attract new demand. This strategy has its risks and may entail heavy costs. It is successful if it anticipates or coincides with new demand and natural growth trends or is supplementing other strategies.

Cost-subsidizing strategies include creating industry sites or other prerequisites such as finance or communal services, which are available at favorable rates. An element of hazard is always present. The success of this strategy depends on being able to "pick the winners," which is not invariably the case with subsidization policies. If many neighboring communities resort to this type of strategy, the result may be throat-cutting competition between local authorities.

Niche-strategies concentrate on local resources and strong features and resources of the particular locality. On the marketing side, potential niches are explored which are either shielded from hard competition or in which the strength factors suffice to secure a competitive advantage. This was originally a microeconomic strategy of competition for a firm: that is, to establish a "core" business consisting of a unique combination of factors, both material and immaterial, which cannot be imitated by competitors. If market niches are made part of selective industrial policies of the country, they can become part of the domain of the central rather than local authorities. But it is controversial whether the government policies succeed more than the companies in identifying niches. Governments tend to think in terms of expansive, stagnating sectors—which are statistical categories. In contrast, the business community—whatever the sector—views potential niches as consisting of "good and bad firms," opportunities seized or foregone, and innovative or bureaucratic organizations. Both government and business sector thinking in this regard has limitations.

A *marketing campaign strategy* can be used to attract new activities: that is, "selling" the locality to new entrepreneurs and companies. The results may be haphazard, however; commitment to accept and support any activity may turn out to be too risky. Another consequence, as in the preceding case, may be a frustrating nonproductive competition between localities.

Finally, a *long-term supply-side strategy* of promoting entrepreneurship (also called small-scale strategy) consists of identifying, encouraging, fostering, and creating the prerequisites for potential entrepreneurs; of finding and activating market niches, local know-how, and resource and material bases, subcontracting possibilities, and facilities for training; and of creating and maintaining an atmosphere conducive to entrepreneurship. Stock is taken of local demand and local potential producers. Government institutions aim at promoting a network of services for small industry (computer services, bookkeeping, consultancy).

REGIONAL DIFFERENCES AND ENTREPRENEURSHIP IN FINLAND

The choice of local strategy also depends on a number of characteristics of the locality or region. A commune with few large companies, another with a deep-rooted entrepreneurial tradition, or one endowed with primary industries, or neighboring on a growth center, are well advised to choose strategies appropriate to their initial conditions.

With regard to entrepreneurship and industrial climate, the initial conditions also vary from province to province. This situation is also reflected in local strategies. The coastal Ostrobothnian regions by the Gulf of Bothnia in the West, headed by the Province of Vaasa, are by tradition most devoted to entrepreneurship. (The share of entrepreneurs in the economically active population was 17 percent in the 1980 census, whereas the national average was 11 percent.) Commerce was one of the main livelihoods as early as the fifteenth century because the region has good inland waterways and shipping facilities to Sweden. Merchants and farmers competed in entrepreneurial projects. By the eighteenth century, trade in tar depleted the region's forest resources, making the role of the tradesperson all the more important.

Presently, the following factors are considered to favor entrepreneurship: (1) the traditionally small size of average farms, with about half of the incomes coming from sources other than agriculture; (2) a rural pattern of settlement, which has made it easier to establish handicraft workshops and other makeshift businesses; (3) a certain openness and equality between people, making it easier to compete on equal terms; (4) religious movements, rooted in homogeneous village cultures, which help to maintain industrial peace; and (5) returning emigrants from the United States and Sweden, who import new capital, ideas, and management styles.

A strong business culture also permeates local governments. A national comparison indicates that, since 1973, local governments in the Province of Vaasa have business promotion budgets more than double those provinces that lie next in line—mainly those provinces that make factory floorspace available to businesses. Large-scale factory facilities are the first prerequisite of most local authorities.

The image of entrepreneurship is positive in the Province of Vaasa, but this does not seem to be the case in the Eastern Province of Kymmene where Finland's industrial growth on a nationally significant scale was started. Pulp and paper mills and sawmills were established along the Kymmene River. The existence of large production units in this region has not encouraged small entrepreneurs. In addition, industrial relations have been dominated by a "working-class" ideology. Some scholars go so far as to suggest that the image of entrepreneurship has been negative in Kymmene. Entrepreneurs are identified as unsympathetic bosses belonging to the "ruling class." This view may be propagandistic, however, and cannot easily be corroborated.

This situation changed in the 1970s, as the large companies found it necessary to downsize while no new opportunities were in sight. A tradition of entrepreneurship had to be created quickly. Working groups composed of business leaders, local authorities, and union people, all of whom shared a common interest, were organized with the aim of finding out what new business could be developed and how large companies could increase their purchases of inputs from smaller companies. Stock has been taken of all feasible ideas, and a great number of new small establishments have been created.

All communities in Finland have a trade and industry officer who serves as a link between administration and business. This officer needs to have the absolute confidence of business, while formally serving as a local civil servant. Often he or she reports directly to the mayor and is able to cut through red tape and bring new ideas to implementation quickly.

ENTREPRENEURIAL INCENTIVES IN REGIONS

Today the central government's budget contains fewer appropriations for business promotion purposes: more decision making is delegated to the provinces and to local authorities. It all started with the northernmost Lapland province in 1980, where grants were made available to inhabitants for innovative purposes without any preconditions. The response by the population after a time lag of up to one year was very positive. Later, this practice was extended to other provinces, and dole payments were made available for starting an enterprise.

Many communities have adopted comprehensive projects that involve an effort by all available community resources. For example, the Padasjoki project involves the entire populace in the search for new or better livelihoods, and the Suomussalmi Ecological Experiment, adapts human activity to the ecology of the area with a goal of producing regenerative natural resources and of preserving the viability of the villages. This is a search for "dormant possibilities" through joint discussions by all interested parties in Sumiainen and Konnevesi.

Solutions have also been proposed in older, problematic industries. For example, Imatra has industrial and training facilities. Guarantees are given to prospective entrepreneurs that their employees will receive whatever training they need. Outokumpu, with its exhausted copper veins, is turning its mining know-how into an independent resource. In many towns, efforts are made to establish small firms to make use of equipment, skilled labor, and previous markets before these assets evaporate or become outdated.

Universities and research institutions in provinces have been geared to local and regional needs. The University of Kuopio, for example, conducts research on fur and fish farming. An industrial high-technology park houses forty small and medium-sized firms and functions in cooperation with the Engineering Department of the University of Oulo.

Universities run entrepreneurship courses financed by employment funds. The participants in the courses are managers of small firms, people who hope to establish their own businesses. They include those with special skills or training who are unemployed or threatened by unemployment. An important part of the tuition is a supervised development project in the company which involves a manager who takes part in the course. An unemployed person has a good chance of permanent employment in the company where he or she has completed this practical experience.

Village committees, revived in the mid–1970s, provide outlets for initiative and independent action in the rural areas. They foster attitudes toward cooperation and discuss the need for and possibilities of subsidiary occupations, training, new industry, and so on. Local skills have been revived: genuine, old-fashioned tar pits have turned out to be a great commercial success, and village smithies have reappeared on the economic scene.

Village committees are more active in the northeastern Carelian provinces than in other parts of the country. The need for cooperation has received much attention. Companies competing with each other on market conditions also have a substantial common interest. Cooperation has not historically been a prominent feature in Finland. One famous Scandinavian model of cooperation comes from Gnosjo, a small community in Sweden. Small companies there cooperate very effectively to overcome bottlenecks and other problems. This may signal a lesson to the government: cooperation between companies may well start at the local level and on a small scale. In this respect, Gnosjo provides a model for future entrepreneurial possibilities.

POWERS AND RESPONSIBILITIES FOR THE FUTURE

Those who pursue a consistent growth and entrepreneurial strategy are likely to be successful if they select and maximize one set of goals, while treating other aims as constraints of "maxima and minima." Thus, the Ministries of Labour can aim at maximizing employment, subject to a minimum of commercial viability and a minimum of distortion in the competitive conditions; or they can attempt to maximize the number of viable small enterprises and hope for the best employment effect.

Lest expectations for reviving and creating businesses are raised too greatly, an inventory should be made of the various organizations and interest groups to promote local industrial initiative. Human and material resources can then be made available from various sources. Best results are achieved in cooperation and synergy from every agent, concentrating on what best belongs to its domain and power.

Table 7.1 summarizes the available resources and requirements necessary to promote entrepreneurship at the regional level. Generally, resources are needed for the following purposes:

1. To survey market possibilities and community needs.
2. To put in place the basic prerequisites for enterprise creation.
3. To generate and establish local solidarity.
4. To promote cooperation.
5. To reorganize available underused production resources.
6. To create new production resources.
7. To innovate: additional demand and new products.

These requirements are not mutually exclusive. Every activity includes a variety of elements whose relative importance differs in degree from case to case. In this summary table, the resources are marked according to where their main thrusts lie.

Commercial viability is a very delicate flower. More economic activity means more economic risk. Although some parts of the risk can be internalized into the cost structure of the society and be jointly borne

Table 7.1
Resources Available for Promoting Entrepreneurship

	1. MARKET COMMUNITY SURVEYS	2. PRE-REQUISITES	3. SOLIDARITY	4. COOPERATION	5. REORGANIZING RESOURCES	6. CREATING RESOURCES	7. INNOVATIONS (DEMAND, PRODUCTS)
POLICIES OF LOCAL AUTHORITIES	X	X					
REGIONAL ASSOCIATIONS	X	X	X				
MINISTRIES		X			X		
CHAMBER OF COMMERCE AND OTHER ORGANIZATIONS	X	X			X		
UNIVERSITIES, RESEARCH, INSTITUTIONS	X				X	X	X
CREDIT INSTITUTIONS	X				X	X	X
LOCAL PROJECTS			X	X	X	X	
TECHNOLOGY PROJECTS					X	X	
ENTPREPENEUR COURSES					X	X	X
VILLAGE COMMUNITIES			X	X	X	X	X
EMPLOYMENT OF HANDICAPPED					X	X	
YOUTH EMPLOYMENT		X			X	X	

by the taxpayers (e.g., costs of patents or innovative but risky product developments), the principal and final risk has to be assumed by the entrepreneurs themselves. If they are encouraged, even induced, to undertake an economic activity in the interest of creating employment, the sponsoring authority may come to assume a part of the commercial risk.

CONCLUSION

Most important policies for local development—and most productive social investments as well—are those that foster the initiative and entrepreneurial spirit: willingness to work, faith in the future, creativity, learning, and training. The Finnish society needs to show courage to invest selectively in creative resources. Local initiative and solidarity are the key factors.

Mobilization of human resources—an inexhaustible reserve—will call for a reorientation of government policies: away from macropolicies targeted at collective groups, social classes, or statistical income brackets, to business-related, cooperative policies geared to individual needs at regional and local levels, designed to provide a fair and encouraging environment for persons to pursue their livelihoods and make their aspirations or dreams come true.

New and improved attitudes favoring cooperation are needed between the local authorities and other social partners to make the local development a joint project to be cultivated by the whole community. This change requires an active capacity for cooperation, as well as an awareness that a company is not merely a source of revenue to the community but a long-term growth asset.

An active policy in favor of enterprises is a productive investment. Generating new entrepreneurship provides us with a learning process that enhances the stock of skills, training, and experience in the society and brings human resources to an intelligent use. The more people employ themselves and others, the lighter the burden of unemployment on all.

8

Local Cultures and Management:
The Case of Switzerland and Its Societal
Management Model

Max Daetwyler

This essay was inspired by the writings of Professor Joseph Weiss and André Delbecq on Silicon Valley and Route 128.[1] The question arose: Are there any Silicon Valleys or Route 128s in Switzerland? Does Switzerland have local cultures which have an impact on the way business is managed?

One major and undeniable fact must be mentioned immediately. Switzerland is a small country. Some 2,500 miles separate Silicon Valley from Route 128, but from east to west, Switzerland measures only 250 miles, and from north to south a mere 130 miles. California has a population of 26 million, whereas Switzerland has 6.4 million. Switzerland is even difficult to find on a world map. It is legitimate to ask whether a country of such small size can really contain regions and local cultures of importance.

On closer scrutiny, one discovers that Switzerland is made up of a surprisingly large number of regional cultures. Some highly successful businesses can be traced back to small parts of the country where the local culture made it possible for these businesses to develop. The watch industry is one example. At the same time, within the country as a whole, a number of homogenizing forces are at work which have a tendency to create an overall Swiss culture. It will be argued here that a Swiss "societal management model" exists and that this model has evolved over time. The model is a combination of local cultural forces and values that have been forged into a decentralized, integrative system of management practices. This so-called model can best be discussed by examining the historical experiences that have influenced its development, and by discussing specific industrial practices that exemplify its diversity. Since the Swiss management model cannot be as narrowly or particularly defined as either the Japanese or Silicon Valley examples, it has not been popularly portrayed. Perhaps more like the Route 128 experiences, the Swiss model has evolved quietly and more gradually. This exploratory and historical essay attempts to depict the cultural influences that have shaped this rather illusive but powerful management system.

Because this chapter is directed to a non-Swiss, mainly American, audience, the first part will present some background information on Swiss history and the political system. The second part will deal with selected regional characteristics. In the third part the homogenizing forces of the Swiss management model will be discussed. The fourth part will raise the question of what this means for management. Finally, since Switzerland is often regarded by non-Swiss audiences as one of the happiest or at least wealthiest countries, the last part will ask whether anything can be learned from "Swiss management."

This essay is not based on specific research, interviews, or surveys. It reflects the thoughts and lifetime professional consulting and educational experiences of a Swiss who has held management positions both within and outside Switzerland, and who also has been active in international management education.

THE SWISS BACKGROUND

Switzerland is preparing to celebrate its 700th anniversary. In 1291 three local communities in what is now the central part of the country signed a pact of mutual assistance against undue external interference. Their valleys had become important as a result of the opening of the St. Gotthard mountain pass, the most direct link across the Alps between Northern and Southern Europe. The signatories of this pact were ambitious; they declared that this newly founded league should last forever.

Other communities soon joined the original three, and they had to repeatedly defend their independence by armed force. By the time of the French Revolution, five centuries later, after a history of wars, development, and occasional internal struggles, the original league had grown into a complex and fairly loose structure of cities, valleys, and regions, each with its own traditions and characteristics. Some members of this community, like the city of Bern, were powerful. Others were what one may call local colonies, governed and administered by the more powerful members of the league.

The Swiss were unable to keep out of the European turmoil that started in 1789. At one time, French, Austrian, and even Russian troops fought on their soil. The existence of Switzerland—and what is regarded as a key characteristic by all Swiss, its neutrality—was confirmed by the Congress of European Nations in Vienna in 1815. After a period of trial and error, the country found, roughly, its current political shape in 1848. This did not happen without one last civil war—fortunately, a short one—between progressive and more conservative forces. This division also followed religious boundaries between Catholic and Protestant regions. Since then, Switzerland has not been involved in any war. As one would expect, there were times of internal tensions, in the difficult years of 1917–1918, for example, or in the 1930s, but the problems were solved by negotiation and compromise. Switzerland is thus in the unique position of being able to look back on 140 years of uninterrupted internal and external peace, during a period when the rest of Europe went through a series of traumatic experiences.

The Swiss political system is complex and difficult to understand. It is, of course, rooted in the seven centuries of Swiss history. Several characteristics stand out.

First, the Swiss Confederation has three levels: the federal level, covering the country as a whole; the level of the 26 local states, called cantons; and the level of the municipalities, of which there are some 3,000. The local units carry substantial weight.

Second, at all three levels, there is a great predominance of collegial decision making. There are parliaments at all three levels. At the federal level, the country has two chambers, much like the United States which provided the example, but unlike the United States and many other countries, it has no president or prime minister in the accepted sense. The executive power is held by a Federal Council of seven members, elected by Parliament. Decisions are taken by this body as a whole, collegially, if necessary by voting. The four major parties usually represent over 80 percent of voting strength and share these seven seats according to what is called the magic formula of 2–2–2–1 which has been in place for the last twenty-five years. Each member of this council takes a turn at being chairperson. He or she is called the president of the Swiss Confederation and is elected by Parliament every year for a one-year period of office. To the surprise of foreign visitors, because the president changes so often, many Swiss do not know who it is at any specific time.

Third, the Swiss have developed a very special brand of direct democracy. It is based on the simple idea that decisions should be left to those most directly concerned—the people. At all three levels, the people vote perhaps three or four times a year on a wide range of subjects. In addition, by collecting signatures—100,000 at the federal level—it is possible to initiate a vote on a constitutional change. It is one of the reasons why the Swiss Constitution is loaded with issues that one would not normally expect in a Constitution. In addition, laws passed by the federal Parliament must be submitted to a vote if a certain number

of signatures is collected—a threat that hangs like the sword of Da-
mocles over the work of Parliament.

Fourth, the Swiss political system is slow and does not encourage
change. In today's rapidly changing world, many Swiss are asking themselves if the country can still be governed efficiently.[2] The answer of
most, but not all Swiss, is usually affirmative.

SWISS REGIONS

Of Switzerland's 6.4 million inhabitants, some 75 percent have German or, more correctly, a German dialect, as their mother tongue, 20
percent French, and 5 percent Italian. There is an even smaller minority
speaking a fourth language, Romansh. About half the population is
Catholic and the other half Protestant. During the boom years after
World War II, Switzerland attracted large numbers of foreign workers.
Today, the non-Swiss population amounts to some 15 percent. Some
60 percent of Swiss territory is taken up by the Alps which have become
a highly developed tourist area, both in summer and in winter, some
10 percent by the Jura mountain range in the West, and the rest by the
relatively flat area—by Swiss standards—in between, called the plain,
where most of the larger cities and industries are located. Water from
Switzerland flows north, east, south, and west, thus underlining the
country's central location in Europe.

The mix of different cantons, municipalities, languages, religions,
mountains, lakes, valleys, majorities, and minorities, all contribute to
a great variety of local cultures. Rather than trying to convey an accurate
overall picture, which would be beyond the scope of this chapter, we
will try to capture briefly the main characteristics of the four largest
cities.

Zurich

Although well known internationally, Zurich is not the political capital of the country. It lost that struggle to Bern, but most Swiss would
agree that it has become the economic capital. At one stage, it had a
smaller population than Basel, Bern, or Geneva but, with about 350,000
inhabitants in the city and 1 million in the agglomeration, it is now
the largest Swiss city. It joined the Swiss league as early as 1352 and
has not only a rich history, but also a distinguished cultural past, with
many writers, musicians, philosophers, and scientists living here at one
stage or another including, for example, Albert Einstein and Richard
Wagner.

Zurich was also an international center of Protestantism. It had its
"Silicon Valley phase" in the nineteenth century when entrepreneurs

created railways, banks, insurance companies, international trading houses, and industrial enterprises. Two of the country's largest banks are located there. The Union Bank of Switzerland (UBS), the largest one, celebrated its 125th anniversary in 1987. In the 1970s envious rivals in London coined the expression the "Gnomes of Zurich." Some Swiss would agree and others would violently disagree with the following description which was given by a Swiss writer and professor of literature:

Zurich has a secret that everybody knows. This is where money lives, with a view to its quiet multiplication. Here it is waited on with all this city's indigenous virtues: security, discretion and capability. Here the proof of divine grace has remained pure to the pure in heart, and even if it should exhale an all too human odour—here it can be washed.[3]

The Swiss authorities and banks point out strongly that this discretion is not allowed to serve as a cover for illegal transactions, and that they always cooperate with foreign authorities whenever there is a possibility that illegal transactions might have been involved.

Basel

The "Chemical Valley" of Switzerland, Basel is the home of three of the world's leading chemical firms: Ciba-Geigy, Sandoz, and Hoffmann-La Roche. Basel is located on the Rhine River which is navigable up to the city. It is thus the only Swiss port city and the entry point of a large amount of bulk commodities. This is also where the borders of three countries meet: Germany, France, and Switzerland.

Some like to say that Basel is looking down the Rhine River and turning its back on Switzerland. It is indeed known for having been particularly open to innovators, creators, and thinkers. The first entrepreneurs in the chemical industry came from abroad. Basel is also well known for its annual carnival, the sense of humor of its citizens, and its cultural tradition. To illustrate its cultural tradition, people from Basel like to cite an example that dates back to 1967. The local government had allowed a credit of some 6 million Swiss francs, which at today's exchange rates is equivalent to some $3 or 4 million, to acquire from a private owner two works by Pablo Picasso. A group of citizens tried to stop it, as was their right, which meant that the local electorate had the final say in a public vote. It did allow this credit. The artist, then still alive, was so delighted that he donated another four of his major works to the city.

Late in 1986 Basel fell on harder times when the industry, the authorities, and the population were shocked by a major fire in a Sandoz warehouse which attracted European and even worldwide attention as a result of the major pollution it caused to the Rhine River. It touched off a major reassessment of the position of the local industry and its relations with the population and the authorities.

Basel is also the home of the third of the three largest banks in Switzerland: the Swiss Bank Corporation (SBS). At one stage, Basel was in fact a more important and older financial center than Zurich, but it was overtaken in the nineteenth century.

Bern

German speaking like Zurich and Basel, Bern is the third largest city in Switzerland. It has been the political capital ever since the current Constitution was introduced in 1848. It is more centrally located than Zurich and Basel, and it is close to the border between the French- and German-speaking parts of the country. It joined the Swiss league very early and played a key role in its development. It has a glorious past, and possessed and governed territories that later became independent cantons of the Confederation.

Bern also became Protestant, but, unlike Zurich and Geneva, it never was an international religious center. The people of Bern are said to be slow, heavy-handed, and conservative. The city did indeed miss the first Industrial Revolution and never became a large center of industry, banking, or trade, but as the seat of the federal Parliament and much of the federal administration, it plays an essential role in the country. This is where much of Swiss societal management, as opposed to corporate or business management, is taking place.

Geneva

French-speaking Geneva is the "international valley" of Switzerland. It was the seat of the League of Nations after World War I and is host today to the European offices of the United Nations as well as some 200 other international organizations. It was mentioned in written history for the first time in 58 B.C. by Julius Caesar, a visitor at that time, when he wrote his report on the Gallic wars. Its formal entry into the Swiss Confederation, in 1815, came late and only when Europe was being reshaped after the Napoleonic wars. Geneva is almost completely surrounded by France. Its border with Switzerland measures about 4 miles, and that with France some 40. With some 150,000 inhabitants in the city and an equal number in the surrounding Swiss countryside, it is a small city by today's standards, but measured by the impact on the world of ideas coming out of Geneva, it is a colossus. The only other small city with comparable influence on the world which comes to mind is Jerusalem.

Geneva is where Jean Calvin worked and preached. He was not even Genevese but a Frenchman who took charge soon after his arrival and made Geneva into what some people call the Protestant Rome. Calvinism exerted great influence in Holland, Great Britain, and elsewhere, even in North America; the pilgrim fathers brought with them Geneva bibles when they landed in 1620 and used the Genevese motto of *Post Tenebras Lux*. Whole bookshelves exist on the close links between Calvinism and capitalism, business and the approach to work, money and interest.

Jean-Jacques Rousseau is another Genevese giant, active two centuries after Calvin. Whereas Calvin came from the outside and established himself in Geneva somewhat like a dictator, Rousseau was born in Geneva and liked to call himself a citizen of Geneva. But some of his thinking was so radical that at one stage his books were burned and he had to leave town.

The nineteenth century saw the foundation of the International Red Cross. The initiator was another Genevese, Henri Dunant. The Red Cross emblem is the reversal of the Swiss colors and was adopted, at the suggestion of General Henri Dufour, another great Genevese, as a gesture to the host country of the first international conference which led to the foundation of the organization. Henri Dunant was originally a businessman. When he went bankrupt—a deadly sin in Geneva at that time—he had to leave town, never to return. He was forgotten during two decades and lived in poverty until he was rediscovered by a journalist some years before his death. In 1901 he shared the first Nobel peace prize (with the French economist Frédéric Passy).

Geneva has been and continues to be an open city. At different times in its history, it received large numbers of refugees many of whom made substantial contributions to the development of the local economy and then gradually became old Genevese families. Today, Geneva is going through another phase of rapid development. During the last ten years, the number of workplaces has increased by some 40,000, equivalent to some 20 percent. Some 15,000 persons are working in the financial and insurance sector, an increase of nearly 50 percent over the last ten years. Geneva is one of the largest construction sites in the country. This rapid development is also taking hold of the neighboring territories in France where conditions are less cramped than in Geneva. In some ways the area resembles one huge Silicon Valley.

These four cities are only part of the colorful mosaic of local cultures in Switzerland. Much more could be said of other parts of the country, for example, of the last canton stubbornly refusing to grant women the right of vote on the local level. Its rather strange excuse is that the square where the men transact political affairs once a year does not have enough space to accommodate women. The importance of local culture was also illustrated by a story recently published in the reputable *Financial Times* of London:

A group of boys from several countries wanted to know where babies came from. Each boy had his say—stork, gooseberry bush and so on. At the end the little Swiss, looking rather sheepish, explained: Where I come from, it's done differently in each canton.[4]

HOMOGENIZING FORCES

Against this rich and colorful background of local diversity, we will select some of the more important integrative or homogenizing forces that ensure an overall Swiss culture. They have to do with the political system, the system of education, the social environment, and the Swiss Army, among others.

As mentioned earlier, the Swiss developed a special brand of direct democracy which requires much voting from the citizens on the three different levels. Prior to each vote, the issues are widely debated in the media. Television often invites spokespersons representing different points of view for roundtable discussions. The political parties and many other groups adopt recommendations after having gone through an internal decision process. Some days before the more important votes, many newspapers publish tables summarizing the recommendations of perhaps twenty or thirty different organizations and groups. Posters in the streets advocating one point of view or the other often create the atmosphere of open-air art exhibitions. The citizens then have to make up their minds. This is not always easy, and participation is often low. The system resembles a kind of long-term persistent self-education process. The result is not always to the liking of the authorities. For example, most people outside Switzerland are not even aware of the fact that it is one of the very few countries in the world that does not belong to the United Nations. To join or not to join is a question that must be submitted to the voters on the federal level. The government and most political parties have tried hard to make the citizens see the value of joining, but, at the last vote in 1986, the proposal was turned down massively, even in Geneva with its international dimension and its numerous United Nations organizations. Some of the Swiss leaders were embarrassed, but who knows how many other countries would have acted likewise if the citizens had had the opportunity to express their views?

Contrary to the U.S. system, Swiss education is dominated by state institutions and is run largely by the twenty-six cantons. This is not surprising when we recall the linguistic, religious, and cultural diversity of the country. The system does include certain integrative aspects, however. The Confederation harmonizes and coordinates the programs at the primary and secondary levels. The country also has a widely developed apprenticeship system that is run on countrywide standards. A large number of young people finish their eight or nine years of compulsory schooling at the age of fifteen or sixteen and then start an apprenticeship in a business or other organization. The apprentice receives a small salary and goes to school two or three days a week. After three or four years, he or she receives a diploma meeting federal standards and joins the country's workforce.

The universities are the responsibility of the cantons, but the Confederation has charge of the one Federal Institute of Technology, a high-level institution that receives students from all over the country, thus also playing an integrative role.

Trade unions and employer and industry associations are also organized on a national level. When new legislation is being created, the federal government includes them in a formal consulting process that is typically Swiss.

Another important integrative role is played by the Swiss Army. It is not easy for anyone outside Switzerland to understand it. One who did was John McPhee, the American author of a 120-page article in the *New Yorker Magazine*.[5] He had spent some time with a small army unit and starts by explaining:

Switzerland is twice the size of New Jersey. New Jersey has by far the larger population. Nonetheless, there are 650,000 people in the Swiss Army. At any given time, most of them are walking around in street clothes or in blue from the collar down. They are a civilian army, a trained and practiced militia ever ready to mobilize. They serve for 30 years. All 650,000 are prepared to be present at mobilization points and battle stations in considerably less than 48 hours. If you understand the New York Yacht Club, the Cosmos Club, the Metropolitan Club, the Century Club, the Piedmont Driving Club, you would understand the Swiss Army.

Switzerland has a military tradition that dates back more than 600 years. Most Swiss are convinced that the army played an important role in keeping the country out of World Wars I and II. In the Swiss system, all able-bodied men—which is about 90 percent—have to undergo four months of initial training. Once they have done that, corporals are selected. They also undergo training and then serve in their newly acquired rank with the troops, and so on for the next higher ranks. Every able-bodied, male Swiss serves in the army for thirty to thirty-five years. An ordinary soldier would return after the initial training period every year for three weeks, and gradually for less time at a later period. Serving in the army is an experience which most Swiss men share. They make new friends and often spend time in other parts of the country.

George Mikes, the British humorist of Hungarian origin, wrote some years ago that the best kept secret of the Swiss is that there are no Swiss.[6] The forces mentioned here, and some others, including the shared history, do help to hold the country together and ensure that after all there are some Swiss. The idea of the German-, French-, and Italian-speaking parts of the country joining Germany, France, and Italy, respectively, is absurd and just does not arise. Recently, a small group of Genevese journalists did launch the idea that Geneva should leave the Confederation and revert to its former status of an independent republic, along the model of Monaco, but the homogenizing or integrative factors mentioned here are sufficiently strong to make sure that this idea is not taken seriously, at least at this stage.

THE SWISS SOCIETAL MANAGEMENT MODEL

Over time, the Swiss have developed a kind of societal management model. This model can be described as a process which has gradually combined diverse regional cultural characteristics into a set of unifying values that have motivated Swiss business leaders to start and maintain successful industrial enterprises. The values of hard work, long working hours, independence, self-discipline, and tolerance are examples of values that drive this model. The main historical and cultural characteristics that underlie this model can be summarized as follows:

1. The Swiss system is designed to allow local cultures to survive and prosper. The United States is sometimes called a melting pot; Switzerland definitely does not want to be a melting pot.

2. At the same time, certain shared values have developed. The Swiss attach importance to personal and national freedom and independence, and are willing to pay the price for it in the form of the army. They accept the fact that their country is small and that it would be foolish to have territorial ambitions or to try and impose their ways on others. They are used to the notion of neutrality which has evolved over several centuries. They have also developed a certain sense of discipline which is necessary if democratically achieved decisions are to be accepted. They also accept the fact that their system is often slow.

3. Switzerland is decentralized, in sharp contrast with neighboring France. No city in Switzerland occupies the position Paris does in France. The twenty-six local states are autonomous, except in those areas where the power has specifically been delegated to the central government, such as national de-

fense, social security, or monetary policy. Only those tasks that cannot be dealt with by smaller units are taken on by larger ones.

4. The Swiss system is based on power sharing. As opposed to the United States where two parties take turns at exercising power, Switzerland has a multiparty system that allows those parties who reach and maintain a certain strength to participate in power sharing. This leads to consensus-seeking and compromise. The current British system of majority elections where, with some 40 percent of voting strength, it is possible to achieve an overwhelming majority in Parliament was abandoned by the Swiss seventy years ago and would be unacceptable today.

5. There is much collegial decision making, as explained earlier. To have a president in the accepted sense, or a king or dictator, is unthinkable in Switzerland. There is a certain aversion to great leaders and a tendency to think that those who are in governance positions are one's employees.

6. There is direct democracy in the sense that as many decisions as possible are left to the voters at all levels who also have the right to take certain initiatives.

7. Finally, the Swiss believe in a free market economy and a stable currency, although they do have a tendency to create and tolerate cartels and are sometimes slow to accept change and innovations.

These, then, are the major influences that have helped develop a decentralized model of management which incorporates a wide range of societal values. While not as homogeneous as the Japanese management model or as singularly narrow as the Silicon Valley one, the Swiss have developed a model that is more integrative of numerous regional cultural forces—indeed, now international forces— while still reflecting the homogenizing texture of societal influences.

The remainder of this chapter discusses examples of Swiss companies and business practices which illustrate the Swiss management model.

SWISS CULTURAL INFLUENCES AND CORPORATE PRACTICES

Switzerland has been a poor country for centuries. It has practically no raw materials and no direct access to the sea. It has become wealthy because of fortuitous circumstances, good luck, and economic activity. It provided an environment in which business could blossom, and it had entrepreneurs who took advantage of it. It would be tempting to assume that certain cultures more than others within the country have contributed to Swiss wealth, or to pretend, in line with preconceived clichés, that the Protestants were more entrepreneurially oriented than the Catholics, or that the Germanic part was more hard working and serious than the Latin. Such assumptions would be presumptuous, and several facts stand out today. Income in Switzerland is fairly evenly distributed by international standards. Switzerland belongs to those countries with the lowest disparity between the cities and regions with the highest income and those with the lowest.[7] In 1985–1986, a wave of family companies and newly established enterprises went public. If one checks in which cultures and regions they have been founded, one finds, according to Professor Vijay K. Jolly of International Management Institute (IMI)–Geneva, a rather even distribution over the whole country.

One is also struck by the fact that the development of selected industries was often a combination of coincidence, luck, and other factors. A good example is the watch industry. Calvin himself accepted the watch as a useful instrument, even though he disliked ornament and distraction. The following is a quote from the fascinating book by David S. Landes on *Revolution in Time*:

In France, overwhelmingly Catholic, but with a small, active community of Protestants, a disproportionate share of the leading watchmakers of the sixteenth and seventeenth centuries were Protestants. No one to my knowledge has done a quantitative sample, but a quick look at the standard biographical dictionary of French clock- and watchmakers by Tardy reveals the high frequency of makers with Old Testament names: the Davids and Daniels and Isaacs and Samuels that were then characteristic signs of Protestant faith. So when Louis XIV reversed a near-century of tolerance and revoked the Edict of Nantes in 1685, he drove two hundred thousand Protestants from the country and devastated the French watch industry. Some of the best of these refugees went to England, where the trade needed little help; but others went to Switzerland where they did much to establish the mountain manufactures that would one day dominate the world.[8]

So, if Louis XIV had not reversed the Edict of Nantes, it is quite possible that Switzerland would not have achieved its predominance in the watch industry which it held a long time.

What factors contributed to the success of Swiss businesses? Generally, these factors can be described as the business environment, the strategies of Swiss firms, their structures, and the performance of the Swiss as workers.

The political stability of the country was certainly a positive aspect. The fact that Switzerland had a stable currency and comparatively free trade also helped. In addition, the social environment was stable. For example, there have been practically no strikes during the last fifty years, owing largely to what is called the "peace agreement" concluded in the difficult 1930s by employee and worker organizations that decided it was better to resolve conflicts by negotiation rather than by strikes.

Another factor that runs through the Swiss economic history like a red thread is a certain openness to the world, if not at all times, at least at certain periods and on certain occasions. Some of today's leading firms were not established by Swiss nationals. Obviously, neither Mr. Brown nor Mr. Boveri were Swiss. Mr. Diesel, who had a considerable role in the development of Sulzer, was German. Mr. Nestle who founded what was to become today's largest Swiss firm was also of non-Swiss origin. The current chief executive of Nestle, who took the company through a repositioning phase, is German. Other such examples abound among the Genevese private bankers and the teaching staff of Swiss universities in the nineteenth century.

There is no literature on what distinguishes the strategies of Swiss companies from that of other companies, but three characteristics stand out. First, since Switzerland is a small country, with no raw materials and a small home market, it was essential for the Swiss to export. Swiss companies, therefore, were export-oriented and from the earliest beginnings had to consider the world as their market. The extreme example today is that of Nestle. In 1986 the Swiss market represented no more than 0.8 percent of its total sales of 38 billion Swiss francs.

This worldwide orientation refers to medium-size and smaller firms as well. It is not well known, but certain smaller Swiss companies have managed to create certain "niches" for themselves in which they hold 50 percent or more, sometimes even 100 percent, of their markets. For example, over 50 percent of the world's flour mills are supplied by a medium-size company in a smallish town, Buhler of Uzwil. This type of success was possible only because these companies responded very closely to their clients' needs and paid great attention to quality, service, and reliability. The notion of first-class quality has indeed been long associated with Swiss products and services.

Swiss corporate structures have much in common with those of companies in other parts of the world. As is the case everywhere else, the share company proved a marvelous instrument to organize industrial activity. Questions concerning who holds the power in the larger companies—management, the board, or the shareholders—arise in Switzerland as they do anywhere else. New stakeholders, such as environmentalists, also took on a certain strength in Switzerland. The fact that corporate boards do have problems was raised as early as 1983 in a speech by UBS chairman Dr. Robert Holzach at the annual shareholders' meeting. No substantial studies exist, but it is likely that, among other things, Swiss boards have more interlocking directorships than boards in other countries.

Swiss corporate structures have yet another characteristic that is typically Swiss. Almost all the larger Swiss companies have taken measures to preserve Swiss control by creating different types of shares—bearer shares, nominal shares, and participation certificates—with different voting power. It means in many cases that takeovers, such as exist in the United States, are made practically impossible. It cannot be proved, but this is probably linked to the undeniable fact that Swiss share prices, as compared to book, equity, or substance values, are very low by the international comparison.[9] For example, the stock market capitalization of Brown Boveri (BBC), the third largest Swiss company, is currently about one-third of the book value. In the United States, such a situation would probably have led to takeover bids long ago. In Switzerland this did not happen, partly because of the way the share ownership is structured. This aspect is usually regarded as positive, but one could also argue that it is a weakness of the system. BBC is now going through a painful turnaround phase, and it might have been much better if the management had been alerted some years ago by takeover bids. It might also have been in the interests of the shareholders and the economy as a whole.

Here and there one finds other typically Swiss structures. For example, the second largest bank in the country, the Swiss Bank Corporation in Basel, for a long time had a top management that was organized along the lines of the Swiss Federal Council. A group of executives took collegial decisions, with a revolving chairmanship. The bank gave up this structure in 1986 and reverted to a more traditional permanent chief executive.

In addition to the environment, the strategies, and the structures, there is, of course, the workforce. The Swiss accept that fact that hard work is necessary. The Socialist party and the labor unions have proposed on several occasions that the official work week be shortened, the last time to forty hours from the then still existing forty-four. To the amazement of foreign observers, the answer of the Swiss voters was negative. A majority of Swiss voters obviously thought it was in the country's best interests to work longer hours. This explains why, together with Portugal, Switzerland still has the longest work week in Europe.

Another typically Swiss situation is the influence of the army, both on the management level and that of the workforce as a whole. Many managers of Swiss industry, banks, and insurance companies, whether they like it or not, belong to the army during thirty or thirty-five years of their life and hold military commands along with their management responsibilities. Many Swiss boards include a majority of colonels. (There are no generals in peacetime.) John McPhee quotes the case of Robert Jeker: "During his parallel rise from soldier to colonel and from trainee to chief executive of Credit Suisse, he served for more than 1,500 days in the Army, an average of some 50 days a year for 30 years."[10] Non-Swiss executives who often cannot spend even one or two weeks a year away from their desk on a management seminar find this schedule almost impossible to believe, but it is Swiss reality.

This may be some kind of management education which, in the more traditional sense, is not highly developed in Switzerland, in spite of the presence of two of the leading European elite international management schools which receive hundreds of participants every year from all over the world: IMEDE in Lausanne, founded by Nestle, and IMI in Geneva, originally started by Alcan. John McPhee quotes a Swiss officer on the training he received to become a member of the general staff: "It was the most stressful time of my life. I would do it again. You are under pressure. You have to learn. It is good executive training. It is more rigorous than Harvard."[11]

It is a controversial topic even in Switzerland, but there is some validity in the view that the biggest, most effective, and influential management school in the country is the army.[12]

Finally, this section would be incomplete without mention of one major enterprise which is so typically Swiss in its structure and so deeply rooted in Swiss culture and history that it cannot be understood by those who do not have some knowledge of Switzerland—Migros, the leading retail organization. It was founded in 1926 by Gottlieb Duttweiler, one of the outstanding Swiss entrepreneurs of the twentieth century. After two ventures in his life had failed, he created his own company and began to revolutionize food retailing against the stubborn resistance of cartelized competitors, industry associations, and hostile political authorities.

Today, Migros offers 58,000 workplaces, equivalent to about 40,000 full-time jobs. It operates only on the national level. Yet with a consolidated turnover of some 11 billion Swiss francs in 1986, currently equivalent to some U.S. $7 billion, it holds fourth position after Nestle, Ciba-Geigy, and Brown Boveri. A quarter of its sales are products manufactured in company plants, of which many were built or bought to counter suppliers' boycotts in the early days. Migros has some fifty subsidiaries, including the second largest travel agency in the country, a bank, two insurance companies, and a publisher.

Migros, like any other firm, was originally a family company, of which Gottlieb Duttweiler held the majority of shares. In June 1940 he announced that he would, in today's parlance, "go public." But he did it in an unusual way. He started to convert his company into a cooperative type of organization patterned largely after the Swiss political system. Today, some 1.3 million Swiss households belong to the Migros community. They receive a weekly paper and have certain advantages but do not get any dividends. They do have the right to elect the members of some of the local boards as well as some members of the main board, including the six top executives and the chairperson.

Gottlieb Duttweiler changed the organizational structure in 1940 not because he needed capital, but, on the contrary, according to his longtime private secretary Ernst Melliger, because of his family situation, his patriotic feelings, and his ideas about the role of the enterprise in the Western world. Duttweiler and his wife, who played an important role in his life, had no children. When he announced his decision in 1940, Nazi Germany had taken over Denmark and Norway, and had invaded Holland, Belgium, and Luxembourg. France was collapsing. The evacuation of Dunkirk was in progress, and Switzerland, now surrounded by Nazi powers, was likely to be the next victim. Duttweiler felt that by converting his enterprise into a cooperative, it would be closer to the people, more deeply rooted among his clients, and thus more difficult to take over and control by the Nazis in case they invaded Switzerland.

At the same time, Duttweiler also developed his own ideas on values, and the role and responsibility of the enterprise. He did smoke cigars, but following the policies he introduced, Migros today sells neither alcohol nor tobacco. It also spends some 1 percent of its retail turnover on cultural and social activities. In 1986 this amounted to some 83 million Swiss francs or, since the rule was introduced, to a total of over 1 billion. It has created adult education centers and language training schools in several countries of Europe. It is also typically Swiss in that it is bilingual. At board and other meetings, each participant uses either German or French, whichever he or she prefers. Duttweiler also felt that the enterprise had great social responsibility. Today, Migros is probably the world leader in social reporting.

Gottlieb Duttweiler's ability to change the structure of his enterprise and his decision to give it away, so to say, brought it closer to the people and established strong roots in the country, but there is another side to it. Migros has at present such large market shares in many sectors that it cannot grow much more. When it was founded, some 35 to 40 percent of family budgets were spent on food against some 12 percent today. The world is becoming more international all the time, but when the Migros members voted, as they were entitled to, on whether the company should expand internationally, the answer was no.

SWISS MANAGEMENT AS A MODEL?

The management literature has recently reflected on what can be learned from the Japanese way of management or from the Silicon Valley experience. Since Switzerland is usually regarded as a happy and wealthy country, it is legitimate to ask if anything can be learned from the way the Swiss manage their affairs. To answer this question, it is necessary to distinguish between business management and what we earlier called "societal management."

Hardly anyone outside Switzerland pays any attention to the way the Swiss manage their companies. In the management literature it is a nonissue. This is understandable. Swiss industries and companies have found it as difficult as their non-Swiss counterparts to remain competitive. Some books on management from abroad have become bestsellers as much in Switzerland as anywhere else. In their efforts to reposition themselves, some of the leading Swiss companies have engaged American management consultants or have flown business school professors across the Atlantic at very high fees. Rather than exporting their management model, if there is such a thing, the Swiss have had to try and learn from others.

The way the Swiss manage their country and thus the environment in which their companies operate, however, continues to attract attention. In a world made up of different nations, cultures, and peoples whose interests often clash, it is tempting to argue that the Swiss model of societal management, explained earlier, might include lessons for the rest of the world. Most of the Swiss feel, however, that this model cannot be adopted elsewhere simply because it is based on a set of specific circumstances—such as the country's geographical location and its lack of natural resources—and a slow, gradual, and sometimes painful evolution over centuries. Those who feel that the Swiss model could be applied elsewhere are often non-Swiss enthusiasts who do not really know the country.

One who knows Switzerland well and still thinks there are lessons to be learned from it is Dr. Otto van Habsburg, a highly respected European and the current head of the Habsburg family. In an article published in 1985, he implied that in the long run Europe had the choice between becoming a larger Switzerland or a Czechoslovakia.[13] Dr. von Habsburg's view that certain lessons can be learned from the Swiss experience is particularly poignant to those who know Swiss history. In the thirteenth and fourteenth centuries, the Swiss obtained and preserved their independence by fighting against the Habsburg family of that time. Indeed, the Habsburg home castle is still located on Swiss soil.

Two authors, one from the Hoover Institute at Stanford and the other at the centuries-old University of Heidelberg, even coined a new expression when they placed an article under the heading "The Risky Swissification of Europe."[14] They wrote:

Wittingly or unwittingly neutralists and isolationists on both sides of the Atlantic have come to look to Switzerland as a model. This country—so it appears—looks after its own defense, escapes from entanglement alliances, maintains a prosperous economy and a democratic system. Neutral, it stays out of trouble and makes no trouble. What a marvelous example to follow.

If they call *Swissification* risky, it is because they feel that anti-Americanism and isolationism often go with neutralism. The authors conclude:

Those Europeans who dream of creating a Switzerland must not forget that Switzerland's most important accomplishment historically is its ability to shape several national components into one united people, as the U.S. has done. This is the lesson that ought to be learned from Switzerland.

Switzerland, as a country, and with it Swiss business, has undoubtedly been successful in the past but how about the future?

A survey of the Swiss economy published by the London *Economist* concludes that: "if the Swiss want to maintain their high living standards and keep inflation and unemployment low, they will have to break into an unaccustomed jog just to stand still in a world accelerating economic change."[15]

Indeed, many Swiss do feel a certain unease, and some even talk and write about a threatening decline. One undeniable fact comes to mind. During the longest part of its existence and during the time the country achieved its current prosperity and reputation, Europe was the center of what was regarded as the developed world, and Switzerland was at the center of that center. Now other regions of the world have taken on new importance, and Europe is not what it used to be. The Swiss may not like it, but they cannot change these developments. Being citizens of a small and basically poor country, they will have all the more need to try and remain at the forefront of their various fields of endeavor. The example of the watch industry—although only a small part of the economy—has shown them that successes and reputations that have taken decades or even centuries to build can collapse almost overnight. Continued attention to the competitiveness of their companies and to how Swiss societal management might have to be changed to cope with the developments of our times, coupled with a good dose of modesty and humility, will help the country to continue on its successful path.

NOTES

1. See chapters 2 and 3 in this volume.

2. Georges-Andre Chevallaz, *La Suisse est-elle gouvernable?* (Lausanne: Editions de l'Aire, 1984).

3. Peter Stadler, "The Zurich Mentality and Swiss Identity," *Swissair Gazette*, no. 7 (1986): 13–15.

4. W. H. Luetkens, "The Swiss Character: Different But Not Dull," *The Financial Times* (London), April 28, 1987.

5. The *New Yorker* articles were also published in book form: Jonh McPhee, *La Place de la Concorde Suisse* (New York: Farrar, Straus & Giroux, 1983).

6. George Mikes, *Switzerland for Beginners* (London: Andre Deutsch, 1973).

7. Ernst A. Brugger, "Politique Regionale Suisse: Pourquoi? Comment? Qui?," *Bulletin de documentation economique*, no. 4 (November 1986): 2.

8. David S. Landes, *Revolution in Time* (Cambridge, Mass. and London: Belknap Press of Harvard University Press, 1983), p. 93.

9. Bank Vontobel, "Aktienmarkt Schweiz, Substanzwerte" (Wirtschafts-studien, 1987).

10. McPhee, *La Place de la Concorde Suisse*.

11. Ibid.

12. Max Daetwyler, "Management Education in Switzerland," *Quarterly Review* (Summer 1985).

13. Otto Von Habsburg, "Europa—Schweiz oder Tchechoslwakei?" *Finanz & Wirtschaft*, April 17, 1985.

14. L. H. Gann and Robert Deutsch, "The Risky Swissification of Switzerland," *The Wall Street Journal*, April 18, 1984.

15. *The Economist*, September 6–12, 1986.

9

Regional Culture, Entrepreneurship, and High-Technology Development in India

Raghu Nath

The prime minister of India has pledged to bring India into the twenty-first century by focusing on high-technology development. Probably the most effective way to move toward this goal is to develop a high-technology park in India. The success of this venture will require careful planning, including the identification of the region best suited for it. This essay identifies regions in India which are conducive to entrepreneurial development such as high-technology parks. To that end, this chapter discusses (1) requirements for high-technology development; (2) the nature of entrepreneurship and the needed culture for promoting entrepreneurship and high technology; (3) some of the salient work relating to regional cultures and technology development in the United States; (4) critical factors for locating high-technology plants and activities; (5) the concept of a technology park and factors for successful development of these parks; (6) some key characteristics of developing countries, including a recent interest in high technology, particularly, the role of technology transfer from developed to developing countries; (7) the partnerships conferences organized to discuss issues related to technology transfer from developed to developing nations, including the strategic issues identified during these partnerships conferences; (8) the project for locating a high-technology park in India; (9) the regional identities and major industrial regions in India; (10) the dialogue between government officials, industrialists, and U.S. experts regarding location of the first high-technology park, with particular emphasis on regional culture and required infrastructure; (11) problems associated with fitting entrepreneurial high-technology ventures with Indian regional cultures; (12) prior experience in dealing with some of these problems and some recent promising developments; and (13) the future of high-technology development in India.

HIGH-TECHNOLOGY DEVELOPMENT

High-technology firms and industries are identified by significant research and development expenditures and the employment of a large number of scientists, engineers, and technical personnel.

A definition of high technology should include both production processes and products. Production process technology refers to the large operations embedded within the organizational and locational structures of mature, multiplant firms. Such plants utilize economies of scale and manufacture standardized products. Robotics is one such example. High-technology products are associated with the industries and plants that tend to be small, new, and at the beginning stages of the product life cycle. Such plants are usually independent, face great risk, are informally organized, are labor intensive, and have rapidly changing product lines. Silicon Valley has been characterized as the premier location for start-up operations that introduce new high-technology products with shorter life cycles. Software products are one such example of the high-technology product (Weiss 1987). Some recent areas of high technology are semiconductors, computers, biotechnology, telecommunications, robotics, and super conductors.

ENTREPRENEURSHIP

Entrepreneurship is the phenomenon of starting new projects, plants, and companies. When successful, these new enterprises grow at a rapid pace. Apple Computer and Lotus Development are good examples of entrepreneurial firms that have achieved phenomenal success. These entrepreneurial firms do not have to be in high-technology areas. In fact, some, like Domino's Pizza, are in the low-technology area, whereas others might be in medium technology. The two examples of Apple Computer and Lotus Development are, of course, from the high-technology field.

Entrepreneurial management style is highly valued. Indeed, many of today's fastest growing and most profitable businesses in the United States were founded on the vision of an entrepreneur and continued to be managed in the entrepreneurial mode. As an entrepreneurial management style has long been associated with business success, many managers regard it as inherently good (Collins and Moore 1970).

Although entrepreneurial style is usually found in small start-up firms, several large firms like IBM, Sony, 3M, and Hewlett-Packard have been able to sustain their high level of performance by behaving in an entrepreneurial manner (Stevenson and Gumpert 1985). Peters and Waterman (1982) have indicated that larger firms encourage entrepreneurship through a process called intrapreneurship. People within the organization are encouraged to develop proposals for new ideas that may involve either product or process innovation. These projects are funded by the firm; thus, the project advocate plays the role of the entrepreneur who is engaged in developing new ideas up to a start-up phase. As we know from the entrepreneurship literature, entrepreneurial activity requires risk-taking behavior. Not all ideas pan out, and there is usually a high degree of failure along the way. Larger firms that are successful in the intrapreneurship activity encourage their people to engage in risk-taking behavior and develop reward systems to encourage such activity.

REGIONAL CULTURE

There are many definitions of culture. Narrowly defined, it is simply a system of beliefs. Broadly defined, culture involves beliefs, value systems, norms, mores, myths, as well as structural elements of a given organization, tribe, or society. Thus, culture acts as an integrating force for a given system. It provides glue to hold together the cognitive, affective, and structural components of the system. Of course, degree of integration depends on how strong a given culture is. The stronger the culture, the better the integration. Weak cultures provide little integration.

Culture can exist at various levels of the system, that is, group, organizational, and society. For a long time, the focus of culture studies has been at the national or societal level (Hofstede 1980). During the last few years, there has been a great deal of interest in corporate culture (Deal and Kennedy 1982; Schein 1985). In recent years, Weiss and Delbecq (1987) have advanced the notion of regional cultures. Just as a given corporation may contain many subcultures, Weiss and Delbecq have argued that several regional cultures may be present in a given nation. In particular, their work has demonstrated the existence of distinct regional cultures in Silicon Valley and Route 128 in Boston. For example, through empirical research Delbecq has shown that Silicon Valley has a distinct culture that encourages entrepreneurship, particularly in the high-technology area of microelectronics. In their definition of regional culture, Weiss and Delbecq have utilized the broader definition of culture as depicted in table 2.1 in chapter 2 of this book.

As table 2.1 shows, the regional characteristics lead to regional industrial culture, which in turn leads to organizational and management manifestations. The five aspects of regional industrial culture identified are: entrepreneurial/conservative, formal/informal, looseknit/tightly coordinated, cooptative/collaborative, and norms governing business practices. As indicated in the prior section, entrepreneurial culture encourages risk-taking, whereas the conservative culture encourages risk avoidance. In the entrepreneurial culture, the emphasis is on trying new things, exploring new avenues, valuing innovation, and not punishing failures. Conservative culture does the opposite. It is obvious, therefore, that entrepreneurial culture would be more conducive to high-technology development that depends heavily on knowledgeable workers who prefer innovation, change, and experimentation to the status quo.

Regional Cultures in the United States

As indicated earlier, recent interest has been shown in the study of regional cultures in the United States. As Japan has started challenging traditional industries in the United States, many state governments have attempted to encourage the development of high technology in their states. In fact, it has been argued that the United States' comparative advantage in the world economy is in the area of high-technology industries because its culture and infrastructure are best suited to development of high technology. However, only a few areas in the United States have become centers of high-technology; among these are Silicon Valley, Route 128 in Boston, and the North Carolina triangle. In recent years, Austin, Texas, as well as areas of Maryland adjoining Washington, D.C., have started developing concentrations of high-technology companies. As Weiss and Delbecq found, a distinct regional culture exists in Silicon Valley and Route 128 in Boston. Although these two regional cultures share some similarities, there are also significant differences between them.

Even regions in the United States that are known primarily for traditional industries such as steel are trying to become centers of high technology. For example, the western Pennsylvania region centered around Pittsburgh is aspiring to become a high-technology center through a planned development effort. This effort, known as "Century 21 Project," is being managed by regional organizations with the help of the state government of Pennsylvania. An important feature of this project is partnership between government, industry, and universities. Central to the project is the belief that, through appropriate incentives and the creation of necessary infrastructure, regional culture can be changed from one of conservatism to entrepreneurship. Already this planned effort is succeeding. Several high-technology firms have sprung up in recent years. The Pittsburgh High Technology Council has approximately 350 member firms, and a study conducted by the Center

Table 9.1
Factors Influencing Location of High-Technology Plants

===

FACTOR	RANK
Labor	1
Transportation availability	2
Quality of life	3
Markets access	4
Utilities	5
Site characteristics	6
Community characteristics	7
Business climate	8
Taxes	9
Development organizations	10

Adapted from Stafford (1983).

for Urban Studies of the University of Pittsburgh reports that there are over 1,000 high-technology firms in western Pennsylvania.

CRITICAL FACTORS FOR SUCCESSFUL DEVELOPMENT OF HIGH TECHNOLOGY

One way we can identify critical factors for success is through surveys that try to identify why executives locate high-technology plants in different areas of the United States. The results of two such surveys (Stafford 1983 and Joint Economic Committee 1982) are summarized in tables 9.1 and 9.2. As can be seen in table 9.1, Stafford's survey identifies ten factors for influencing the location of new manufacturing high-technology plants. In the table, these ten factors are ranked one to ten in order of their importance.

The Joint Economic Committee's survey of the selection of high-technology plants reports factors for selection of region as well as factors for selection within region. Again, there are ten factors ranked from one to ten in order of their importance.

As the two surveys show, labor skills and availability is ranked number one in both. Other factors common to the two surveys are transportation, market access, taxes, and utilities or energy cost.

Table 9.2
**Factors for Selection of Region and Within-Region Location
for High-Technology Plants**

==

SELECTION OF REGION	SELECTION WITHIN REGION	RANK
Labor skills/availability	Labor availability	1
Labor costs	State/local tax structure	2
Tax climate within region	Business climate	3
Academic institutions	Cost of property/building	4
Cost of living	Transportation (people)	5
Transportation	Area for expansion	6
Market access	Proximity to good schools	7
Regional regulatory practices	Proximity to amenities	8
Energy cost/availability	Transportation (goods)	9
Cultural amenities	Proximity to customers	10

Adapted from Joint Economic Committee (1982).

The two surveys also exhibit some differences. For example, quality of life is ranked very high in the Stafford survey but is not specifically mentioned in the Joint Economic Committee survey. Cultural amenities that contribute to quality of life are ranked number ten in the Joint Economic Committee survey. The Stafford survey lists community characteristics as an important factor. Although the other survey does not mention this factor, such factors as proximity to good schools may be considered as community characteristics. Furthermore, the Stafford survey mentions developmental organizations as a critical factor, but the Joint Economic Committee survey does not list it.

In their study of high-technology cultures in Silicon Valley and Route 128 in Boston, Weiss and Delbecq (1987) found that the Silicon Valley culture values individualistic competition, informality, and experimentation. The result is a general business culture characterized by job-hopping, a free-form type of organizational structure, and emphasis on short-term planning and product innovation. The high-technology regional industrial culture in Silicon Valley is, therefore, characterized as entrepreneurial, informal, intense, dynamic, cooptive, materialistic, individualistic, tightly knit network between employees across firms;

and belief systems centered on self-fulfillment, wealth, and profession-alism. In comparison, Boston's Route 128 has a high-technology re-gional industrial culture characterized as formal, conservative, calculated, innovative, looseknit relations between firms, analytic and control oriented, group oriented; and belief systems centered on loyalty, commitment, and diligence. Whereas job-hopping is a norm in Silicon Valley, it is considered unacceptable in Route 128. In summing up their study, Weiss and Delbecq (1987) report:

This study, for example, showed not all high technology cultures are alike, nor the effects of regional environment on business practices necessarily the same. The findings also indicate that variables presented here in addition to those most frequently used, such as presence of research universities, agglomeration of economies, technology, and the like [Dorfman 1982; Miller and Cote 1985], may also be important determinants of high technology management practices and ways of doing business.

As is obvious from the above studies, empirical research has not led to identification of a common list of critical factors for successful de-velopment of high technology. Although some regional characteristics are common among high-technology areas, there are also significant differences among these areas. In addition, the example of Pittsburgh cited earlier indicates that high technology can be developed in a region that was characterized by traditional industries and conservative cul-ture. This, however, requires a planned effort involving a partnership among government, industry, and universities.

TECHNOLOGY PARKS

High-technology development in a traditional region can be facili-tated by the catalytic role of a well-developed technology park. Devel-opment of technology parks is, therefore, a proactive strategy to bring about desired high-technology development through a planned change process. The major advantage of this strategy is that available resources can be initially concentrated in a single location. The technology park brings together at one location those who conduct research and generate knowledge and entrepreneurs who develop products based on these knowledge-based technologies. There are also other advantages. First, by sharing common facilities, the costs of operating a single enterprise can be reduced substantially, thus insuring a better survival rate for start-up companies. Second, and most importantly, the location of lab-oratories and companies in the vicinity of each other provides synergy to develop viable technologies and products. Third, needed social, eco-nomic, and management services can be provided to individual com-panies on a cost-effective basis.

Development of a successful technology park requires partnership among government, industry, and universities. For example, in western Pennsylvania the Century 21 Project involves development of a high-technology park through cooperation among city and state governments, local industry, and the two world-class universities. The Urban Redevelopment Authority is providing land, and the state government is providing required financial resources through grants. Universities would manage research and development facilities at the location and provide knowledgeable workers and future entrepreneurs.

In summary, a successful technology park requires that the following critical factors be present:

1. The existence of world-class universities in the region which can be a source of ideas and provide scientific, technical, and managerial personnel.
2. Availability of venture capital through either state-funded sources and/or banks and venture capitalists.
3. Developed site that can provide necessary infrastructure as well as quality of work life.
4. A spirit of collaboration among government, industry, and universities.

DEVELOPING COUNTRIES

In recent years a number of developing countries such as Brazil, China, India, and Singapore have expressed interest in developing high-technology industries. The primary strategy for developing high-technology industries has been to entice multinational companies to locate their high-technology facilities in developing countries or license their technology to firms of these countries. This strategy has had very limited success for the following reasons.

Multinational firms have moved their manufacturing facilities to developing nations for primarily two reasons: availability of cheap labor and scarce raw materials. In either case, it is not the high-technology end of the industry that has moved to developing countries. Instead, it is the manufacture of standardized commodity products that have been located there. For example, in the case of the electronics industry, what has been moved to developing countries is the manufacture of standardized chips, which is the low-technology end of this high-technology industry. Very few multinationals have moved their state-of-the-art research and development facilities to developing nations because developing nations are not perceived to have a comparative advantage for research and development work.

Attempts to transfer high technology from developed to developing nations through licensing arrangements have also failed. Proprietary and control considerations require that high (the latest) technology be kept in the home nation where it is invented. Therefore, when technology has been transferred from developed to developing countries, it is usually the established technology rather than the new technology. In most cases, the mature technology has been medium or low technology rather than high technology.

PARTNERSHIPS FOR DEVELOPMENT DIALOGUE CONFERENCES

Two partnerships conferences were held in Pittsburgh during October 1983 and May 1985. These conferences brought together leaders of government, industry, labor, academic institutions, and media from developed and developing countries to consider and deliberate on issues of mutual interest. Because the climate prevailing in these conferences was open and friendly, many serious issues were debated and discussed. The general consensus was that multinationals have by and large done a good job in developing countries. On the other hand, both sides recognized that technology transfer from developed to developing nations has not been up to the expectation of developing countries. Although it has been partly the fault of multinational firms from developed nations, a number of constraining factors emanating from developing countries have prevented the desired transfer of technology. The most important constraining factors are lack of proper infrastructure facilities, including required human resources as well as the absence of incentives for the development of high technology.

The second conference, therefore, recommended that developing nations adopt a partnerships approach which involves collaboration among government, industry, and universities from both developed and developing countries (Nath 1985). Some of the ideas and recommendations from the second partnerships conference were further discussed at the specially convened meeting in Beijing during April 1986 on the topic "Strategic Orientation of Science and Technology for Development." This meeting was attended by eminent scientists and government and industry leaders from leading developed and developing countries.

As a result of these conferences, a working group was set up in Pittsburgh to develop a viable plan for developing high-technology industries in developing nations. This working group has identified the establishment of high-technology parks as the most appropriate vehicle for catalyzing the development of high technology in developing countries. Since India had expressed keen interest in high-technology development, it was decided to try this strategic idea in India.

INDIA AND HIGH-TECHNOLOGY DEVELOPMENT

From its inception as an independent country in 1947, India has been interested in the development of science and technology. Its first prime minister, Jawaharlal Nehru, was deeply interested in science and technology and personally assured that it received high priority in India's development plans. This interest was further pursued by his daughter Indira Gandhi who became India's prime minister in the 1970s. Upon her assassination, her son Rajiv Gandhi became the prime minister of India. As soon as elections were over in December 1984, Rajiv Gandhi made it known that his top priority was to catapult India into the twenty-first century by encouraging the development of high-technology industry in the nation, particularly the electronics-based industry. In order to implement this policy, the prime minister liberalized the import of needed electronic equipment to allow rapid development of software industry in India.[1] Export incentives were also provided. As a result, during the last few years several software development firms have been set up by local entrepreneurs as well as by multinational firms in India. It was, therefore, natural to think about setting up the first high-technology park in the country centered around software development. Before discussing the location of this park, it is necessary to describe the regional diversity prevailing in India and the leading industrial regions of the country.

INDIA: A COUNTRY OF REGIONAL DIVERSITY

India is a country of great regional diversity.[2] Geographically, there are the great mountain walls of the Himalayas in the north, bush plains in the central region, the Plateau of Deccan in the south, and coastal areas in the east and the west. It is the seventh largest state in the world and the second most largely populated.

The People

From north to south and from west to east, the complexion of the population in India changes by several shades, from the fair northwesterners to the very dark southerners. Ethnologically, the population can be divided into six categories: Negroids; the Proto-Astroloids; the Mongoloids; the Mediterraneans; the Alpo-Dinaries; and the Nordics. The dominant racial strain is the Mediterranean. The Aryan culture prevails in the north, whereas in the south Dravidian culture predominates. It is small wonder that some anthropologists have characterized India as the ethnological museum of the world.

Historically, Indian civilization dates back to several thousand years before Christ. In addition to local inhabitants, many people, including Aryans, Greeks, Moghuls, Parsis, and Jews, invaded and migrated to India from other countries. Thus, India is a land of many religions and ethnic groups that have maintained their ethnic identities including religious practices. Most have learned to live together in relative harmony. From time to time, communal conflicts do develop in India, but these are always shortlived. Finally, the 300 years of British rule have greatly influenced the infrastructure in India, especially the educational system, the legal system, and the transportation network. The Indian civil service is also patterned after the British civil service.

India is approximately one-third the size of the United States, yet its population is about three times larger. As a result, the population density is very high in India, particularly in urban areas where industry tends to be concentrated.

The Industrial Regions of India

Although industries have sprung up in most of India's urban areas, we can identify five major industrial regions with a high concentration of industry:[3]

1. Calcutta
2. Bombay–Pune
3. Delhi–Ghaziabad–Faridabad
4. Ahmedabad–Baroda
5. Bangalore

The following sections briefly describe each of these regions.[4]

Calcutta

Calcutta is the chief metropolitan area in the state of Bengal. It is located in the east of India. The climate is tropical with high humidity and temperature which gets exceedingly oppressive during some parts of the year. Because Calcutta is located 60 miles inland from the sea coast, it does not get the cooling effects of sea breezes.

Calcutta was probably the first city to be industrialized by the British. The first few industries that developed in this region involved the processing of agricultural raw materials such as jute and indigo. Furthermore, a part of Calcutta was used to send tea to the United Kingdom. As a result, Calcutta became the headquarters of British trading companies. The availability of coal and iron ore really gave impetus for industrial development in this region. Today, greater Calcutta has a diversified industrial base comprising light engineering, shipping, textiles, and printing.

After the partition of India and Pakistan in 1947, there was a great influx of refugees from east Bengal (now Bangladesh) to Calcutta. Because of poor planning and limited space, this influx was not absorbed appropriately, leading to poor living conditions for many of these refugees. In addition, the city could not handle the vast expansion in population as a result of migration from rural areas to Calcutta. The present control of the state government is in the hands of the Marxist party. Severe labor unrest arose in the 1960s and 1970s, resulting in the closing and relocation of some existing factories and offices to other areas of the country (*India Today*, July 31, 1987). There is also a power shortage in Calcutta. Therefore, few new industries have been established in this region during the last decade. The present chief minister, Mr. Jyoti Basu, has offered many incentives to attract industry to this region. It is too early to determine whether his efforts will bear any fruit.

Calcutta has been and continues to be a center for art, music, and culture. The Indian Institute of Technology is located just 80 miles away at Kharagpur and has been a premier source of engineers even for the National Aeronautics and Space Agency program in the United States (*Time*, July 7, 1987). In addition, an Indian Institute of Management which was set up in collaboration with the Massachusetts Institute of Technology is located here. Other famous institutions are the Indian Statistical Institute and the Bose Institute (Physics).

Bombay–Pune

This region is probably the most highly industrialized region of the country. Like Calcutta, Bombay developed early during the British occupation of India. Bombay is a major port city. Although its weather is hot and humid during most of the year, it benefits from being a coastal town. Unlike Calcutta, sea breezes moderate the weather in Bombay.

Bombay is a renowned center for education and research. Bombay University is considered one of the best universities in India. In addition, the city has many research institutes such as the Atomic Energy Commission Laboratories and Tata Institutes of Fundamental Research and Social Sciences.

Bombay has always been a progressive metropolitan area and has a cosmopolitan outlook. As a result, people from different parts of India have migrated to this city. The local governments of Bombay have always been very progressive. Moreover, the business community there is highly developed and relatively forward looking. In many ways, Bombay is the free enterprise capital of India.

During the last decade, the Bombay metropolitan area has become very crowded. Nevertheless, its transportation system efficiently handles more than 8 million passengers daily. Although a twin city linked by a bridge to the mainland has been planned, it has only now taken off after the state government moved many of its departments there. The infrastructure in Bombay is stretched to its limits; therefore, new industrial development in the Bombay metropolitan area has slowed down in recent years. As a result, Pune, which is about 200 kilometers from Bombay, is now becoming a major industrial center, as is the area along the Pune-Bombay Highway.

Delhi–Ghaziabad–Faridabad

Delhi is the seat of India's central government. Historically, it was the seat of Moghul and British empires. As a result, Delhi has many historical buildings and monuments.

New Delhi was designed as a modern city with an excellent transportation system. Unfortunately, Delhi has expanded enormously as a result of the population influx from West Pakistan as well as other states. Therefore, its infrastructure facilities are highly strained. This situation was somewhat improved during the Asian games held in 1982.

Industrial development in Delhi has been planned in such a way that most of the industries are located in areas specified for industrial development. In addition to several locations in Delhi, two major industrial townships surrounding Delhi are Ghaziabad, which is in the state of Utter Pradesh, and Faridabad which is in the state of Haryana. In addition to special incentives provided by the respective states, these two townships benefit greatly from the fact that they adjoin Delhi.

Delhi has an excellent educational system. The University of Delhi is regarded as one of the premier institutions in the country. In addition, several central government research and development facilities are located in Delhi.

Ahmedabad–Baroda

In recent years the state of Gujarat has aggressively promoted industrial development. Industrial development has been concentrated in two metropolitan areas in this state, Ahmedabad and Baroda. Ahmedabad was the seat of the textile industry. However, in recent years its industrial base has diversified somewhat to chemicals, owing to incentives provided by the government of Gujarat. The prestigious Indian Institute of Management, started in collaboration with Harvard University, is located here. The internationally acclaimed SITE program, the Physical Research Laboratory and the Indian Space Research Organization, has one of its main centers in Ahmedabad. Initially, it was known primarily for its chemical industry.

In recent years, Baroda has also developed a diversified industrial base. The Sarabhai group has established a number of progressive enterprises in Baroda. In addition, major petrochemical complexes have been set up near this area. The people of Gujarat are entrepreneurially oriented. For example, Gujaratis have set up major firms in East and West Africa, and they are active in the motel industry in Florida, California, and the United Kingdom. They also adapt quickly to new techniques such as the cooperative system in the dairy industry and agriculture.

Bangalore

Bangalore, the capital city of the progressive state of Karnataka, is called the Garden City of India.[5] The quality of life in this city had been exceedingly good. The climate is ideal, with the temperature most of the year staying in the 70s. Hence, it has always been considered a resort town. As a result, people from all over India have moved to this city, making Bangalore a very cosmopolitan city.

This city has an excellent educational infrastructure. More importantly, it has not experienced student unrest as other places in India have. In fact, the entire state of Karnataka has had no student unrest. Bangalore has a world-class Indian Institute of Science that has links with many distinguished institutes in the developed countries such as MIT in the United States and the Imperial College of Technology in London. Also located here is the Raman Institute, named after the famous Nobel Laureate Sir C. V. Raman.

The state of Karnataka was formerly the princely state called Mysore. The Maharaja of Mysore, Sir Jaya Cham Rajendra Vodeyar, was an educated king and, therefore, donated liberally to the establishment of fine educational institutes. Mysore also had able prime ministers called Dewans. One of these Dewans was Sir Vishweshwarayya who was an engineer par excellence and was responsible for the establishment of the National Institute of Engineering. He built the famous Sharavati Dam which gave a great boost to the industrialization of the state.

Although Bangalore was a seat of engineering education for a long time, the industrialization of Bangalore really started in the 1960s and accelerated in the 1970s. Because of unrest in many parts of India, several entrepreneurs moved into Bangalore and are still moving there (India Today, July 31, 1987). For example, Gujarati and Tamils came in the 1960s and 1970s. These highly educated and industrially oriented people have been responsible for industrial development in the state.

In addition, local groups such as Pais developed not only banking but also medical and engineering colleges.

Given the area's excellent climate, leading engineering institutes, as well as a progressive environment, the government of India started moving its major high-technology industries to Bangalore in the late 1950s and 1960s. First was the establishment of Hindustan Aeronautics Ltd. (HAL) and Bharat Electronic Limited (BEL). These were followed by establishment of Defense Electronic Laboratory (DEL) and Indian Scientific Satellite Project (ISSP). As a result, Bangalore developed into a major center for the electronics industry during the 1960s and 1970s.

This migration of people and industries has created a heavy burden on the infrastructure. Whereas transportation was excellent in this city, it has become relatively clogged in recent years. In addition, the water and electricity supply has become scarce. Fortunately, the present state government is taking steps to restore Bangalore to its prior garden city status by encouraging the planting of trees. It is also providing commissions to bus drivers so as to provide free market incentives to improve the transportation system. The state government is headed by Chief Minister Ramakrishana Hegde who is very progressive and is committed to restoring Bangalore's reputation as India's most desirable and most livable city.

In recent years, many multinational firms such as Texas Instruments and Philips have moved their software development facilities to Bangalore. *The Wall Street Journal* (1986) has described Bangalore as the Silicon Valley of India.

DISCUSSIONS WITH GOVERNMENT, INDUSTRIALISTS, AND U.S. EXPERTS

In order to select the appropriate location for the first high-technology park in India, the author took an extensive trip to India during the fall of 1986. During this trip, he held discussions with government officials at the state as well as the central government level, leading industrialists from India, and many U.S. experts including professors, scientists, and Agency for International Development personnel. These discussions were further carried on with relevant people in Washington, that is, the National Academy of Sciences, the National Science Foundation, as well as other relevant experts familiar with the situation in India.

Based on these discussions, Calcutta was early eliminated as the possible site. Of the remaining four sites, two leading candidates emerged: Bangalore in Karnataka and Pune in Maharashtra. In the following sections, therefore, we will discuss regional culture as well as the infrastructure of these two regions in India.

Some Similarities

There are many similarities between Bangalore and Pune. Both have excellent climates, with the temperature in both cities staying in the 70s most of the year. Both have relatively humidity-free climates. Pune is located in the hills, whereas Bangalore is located on a plateau about 2,000 feet above sea level. Both have been the seat of military establishments; therefore, military personnel have settled in both cities, resulting in excellent cantonment areas. Thus, both regions offer excellent quality of life, which is an important consideration for professional people engaged in high-technology work.

Both cities have very progressive state governments that provide a number of incentives for development of high-technology industries. These incentives include grants of land at concessional rates and tax incentives for development of high-technology parks. U.S. experts who have visited these two cities speak highly of both regions.

Both cities have a well-developed industrial structure and a broad industrial base. However, there are significant differences in the type of industries located in each area. These differences will be examined later when we discuss the key differences between the two areas.

Both have a cosmopolitan outlook that is very conducive to the establishment of a high-technology industry that requires professional employees and knowledgeable workers. Finally, both cities have highly developed educational systems. Bangalore has fine engineering, science, and management institutes. Not only does Pune have an excellent university system, but it can also draw on the fine institutions of Bombay which are only 80 miles away. As indicated earlier, Bombay has an excellent university system and premier research institutes in social as well as fundamental sciences.

Key Differences

Having discussed some of the similarities, we will now highlight the differences between these two cities. The first major difference is the type of industry located in each. Whereas Bangalore has primarily public sector enterprises (such as BHEL, HAL, and DEL) which are mostly in high-technology areas, Pune has mostly private sector companies (e.g., chemical, light electricals, trucks, and two-wheelers) that are in medium-technology areas. Moreover, several Indians who have returned from abroad have set up small entrepreneurial firms in Pune. In recent years many foreign companies such as Texas Instruments and Philips have set up their facilities in Bangalore. In sum, Bangalore has more of what we call high-technology industries such as those relating to space and electronics. Pune, on the other hand, has industries that may be classified in the medium range involving mostly mature technologies. Finally, whereas Bangalore has primarily a public sector culture, Pune has mainly a private sector culture.

Bangalore houses the Indian Institute of Science (IISC) which is one of the premier institutes in the country graduating scientists of high caliber. These are knowledgeable workers who are well suited for high-technology industries. Although Pune has fine educational institutions, it does not have a world-class institution like IISC. Another important difference is that Bangalore has not been troubled by student unrest, whereas Bombay and Pune have been affected. In addition, the Bombay–Pune region has more strike-prone and militant trade unions. Thus, the workforce is probably more stable in Bangalore than in either Bombay or Pune.

Although both state governments have provided incentives for industrial development, the state government in Bangalore is currently perceived to be more responsive and has a better reputation for delivering what it promises.

In regard to transportation facilities, Bangalore is experiencing difficulties. Apparently, the present incentive program offered to the bus drivers has brought some improvement. Nonetheless, transportation facilities are overstrained, and their improvement would require considerable investment. Pune, on the other hand, has excellent transport service. Similarly, water facilities are under strain in Bangalore, whereas Pune has a relatively abundant supply. Finally and most importantly, Bangalore has an energy shortage, particularly owing to heavy drought conditions experienced in the state for the last several years. This situation should be somewhat ameliorated by the commissioning of the Tungabhadra hydroelectric project. Pune, on the other hand, has no energy problem. It has ample electricity for industrial use, and more is being developed in the state of Maharashtra. Because reliable energy tends to be a critical element in the high-technology industry especially involving computer-related work, Pune definitely has a clear advantage over Bangalore in this regard at the present time. Although the Karnataka state government has undertaken the expansion of its electricity-generating capacity, it will take several years before this capacity comes on line and is available to the industry.

The Decision

Both cities have conducive regional characteristics for the development of high technology, and therefore for the location of a high-technology park. However, Bangalore seems to have a slight edge over Pune provided energy problems can be resolved in the short term. As a result, the decision was made to include an energy-generating station in the

Table 9.3

High-Technology Regional Industrial Culture in Bangalore, Route 128, and Silicon Valley

CULTURE DIMENSION	BANGALORE PROFILE	BOSTON ROUTE 128* PROFILE	SILICON VALLEY* PROFILE
-Entrepreneurial/ Conservative	-Conservative	-Conservative	-Entrepreneurial
-Formal/Informal	-Formal	-Formal	-Informal
-Calculated Innovation/ Experimental	-Calculated Innovation	-Calculated Innovation	-Experimental
-Loose-knit/Tightly Coordinated	-Loosely knit Relations Between Firms	-Loosely knit Relations Between Firms	-Tightly knit Network Between Employees Across Firms
-Individualistic/ Group Oriented	-Individualistic	-Group Oriented	-Individualistic
-Cooptative/ Control Oriented	-Control Oriented	-Control Oriented	-Cooptative
-Norms Governing Business	-Belief Systems Center on Loyalty, Commitment, Diligence	-Belief Systems Center on Loyalty, Commitment, Diligence	-Belief Systems Center on Self-fulfillment Wealth, Profession

*Adapted from Weiss and Delbecq (1987: 47, 49).

technology park so as to have an assured supply for the firms located there. The state government was receptive to the idea and decided to help develop a power-generating station. Therefore, it was decided to try Bangalore as the site for the location of the first high-technology park in India.[6] Pune, of course, is a close second choice region.

Inasmuch as Bangalore is the first choice, it is important to consider the dominant regional industrial culture in Bangalore. Table 9.3 provides a brief summary of the prevailing industrial culture in Bangalore, along with those of Route 128 in Boston and Silicon Valley.

Bangalore, Boston, and Silicon Valley

Table 9.3 shows that the industrial culture in Bangalore is characterized as formal, conservative, calculated innovation, loosely knit relations between firms, individualistic, control oriented, and belief systems centered on loyalty, commitment, and diligence. As can be seen from the other two columns of the table, this industrial culture is closer to the one prevailing on Route 128 in Boston rather than the one in Silicon Valley. It is also apparent that Bangalore has not yet seen the development of small start-up companies in the microelectronic area. It is primarily large companies such as Texas Instruments and Philips that have set up software development facilities. These companies have more in common with the Boston companies (e.g., Digital Equipment Corporation and Wang). Thus, it appears that Bangalore is likely to develop more along the lines of Route 128 rather than of the Silicon Valley. Yet, as indicated earlier, Wall Street has described Bangalore as the Silicon Valley of India.

PROBLEMS ASSOCIATED WITH FITTING ENTREPRENEURIAL HIGH-TECH VENTURES WITH INDIAN REGIONAL CULTURES

A number of problems are associated with developing entrepreneurial ventures in Indian regional cultures, including Bangalore and Pune. We will discuss these problems under five categories: the role of central and state governments, paternalistic organizations, infrastructure deficiencies, financing for research and development, and cooperation among government, industry, and universities.

Role of Central and State Governments

In India, the central government plays a strong role in the development of industry. Although states and regions have autonomy in many respects, the central government exercises a great degree of control in granting licenses, particularly when the import of foreign technology/ goods into the country is involved. In addition, several incentives are reserved for the central government to provide. For example, income tax concessions have to be granted by the central government, which also approves the ratio of foreign to domestic equity.[7] On the other hand, state government has power over sales and excise taxes. Many states like Karnataka regulate the purchase of large parcels of land. Finally, the state has control over infrastructure facilities such as electricity.

Thus, one has to deal with two bureaucracies—one at the state and another at the central level. The government bureaucracy in India is difficult to deal with because cumbersome procedures are in operation. This has been the major complaint of foreign companies investing in India. One needs a lot of patience to deal with the Indian bureaucracy.

Paternalistic Organizations

Indian organizations tend to be organized along paternalistic lines and are usually averse to risk (Hofstede 1980). Indian culture accords great respect to the authority figure. We know that entrepreneurial management style flourishes in an organizational structure that is organic (Covin and Slevin 1987). Thus, the authority structure prevailing in most Indian enterprises tends to stifle entrepreneurship. To the extent that entrepreneurial culture is required for the development of high technology, there is a need to provide entrepreneurial style training to potential entrepreneurs in India. Moreover, management consultation needs to be available so as to develop organic designs for high-technology firms. For this reason, a social high-tech facility should be located in the high-technology park so that hands-on training and consultation can be provided to organizations located within the park. This should help facilitate the successful development of appropriate style and organizational structures.

Infrastructure Deficiencies

As we indicated earlier, Bangalore is experiencing several infrastructure deficiencies. These relate to transportation difficulties, and water and power availability. Although the state is trying to overcome these deficiencies, several years will be needed to resolve these problems. In the meantime, appropriate infrastructure facilities need to be developed within the high-technology park. Such development would, of course, raise the cost of developing such a park. Until subsidized by the state and/or other national resources, the technology park will likely become noncompetitive in the world market. Alternatively, government protection would be necessary to shield local enterprises from international competition. This in the long run would not be very healthy. Therefore ways have to be found to reduce the cost of developing and operating the technology park by providing initial subsidies and/or grants to overcome these infrastructural problems. If high-technology industry has to develop in India and produce goods and services at internationally competitive rates, it is essential that the central and state governments spend resources so as to provide infrastructure facilities that are of world-class stature.

Financing for Research and Development

High-technology entrepreneurial firms require venture capital for research and development. The present financing system in India is not geared toward providing this type of venture capital. Furthermore, there are no venture capitalists in the country. Hence, the financing system has to be reorganized to provide the needed venture capital. Both the central and state governments urgently need to consider this issue.

Cooperation among Government, Industry, and Universities

Appropriate leadership and long-term commitment from government, industry, and universities are needed for developing a successful high-technology park. Of course, state as well as central governments have developed some areas for industrial development (industrial parks, free trade zones), but these have been primarily for manufacturing enterprises. Although the government and universities have R&D laboratories, these facilities have not usually been successful in developing commercially viable products. This failure can primarily be attributed to the lack of meaningful partnerships among government, universities, and industry. Research in India needs an applied focus. Thus, there is an urgent need to develop technology parks through private sector initiative but with the collaboration of government, industry, and universities.

Obviously, then, a number of issues remain to be resolved. In order to develop a prognosis, it is necessary to look at some prior experience and recent developments.

PRIOR EXPERIENCE AND RECENT DEVELOPMENTS

Given the nature of bureaucracy at both the state and central government level in India, a lot of patience is needed to develop and implement any project. Therefore, development of a high-technology park would take a lot of time and resources. On the other hand, India offers tremendous opportunities, particularly with its large potential markets and rather cheap but highly qualified human resources.

As indicated earlier, some healthy developments have taken place in recent years, including strong commitment to high-technology development by the central government as well as the Karnataka state government.[8] It is, therefore, expected that strong support from the central as well as the state government would help overcome most of the problems mentioned in the earlier section.

THE FUTURE

The future of high technology in India is very promising. Several regions have potential for developing high-technology enterprises. It is hoped that the first attempt will be successful, thereby paving the way for similar initiatives in other locations.

It is also hoped that similar projects will be undertaken in other developing countries where regional cultures are conducive to the development of high technology. Use of high technologies to solve their problems would increase the standard of living in developing nations and increase the demand for goods and services. Ultimately, this effect should greatly enhance trade between developed and developing nations, thus leading to world development.

NOTES

1. For further details see "Premier Rajiv Gandhi Makes Impressive Start" (1985).

2. This section draws heavily upon the work of Chopra (1977).

3. In addition to the above five regions, there are two more metropolitan areas (Madras and Hyderabad) which have substantial concentrations of industry. For reasons of space, these are not described in this essay.

4. The description in this section draws upon many sources. Among these are Chopra (1977), OPIC India Investment Mission (1983), "Modern India: A Profile" (1985), Kelkar (1985), Alexander (1986), Khan (1986), and India Today (July 7, 1987).

5. In addition to prior sources, this discussion draws upon two USAID reports. The first is a survey of Bangalore completed by Rao Associates (1987), and the second is the summary of a USAID-sponsored workshop on technology development held at Bangalore, March 5–7, 1987.

6. Arthur D. Little (1987) conducted a study for the USAID. Its purpose was to select an appropriate region in India for technology development. After examining four regions (Pune, Bombay, Hyderabad, and Karnataka), the Arthur D. Little report recommended Bangalore (Karnataka) as the best choice.

7. The ratio of foreign to domestic equity is presently 40:60. This can, however, be modified for projects involving 100 percent exports.

8. There are also nonresident Indians (settled in developed countries) who are willing and able to help in the development of high technology parks in India.

10

Industrial Competitive Development in Three Regions in the Federal Republic of Germany: The Case of Kassel, Bonn, and Duisburg

Horst Albach and Hermann Tengler

Do regional differences exist in West Germany in terms of economic and industrial development? We suggest there are strong differences. This chapter examines these differences and the influences of regional conditions as they relate to the structure and site of industrial development in the Federal Republic of Germany. The following regions are discussed: Kassel, representative of a sparsely populated, rural area; the region of Bonn, an overcrowded region with its predominant service industry; and the region of Duisburg, an old, highly industrialized, overcrowded region. It is argued that the determinants of industrial development are multifaceted; however, many factors have shifted— surprisingly enough—in favor of the rural regions. Still, in the future it will be difficult for the rural regions to keep pace with the development of the industrial overcrowded regions. This essay takes an economic approach in comparing the industrial development of these three West German regions.

There is reason to believe that high industrial density is no longer considered an obstacle to regional growth as it was in the past. In order to support growth, governmental economic policy must be more substantive and positive than in the past, when such policies focused on obstacles to growth rather than on developmental incentives. We also identify those industries that are flourishing and those that are not in each region. Interview results from industry executives are also presented to support these findings. Economists, industrialists, and entrepreneurs may find these results interesting and useful.

INTRODUCTION: COMPETITIVENESS AMONG REGIONS

Regional problems cannot be characterized in the Federal Republic of Germany as they are in most other Western industrial countries, that is, by contrasting developed versus less developed parts of the country. On the contrary, economically well-developed and less developed regions are scattered throughout the Federal Republic. The regional distribution of growth is also not constant but shows a distinctly dynamic character. In general, one region compared to another shows that economic competitiveness is lost or diminished when the following conditions are present:

1. When location conditions deteriorate, that is, the location profile no longer corresponds as well as in the past with the requirements concerning the production of goods.
2. When site factors lose their importance, or, on the other hand, site factors gain in importance.
3. When the production requirements lose their importance with respect to the national economical process of growth, for example, by being superseded by import competition.

Therefore, the usual identification of regional agglomeration with economic power and of rural areas with weakness in structure and location no longer correctly describes the regional distribution of growth. A number of industrial overcrowded regions, which in most cases display less diversified, "old" industrial structures, have also become trouble areas suffering from high unemployment and low growth rates. On the other hand, a few rural pheripheral areas have attained in a comparatively high growth rate. However, compared to their absolute economic power, they are far behind the federal average. The "winners" of regional economical development in the Federal Republic of Germany are, above all, still the overcrowded regions that have a large number of service companies.

Three Regional Types

This analysis of industrial development in Kassel, Bonn, and Duisburg focuses on influences that affect different regional conditions in terms of site and structure factors which lead to growth of industries. It is based on the results of empirical investigations carried out by the Small Business Research Institute (Institut für Mittelstandsforschung) in the districts of the Chamber of Commerce and Industry in Kassel, Bonn, and Duisburg.

Methodology

Official statistics were used as the basis for describing industrial development in these three regions. Data discussing the gross value for wealth creation per inhabitant, the unemployment rate, and the most essential indices of the industry were used for the individual areas. Moreover, global data from 1977 will be presented and compared to overall development in the Federal Republic of Germany.

This essay will not give a detailed description of the "shift analysis" method which was used to determine the extent to which regional development deviated from that of the industrial analysis at the federal level. We state here simply that the first step was to compare the growth of each industry in these three regions with the average growth rate of all industries in the Federal Republic.

The site factor represented in the shift analysis, however, does not specifically indicate the exact site advantages or disadvantages in the respective regions. To clarify that question, an interview query concerning the quality of the individual site factors was carried out, which included 373 industrial companies in Kassel, 252 in Bonn, and 445 in Duisburg. The replies received were converted into "quality indices"; these were represented numerically from $+4$ (i.e., excellent quality) to -4 (i.e., very poor quality). The steps in this analysis were aimed at comparing economic and industrial growth within and across regions, and between each region in the study with the country's average industrial growth rates.

THE REGIONS OF KASSEL, BONN, AND DUISBURG

Kassel: A Depressed Region

Kassel suffers from basic economic conditions that deteriorated massively after World War II owing to the separation of West from East Germany and to its location at the outer edge of the Federal Republic as well as from the European Economic Community. As a result, in the majority of cases even the latest indices for the economic power of this region display a considerably underaveraged level.

With its population density of 144 inhabitants per square kilometer, the economic region of Kassel also belongs to the rural areas of the Federal Republic (247 inhabitants per square kilometer). The gross value for wealth creation per inhabitant is DM (deutsche mark) 21.182, which is 16 percent lower than the federal average. The unemployment rate is 11.3 percent, that is, almost 22 percent above the federal average. The number of industrial employees per 1,000 inhabitants only amounts to approximately 88 percent of the federal results. The sales productivity of labor is remarkably below the federal average. While on federal average approximately DM 204 per employees are turned over, the value for the Kassel region is only DM 133, that is, one-third less. The export rate is 23.5 percent compared to the federal average of 28.7 percent.

The region of Kassel also projects an image of a rather economically weak area and is consequently burdened by an extreme unemployment rate. The data displaying the development of the industry in the past seven to eight years, however, present an improvement on significant items. This is especially evidenced by the success of the export business.

Since 1977, industrial employment in the Federal Republic has decreased by 10.2 percent as compared to 5.6 percent in Kassel. This relatively favorable result of industries in Kassel—it provides one-half of all jobs to the Federal Republic and still remains the largest employer in this region—has significantly contributed to the fact that the unemployment rate has not increased since 1983, a trend opposite that of the federal average.

Bonn: A Prototypical Region

The preconditions for economic growth have been considerably more favorable for Bonn than for Kassel. Bonn has four times the population density of Kassel, it is also more centrally located within the Federal Republic, and it is the capital. This position is reflected in the employment rate, driven by the service sector—more so than anywhere else in the Federal Republic: Bonn employs 63 percent of all labor. In this respect, the economic region of Bonn can be characterized as a prototype of a tertiary dense area that has profited considerably by the strongly expansive development of service businesses in the past years.

The best example of this development is the labor market. The unemployment rate in the region of Bonn is 7.7 percent, 17 percent lower than that of the federal average. However, contrary to Kassel, the unemployment has continuously increased even in the past two years. The main reason for this increase has to do with the development of industries. Despite its traditionally low industrial establishments, the economic region of Bonn suffered more from a continuous deindustrialized process than did most other regions of the Federal Republic. The number of enterprises, above all the number of employees, has decreased by 13.4 percent since 1977—which is considerably more than the federal average. Simultaneously, the overall turnover and the overall turnover per employee were also above the federal average. The turnover productivity of labor was nearly 190,000 DM, a number that is significantly higher than that in Kassel. In comparison to the federal average, however, this amount signifies an increase of the productivity backlogs from 1.6 percent to 7 percent. The development of the export business alone expanded by 87.4 percent since 1977, a bit more than on federal average (76.5 percent). This and the low growth rate of the internal turnover showed that the export rate of the industry in Bonn (after having recently been at nearly the same level as the federal average) is now at 31.6 percent, approximately 3 percent higher.

Duisburg: A Region of the Past

The exact counterpart to the economic structure of Bonn is the Duisburg region. Duisburg, like Bonn, is also characterized as a tertiary dense region. It is also a highly industrialized, overcrowded region. It is part of the "Ruhrgebiet," one of the most significant industrial zones of Europe and West Germany that still has decisively been formed by the dominating coal, iron and steel industry.

Duisburg accounts for approximately 20 percent of the bituminous coal output and 39 percent of the Federal Republic's total steel production. The industrial sector excels from its high share of raw material production, which displays a sensitivity to economic and price fluctuation on the world market.

An additional feature of such old, industrialized regions—besides a high industrial density—is the structure of large-sized enterprises. In Duisburg, the medium size of an industrial company is 273 employees, which is almost 80 percent above the federal average. However, since 1977 this size has decreased by 9.3 percent, whereas it remained nearly unchanged in the Federal Republic. The accompanying below-average decline in the number of enterprises in the region of Duisburg indicates that the number of industrial employees has decreased considerably. In fact, the number of industrial jobs in Duisburg has been cut back drastically—by 17.6 percent. The tense economical situation which the industry of this region is now facing is clearly obvious regarding sales. In addition, both the internal and export turnover have significantly risen in comparison to the regions analyzed here. The sales productivity of labor is approximately DM 208,000, which remains above the federal average but has significantly declined from that of previous years.

The low increase in industrial productivity in Duisburg has its equivalent only in an underaveraged development of the gross wealth creation per inhabitant. However, the effects on the labor market have been most aggravating since 1981. The unemployment rate in the region of Duisburg continuously rises more than the federal average annually, and is now at 14.4 percent—nearly 55 percent above the federal level.

REGIONAL "WINNING" AND "LOSING" INDUSTRIES

The decrease in jobs available in the region of Duisburg is definitely more distinct than that of either the federal average or Bonn. In addition, the region of Kassel has experienced greater industrial growth than on average either Bonn or the Federal Republic as a whole. However, the industrial structure in the region of Bonn presents itself even more favorably. As a result, the lack of companies belonging to an industry with positive employment as compared to the overall economy has not proved to be the cause of job losses in Bonn.

The economic region of Duisburg shows the opposite trend and profile. The employment development in this region has by far been more impaired by the prevailing industrial structure, whereas the regions of Kassel and Bonn have been favored by the growth-oriented sectors within the industry. The questions that emerge are, "What are the industries that are responsible for the positive industrial economic structure in Kassel as well as in Bonn, and what are the negative industrial structures in Duisburg?" Results show that all industries representing the bulk, that is, at least 80 percent, of all employees in the areas analyzed, have faced relatively severe losses in employment in the Federal Republic of Germany since 1977. In particular, the textile industry, the clothing industry, and the iron- and steel-producing industries have suffered worse unemployment. These industries have suffered enormously from the pressing competition by foreign firms from low-wage countries, from a stagnating market, from subsidies granted foreign competitors, or from protective countermeasures. The winners of the sectoral change within the Federal Republic of Germany in the past few years have been automobile production, the plastics industry, and the chemical industry. However, only the automobile and plastics industries generated additional jobs.

By limiting the study to the worst or best industries, we can clearly identify the causes for structural economic power or structural weakness of the industry in the individual regions. In case of the weakest sectors, the employment data of the regions investigated here show the highest unemployment in the iron and steel industry in Duisburg. Note the regions that have no particular industry:

Industrial Branch	Kassel	Bonn	Duisburg
Textile industry	3.7	None	1.2
Clothing industry	3.0	0.5	0.8
Iron- and steel-producing industry	None	None	32.3
Total	6.9	0.5	34.3

The following results show the three strongest sectors with the highest employment in Kassel's auto production and Bonn's chemical industry:

Industrial Branch	Kassel	Bonn	Duisburg
Automobile production	26.2	9.6	None
Plastics industry	4.7	5.2	1.3
Chemical industry	7.4	23.2	5.0
Total	38.3	38.0	6.3

The greatest structural advantage of Kassel's auto industry lies in the fact that the largest growth-oriented industry of the Federal Republic of Germany, the automobile industry, employs more than one-quarter of all industrial employees.

Bonn's greatest economic advantage can be traced to the fact that the three sectors which in the past suffered from the most severe employment problems do not exist here at all. On the other hand, regarding the so-called growth-oriented industries, the chemical industry alone provides approximately every fourth job in this region.

The region of Duisburg is far from being even as powerfully represented in any of the best industries as are either of the other two regions or on federal average. Automobile production does not have a single site there. Vice versa, the iron- and steel-producing industry still provides nearly every third industrial job in Duisburg, even though it has been responsible for half of all personnel releases of the whole industry of the region since 1977.

We can expand the sector-specified study to all industries and arrange the sum of the employment quota in the individual regions accordingly to positive and negative structural factors. The percentage results are as follows:

	Kassel	Bonn	Duisburg
Positive structural factor	57.9	65.4	38.9
Negative structural factor	27.9	15.8	53.0

Consequently, the ratio between positive structural and negative structural factors amounts to 2.1 for Kassel, 4.1 for Bonn, and 0.7 for Duisburg. It is obvious that the tertiary dense area of Bonn has a superior economic industrial structure; the rural area of Kassel also shows an advantageous structure; and the old industrialized, overcrowded area of Duisburg shows an extremely unfavorable economic industrial structure.

REGIONAL SITE FACTOR RESULTS: KASSEL VERSUS BONN

The second determinant used here to classify regional differences is the so-called site factor, that is, the deviation of regional economic development from overall economic development. The results regarding this factor in the individual regions were surprising. Of all regions, the rural peripheral region of Kassel showed better industrial site conditions than the federal average and much better than the dense areas of Bonn and Duisburg. The favorable employment development of industries in Kassel has been attributed to the fair number of growth-oriented industries and to regional site conditions that allow individual enterprises better results. The exact contrary is observed in the economic area of Bonn. Its outstanding industrial structure is obviously overcompensated by unfavorable site conditions that finally result in greater losses in jobs available than on federal average. With respect to the industrial region of Duisburg, the average site factor also presents better conditions for industrial location compared to Bonn, but simultaneously shows slightly below-average specific site features.

These results were surprising since in the beginning of a region's development only the site advantages provoked the creation of overcrowded areas. The chances for economies of scale and external savings from localization of economies (or urbanization of economies) are intensified when adding the element of the lapse of time. For this reason, the economic area of Duisburg stands as the classical example of how the existence of natural site advantages created by large deposits of coal and excellent transportation facilities for bulk goods by the Rhine has led to one of the largest developing industrial zones with a high economic potential. Even today it is assumed that fair site conditions for enterprises are based primarily on such factors that are closely connected to agglomeration advantages. As a result, rural regions present considerable site disadvantages.

The contradiction of this assumption is evident from our results. It is not only manifested in the results of the overall site factors in the three regions, but is also confirmed by the values for the sector-specific site factors. With regard to the economic area of Kassel, nine industries have a positive score and only six a negative site factor; Bonn has five industries that have developed more positively, but eight have degenerated as compared to the federal average; and in the region of Duisburg, six branches have a positive score and nine have negative values. Consequently, the ratio of positive to negative site factors proves most favorable in Kassel, whereas Bonn shows the poorest and Duisburg is only slightly better.

It is informative to learn which industries in the different regions have better or poorer industrial development compared with the federal average. It should be pointed out that the sector-specific site conditions within the individual regions differ significantly from each other. There is some reason to believe this difference exists since only 5 of the 16 most important industrial branches show a common sign in all 3 regions.

WINNING AND LOSING INDUSTRIES IN THE REGIONS

Unfavorable employment development as compared to the federal average has been experienced by industries in natural materials, steel, light metals processing, and chemistry; besides mining, positive site factors are recorded only in the plastics industry. In addition, different site qualities in the three regions are also supported by the fact that these industries are distributed among practically all parts of the industrial sector—from the basic goods and producer goods industry via the capital goods industry to the consumer goods industry.

Without doubt, the employment situation in the region of Kassel has profited mostly from its automobile production, since this is the most significant structural economic advantage in the Federal Republic. The value for the site factor of this branch was exceeded only by the precision engineering and optical industry. Also the second largest employer of the region, the electrical engineering industry achieved a more favorable development compared to the federal average.

Although Kassel excels in optimal site conditions that meet site requirements of superior economic structure-inducing industries, the contrary is observed for Bonn. It is the chemical industry which is the winner in the Federal Republic. This industry employment rate is 23.2 percent in Bonn. A slightly better result compared to the federal average was achieved by the second largest industrial employer of the region, mechanical engineering; however, even this industry had job losses of 2.3 percent. The branch with the absolutely highest site factor in Bonn proved to be the wood processing industry which employs only 1.5 percent of all industrial labor. Only the plastics industry in this region showed employment development above the federal average. In Bonn the plastics industry represented 5.2 percent of all jobs. The employment rate of all industries with negative site factors in Bonn was 51.1 percent, nearly twice as high as that of the region of Kassel.

The mining, iron, and steel-producing industries are the least significant of all industries but have a positive site factor that provides over half of all industrial jobs available in Duisburg. This does not mean, however, that Duisburg did not have enormous job losses. It did.

The structure-inducing and agglomeration-supporting effects of specific site qualities involve another risk. To the extent that old industry, site-favored qualities are still present, then the development of modern, promising industries is impaired. Entrepreneuring planners should take heed of this observation. Since 1977 Duisburg's mechanical engineering, electrical engineering and chemical industries could not compete with the results of these older industries in the federal Republic. In the region of Duisburg, the only branches with a remarkably better development record as compared to the federal average were the precision engineering and optical industry and the plastics industry. However, their employment quota of 2.1 percent is very low. Finally, the dominating and structurally weak industries such as mining and iron and steel have contributed to the quota of jobs with a negative site factor in Duisburg of 35 percent.

INTERVIEWS WITH ENTREPRENEURS

The differences in the rate of growth and speed of the same industrial sectors between one region and the overall economy can essentially be attributed to a region's site advantages or disadvantages. It is possible to assess whether a region provides for optimal development of a single industry or the whole industry, rather than for just good or poor site conditions. On the other hand, no conclusion can be given regarding the identification of concrete site power or weakness in a region.

The theory of regional economic development suggests that the central site advantages of overcrowded areas as contrasted to rural areas are above all based on better chances of realizing external savings. Such external savings originate from (1) infrastructural facilities and services, considered as high value in quality and extensive in capacity; (2) the near vicinity or the modest economical distance to suppliers, consumers, local authorities, and services companies; and (3) highly differentiated labor markets with a respective potential by income and demand. However, progressively increasing itemized and social costs, especially resulting from environmental burden and capacity shortages like landed property and infrastructure, cause diminishing agglomeration advantages, combined with the risk that the external savings can turn into diseconomies.

The adequate availability of low-priced business and dwelling spaces with a simultaneously negligible environmental burden is also of importance here as a potential site advantage of densely populated regions lacking industries. These considerations, however, do not fully explain the observed differences from the site factor results of the shift analysis. For this reason, we carried out interviews with entrepreneurs concerning the importance and quality of single site factors in the three regions. In order to summarize this variety of individual evaluations by a few groups of site factors, we at first performed a factor analysis with the responses from the entrepreneurs concerning the importance of the individual site factors. As a result, those interviewed are essentially concerned about seven site factor groups regarding their chances for development. Table 10.1 summarizes these results.

Labor Market

The availability of qualified labor is not a site problem for most enterprises because the Federal Republic has an employment rate of nearly 10 percent. However, for the regions of Kassel and Bonn, this assumption proves wrong. Managers and specialists cannot be recruited by enterprises to the extent necessary to accomplish the firms' business tasks. Qualified labor is above all missing in a large number of small and medium-sized enterprises performing research, design, and development tasks. These problems are most aggravatingly represented in the rural region of Kassel. This observation complies with the thesis of labor market advantages in agglomerations. Even for the region of Bonn the unfavorable results are not that surprising inasmuch as this region is characterized as a tertiary dense area with a labor supply that is oriented to the demands of service businesses. On the other hand, in the industrial overcrowded area of Duisburg, there is an unrestricted satisfaction insofar as the availability of unskilled labor is concerned. Results show that technologically high-ranking enterprises in growth-oriented industries like mechanical engineering and chemistry cannot cover their requirements for specialists. This could explain the below-average development of these industries in the region of Duisburg. On the other hand, recruiting specialists for the mining and iron- and steel-producing industries has not been problematical. These industries predominantly intend to release personnel, and they can help themselves to the traditionally wide and highly qualified labor market.

The less the labor market corresponds to the requirements of the economy, the more it is important that there be sufficient chances for educational and vocational training to compensate these deficits. These preconditions exist in the overcrowded areas of Bonn and Duisburg. However, the enterprises in the rural region of Kassel do not even consider this a sufficient contribution to solve their employment problems. On the other hand, industries in Kassel show remarkable advantages in capturing an essential component of the labor market—namely, the labor cost level. In Kassel the labor cost level is approximatley 6 percent below the federal average and is evaluated positively by enterprises there. The average wage and salary costs per employee in Bonn and Duisburg are significantly higher and have site factors that are most sharply criticized.

Table 10.1
Quality of Site Factors in the Regions of Kassel, Bonn, and Duisburg

Site factor	Kassel	Bonn	Duisburg
I. Labor Market			
Resources of specialists	-1.4	-0.8	0.1
Resources of managers	-1.5	-0.8	-0.5
Resources of unskilled labor	-0.1	-0.2	0.9
Labor cost level	0.3	-1.6	-0.6
enhances for educational and vocational training	-0.3	0.1	0.2
II. Governmental terms and provisions			
Imposition of environmental protection	-	-0.6	-0.6
Official financial support	-0.9	-	-1.8
Attendance by community	-0.5	-0.4	0.2
Regional space utilization plans favoring economic aspects	-0.7	-0.9	-0.3
III. Home-related infrastructure			
Living quality, recreational quality	0.8	0.9	-0.1
IV. Community rates and energy expenses			
Burden by the local business tax	-2.2	-1.4	-1.3
Energy expenses	-	-1.2	-0.7
V. Market neighborhood and competition positions			
Location to procurement markets	-0.5	1.2	0.7
Location to sales markets	-0.7	1.7	1.4
Competition by regional competitors	-0.1	-0.2	-0.7
VI. Traffic connection			
Connection to railway	-0.2	0.8	0.8
Connection to road network	1.2	2.5	3.0
Connection to waterways	-3.6	-1.3	-0.1
Connection to air traffic	-3.1	1.5	-1.0
VII. Potential of business space			
Prices for business space	0.7	-1.1	-0.2
Chances for space-related expansion	0.5	0.0	0.4

Governmental Terms and Provisions

Governmental terms and provisions are never neutral in their effects. Violators of governmental environmental policy are largely prosecuted in selective situations. Consideration is given to environmental cost with respect to a growing agglomeration trend. It is recognized that negative external effects concerning environmental protection may cause significant cost burdens for firms in overcrowded areas. In Kassel, governmental impositions were minimal as compared to those in Bonn and Duisburg.

The odds are also on the side of the industry in Kassel against Bonn and Duisburg regarding governmental financial support. The region of Duisburg also has the governmental advantage of regional economical promotion. However, the potential investment subsidies amount to a lower percentage. Finally, the economic area of Bonn receives no help from governmental regional financial promotion.

The quality of local economic promotion is, to a large extent, dependent on which politician is governing. For this reason, each region is different. The results of our entrepreneurial interviews showed that Kassel and Bonn were significantly behind Duisburg regarding attendance by the community and regional space utilization plans favoring economic aspects.

Home-related Infrastructure and the External Image of Regions

Home-related infrastructure factors like living and recreational facilities do not immediately affect site quality characteristics, but do so indirectly via their influence on the mobility decision of labor. In Kassel, Bonn, and Duisburg qualified employees are not readily available. The personnel required in the short term have to be recruited outside the region. Kassel and Bonn have a comparative advantage in this regard.

Recruitment is less decisive with respect to living and recreational characteristics as sensed by inhabitants of a region. How the image of a region is presented "outside" is very important for recruitment purposes. Duisburg is considerably handicapped in this regard. Interviews throughout the Federal Republic concerning the attitude of the "Ruhr Territory" reveal that the population living outside this region flatly refused to move in. Results show that the interviewees believed the clichés about intense air pollution and unfavorable living conditions in Duisburg.

CONCLUSION

Overcrowded areas definitely present better business sites relative to their market network and their transportation connections. Regarding the labor market, site advantages assumed for agglomerations such as those in Bonn are deceiving. Why? Labor, especially in the tertiary dense area of Bonn, does not adequately meet the structural requirements of the industry. Second, the rural region of Kassel has considerably greater labor cost advantages. Also compared to Bonn and Duisburg, Kassel has an advantage in business space potential, the amount of available official financial support, and in less imposed environmental regulations. As far as living and recreational characteristics are concerned, Kassel is equivalent to Bonn and exceeds the industrial region of Duisburg according to our interviews.

In the results of the shift analysis, Bonn proved to be the most favorable region, given advantageous site conditions for industries. Duisburg was second, and Kassel was third.

The Most Essential Regional Site Factors

Obviously, the qualitative evaluation of the individual site factors alone is not sufficient to explain the different development of identical industries in different regions. A list of essential site factors classified by companies in the three regions is presented in order of their significance in table 10.2.

Except for home-related infrastructure, all seven site factors are represented as essential by industries. As a result, the quality of an area that acts as a business site does not depend solely on a few determinants. It also proves that in all three types of regions, with only slight deviations, the same site factors are assessed as the most significant. Each site factor given in table 10.2 ranges among the top ten in Kassel, Bonn, and Duisburg.

The site factor which, on average, was considered the most important was the connection to the major road network. The regional differences among the quality site indices remain unchanged with respect to the level of satisfaction. The same applies to the labor cost acting as the second important site factor. The region of Kassel maintained its site advantage over Duisburg and Bonn, although in Kassel the positive qualitative evaluation remains below the significance assigned. Moreover, in all three regions the requirements for a low business tax are not fulfilled. Although the interviewees in Kassel criticized the burden of the business tax more severely than those in Bonn or Duisburg, they did not regard this factor as an aggravating site disadvantage.

Table 10.2

Level of Satisfaction Concerning the Essential Site Factors in the Regions of Kassel, Bonn, and Duisburg

Site factor	Kassel	Bonn	Duisburg
Connection to road network	0.8	1.2	1.1
Labor cost level	0.7	0.4	0.5
Burden by the local business tax	0.5	0.4	0.4
Energy expenses	-	0.5	0.5
Resource of specialists	0.4	0.6	0.8
Location to sales market	0.6	1.2	0.9
Impositions of environmental protection	-	0.7	0.7
Regional space utilization plans favoring economic aspects	0.6	0.7	0.8
Prices for business space	1.1	0.7	0.8
Official financial support	0.7	-	0.5

The high energy prices weigh heavily on the enterprises located in the economic area of Duisburg.

For all other site factors classified as essential by the companies in Kassel, Bonn, and Duisburg, the differences shown in the quality evaluation remain unchanged owing to similar assessments as shown in the index values for the level of satisfaction.

Surprisingly, our results also showed that the rural region of Kassel does not offer more unfavorable site conditions than the overcrowded areas of Bonn and Duisburg. With regard to the most essential site factors, hardly any quality differences among the single types of regions are identifiable. Other site factors like resources of managers, chances of educational and vocational training, location to procurement market, connection to railway, waterways, and air traffic with which rural regions are not well equipped, do not materially influence their chances of development. Therefore, we conclude that the site quality of overcrowded areas compared to less dense regions is generally overestimated.

Other Regional Determinants of Development

David Birch's finding for the United States,[1] that in the past smaller sized enterprises contributed greatly out of proportion to the generation of new jobs, applies to the Federal Republic of Germany. Accordingly, in the period 1978 to 1984, the industrial sector in the largest *Bundesland*, North Rhine Westphalia, was characterized by a drastic labor reduction in large-sized enterprises employing more than 500 laborers. Medium-sized companies showed only minor employment losses, and small-sized enterprises with fewer than ten employees could generate additional jobs to a remarkable extent. Results from other studies indicate that most regions in the Federal Republic of Germany with a relatively favorable job development are characterized by an above-average employment share in small-sized enterprises.

These findings correspond with our results for Kassel, Bonn, and Duisburg and can be further substantiated for specified periods of time by our entrepreneurial interviews. Kassel had the smallest enterprise sizes on average as compared to the other regions. The small and medium-sized enterprises with fewer than 500 jobs increased the number of staff by 2.9 percent from 1978 through 1980. Contrary to other regions, the large-sized industries could expand, but with a 0.1 percent increase in employment, they turned out very poor both percentage-wise and in absolute numbers. In addition, Bonn has predominantly medium-sized companies. The number of jobs in Bonn's small and medium-sized enterprises increased by 3.0 percent in the period from 1982 through 1984, whereas jobs in large-sized companies decreased by 2.5 percent. (The balance of the employment development was positive, +0.6 percent, which can be attributed to the fact that larger enterprises are not well represented in Bonn.) Exactly the opposite situation was found in Duisburg. There, the middle-class economy experienced employment increases of 0.4 percent from 1982 through 1984. However, job losses in large-sized enterprises amounted to 3.5 percent, an overall negative result of −2.7 percent. If an increased number of middle-class enterprises had located in Duisburg, greater stability in the labor market would likely have occurred.

SERVICE SECTOR PRESENCE

Another structural determinant of economic development within regional industry is the employment and physical presence of the service sector. Its influence is obvious when considering the tertiary dense area of Bonn and the industrial overcrowded area of Duisburg. In the past Bonn profited substantially from its low industrial density and its dominance of the expansive services sector. Labor market statistics illustrate

this advantage. But this sector, which dominates Bonn's overall economy, presents disadvantages in its own structural composition. The
reason is that the home-related tertiary sector is overrepresented in
Bonn, whereas the production-oriented services sector is relatively
poorly represented. Services, in close proximity to industries, showed
actual growth in the past and will continue to do so in the future.
However, service industries in Bonn, which has a limited customer
base, cannot fall back on important service functions as is possible in
other regions.

The highly industrialized Duisburg has an additional site advantage
for service industries inasmuch as they are well represented in Duisburg
and Duisburg has a broad customer base potential.

PRIOR INDUSTRIAL HISTORY

These explanations show that the determinants of the economic development of regional industry are multifaceted. As is evident in this
study, the industrialization of a region does not merely present a mort-
gage to its past, but offers a chance for further economic development.
On the other hand, an assumed structural advantage owing to low
industrial density and a high home-related service share can inhibit
future industrial growth. Finally, even a rural area like Kassel should
not be satisfied by the positive results of its past. Past successes were
generated by essential structural and site conditions that had altered
in their favor. For the future, new site factors such as researching infrastructure and connection to communications technologies will gain
in importance. The rural regions may find it hard to keep pace with
the infrastructural equipment of overcrowded regions.

THE FUTURE

The centralization of industrial location selection criteria suited to
problems of individual regions is required. Our study has shown that
regional stereotypes do not hold with time. Decentralizing governmental influence in charge of a regional policy is necessary. With regard to
regional economic policies, decentralizing implies that governmental
promotion programs are increasingly oriented to the problems of the
individual regions but are in fact left to the discretion of central institutions. Institutional decentralizing practices should be shifted to "on
site" authorities because regional bodies are more informed about trouble spots. The risk of an increased dependence on regional policies
given to particular firms' interests has to be faced.

The most essential dimension of decentralizing has to do with the
scope of promotional governmental activties. In the past, the Federal

Republic of Germany's regional policy was characterized primarily by capital subsidies. Granting subsidies was intended as an impetus for job-generating investments within the promotion areas. Above all, impetus was intended for industrial settlements in these regions. Today, the effort to recruit new companies has failed. Even the increasing subsidy race among the communities cannot change this fact. Failures of this kind must be recognized, and changes such as those mentioned above must be implemented. Financial support is granted based on outdated statements of firms. Decentralizing regional government promotion policies means turning away from exaggerated subsidies and considering more significant site factors such as availability of specialized labor and business spaces. The measures chosen should provide support for local enterprises and act as self-help guides for the decision making and growth of firms at the regional level.

NOTES

Professor Joseph Weiss has significantly revised and condensed this essay from a previous, more technically oriented draft, with the authors' approval.

1. David Birch, *The Job Generation Process* (Cambridge, Mass.: 1979).

11

The Entrepreneurial Enterprise of Changing Capitals across Regional Cultures: The Case of Belize

Sam M. Hai

Belize is a small country characterized by sharp cultural distinctions beween regions. Consequently, it is ideal for studying the effects of cultural distinctiveness on managerial, entrepreneurial, and governmental decisions and enterprises. In addition, Belize had the unique experience of having its capital relocated from Belize City to Belmopan, which is situated in a region with contrasting cultural characteristics. The move has not proven successful; in fact, it has fallen short of all earlier projections.

This study illustrates one of the most penetrating means of analyzing a country's regional cultural identities in the context of a large-scale monumental entrepreneurial project (i.e., moving the capital inland) that did not work. We will also compare Belize's relocation of its capital to Brazil's relocation of its capital to Brasilia, and show why the Brazilian case has far exceeded the original expectations. The lessons we may derive from this study emphasize the role regional culture plays in such a social experiment.

METHODOLOGY

This study avoids anecdotal analysis of regional cultural characteristics. Instead, the analysis is based on census data obtained from the government of Belize and on other data obtained from the American Embassy in Belize and the World Bank, to name a few. We analyze the ethnoracial characteristics of various regions just prior to the move in 1970 and again ten years later in 1980. Although the Belizean regional cultural characteristics can be described by a great many factors, our conclusions and findings are based on factors with the greatest significant variance.

The author visited Belize in 1976 and met with many people of diverse sociocultural and economic backgrounds. He met with the Honorable Carl Bernard Rogers, deputy premier and minister of home affairs and health, had lunch at a home of a poor Creole farmer, had dinner with a Mayan Indian, stayed as guest at the home of the country's only pediatrician, was a guest at the home of the city engineer of the new capital, was interviewed by radio and newspaper reporters, and gave lectures at various institutions. Even with this firsthand knowledge, the author based this study on analytical data and information available to him from other statistical sources. Anecdotal points are presented only when already established facts need some amplification rather than as a proof in itself.

THE COUNTRY

Geography

Belize is a small English-speaking country located on the east coast of Central America, bordering Mexico to the north, Guatemala to the west and south, and flanked by the Caribbean Sea to the east. Approximately 172 miles long and 68 miles at its widest point, the total area is 8,866 square miles—about the size of Massachusetts or twice the size of Jamaica. The population of Belize is 154,100 (mid–1983 estimate) compared to the 6 million population of Massachusetts. Islands and cays dot the sea offshore and straddle the second longest barrier reef in the world.

North of Belize City, the country is mostly level. South of that latitude, the land rises sharply into a mountainous area of a general altitude from 2,000 to 3,000 feet, where the Maya Mountains are located. Except for savannah and swampland along the coastal area and the mountains, the country is forested throughout.

It is estimated that over 2 million acres of land are suitable for agriculture, of which perhaps 10 percent is in use in any given year. About half of this land area is under pasture, with the remainder in a variety of permanent and annual crops. Traditional farming follows the *milpa* system which involves annual clearing of new land with a seven-year bush fallow. A growing number of farmers are making permanent use of cleared land, primarily using mechanical cultivation.

The larger landowners have been somewhat skeptical and unwilling to promote large-scale agricultural schemes because they fear losing their skilled forestry laborers to the land. Moreover, the men themselves seem to have preferred the irregular life of working mahogany camps and have shown little desire to turn to farming with its more settled way of life. This frame of mind is still evident among the Creole community, and since farming has remained relatively unattractive, it has added to the difficulties of obtaining suitable labor. For the majority of the population, farming is considered beneath them (Dobson 1973, 259).

Belize has a subtropical climate with a wet season from June to the end of the year. Peak rainfall occurs in July and September, with a slight lull in August. Wheras rain falls during every month, March and May of each year are considered dry. Rainfall increases from north to south, with Corozal experiencing about 50 inches per annum and Toledo over 150 inches per annum.

Average daytime temperatures range from 70 to 90 degrees, with the coolest months being November to March. Average humidity is 80 to 90 percent in coastal areas and about 75 percent inland.

Belize is periodically hit by hurricanes, most recently in 1978 when Hurricane Greta caused over Bz $30 million (U.S. $15 million) of agricultural damage.

History

The Mayan civilization spread into the area of Belize between 1500 B.C. and A.D. 300 and flourished until about A.D. 1000. Several archaeological sites, notably those at Altun Ha and Xunantunich, reflect the civilization of this period. European contact began in 1502 when Columbus sailed along the coast. The first recorded European settlement was begun by shipwrecked English seamen in 1638. Over the next 150 years more English settlements were established. This period was also marked by pirating, indiscriminate logging, and sporadic attacks by Indians and neighboring Spanish settlers.

Great Britain recognized Spanish sovereignty over the territory in several eighteenth-century treaties. It first sent an official representative to the area in the late eighteenth century, but Belize was not formally termed the "Colony of British Honduras" until 1840. It became a Crown Colony in 1862. Since then, several constitutional changes have been enacted to expand representative government. Full internal self-government under a ministerial system was granted in the Letters Patent of January 1964. The official name of the territory was changed from British Honduras to Belize in June 1973. Belize became independent on September 21, 1981. The name *Belize* is derived from a Mayan word meaning "muddy water." After El Salvador, it is the smallest political unit on the mainland of the Americas (Adams 1984).

The People

Belize is the most sparsely populated territory in Central America and one of the least densely populated countries in the world. Its population density of 16.3 per square mile compares with 109 for Central America and 86 for the world. Slightly more than half of the people live in six urban areas located primarily along the coast. Approximately one-third of the population lives in Belize City, the former capital and principal port. Net population growth has been negligible since 1972; the emigration of workers to the United States has offset a natural growth rate of over 3 percent. In recent years Belize has experienced an influx of settlers and refugees from the neighboring Central American states. Comparison of census data between 1970 and 1980 indicates a 44.2 percent increase as a result of births, a 6.2 percent decrease from deaths, and a net migration loss of 17.0 percent (or 20,394 persons), resulting in a population increase of 21.2 percent (Zammit 1983a, 2). If we do not consider the outmigration, according to one recent report, Belize had an annual rate of natural population growth of 3.6 percent, the greatest of any of the 159 countries on earth. The population statistics suggest that during the 1970s perhaps as many as one out of every seven Belizeans emigrated (Davidson 1983, 44).

Most Belizeans are of multiracial descent. About half are of African or partly African ancestry; somewhat more than one-fifth are of mixed local Indian and European descent; another one-fifth is composed of Carib, Mayan, or other Amerindian ethnic groups; and the remainder, about 10 percent, includes European, East Indian, Chinese, and Lebanese strains.

English is the official language in Belize and is spoken by virtually the entire population. Spanish is the native tongue of about 40 percent of the people and is spoken as a second language by another 20 percent. The various Indian groups still speak their original languages, and many others speak a Creole dialect similar to the Creole dialects of the English-speaking Caribbean islands. The rate of functional literacy is over 90 percent. More than half of the people are Roman Catholic; the Anglican Church and other Protestant groups account for the other half. There is also a Mennonite colony of over 3,000 (Adams 1984, 2).

Government

The British monarch is head of state of Belize and is represented in the country by a governor general. The primary instrument of policy is the Cabinet, led by the prime minister (head of government). Following British tradition, Cabinet ministers are members of the majority political party and usually hold seats in the National Assembly concurrently with their Cabinet positions.

The National Assembly consists of a House of Representatives and a Senate. The eighteen members of the House are popularly elected to a maximum term of five years. Of the Senate's eight members, five are appointed by the prime minister, two by the leader of the opposition, and one by the governor general.

Members of the independent judiciary are appointed. The highest court in Belize is the Supreme Court, headed by a chief justice. For administrative purposes, the country is divided into six districts of Belize (in the east), Corozal (in the north), Orange Walk (in the northwest), Cayo (in the west), Toledo (in the southwest), and Stann Creek (in the southeast). Belize District has the highest population and includes Belize City (the old capital). Cayo District has the second lowest population density and includes Belmopan—the new capital (Davidson 1983, 2; Adams 1984, 3).

Political Conditions and Regional Divisions

The political party system in Belize began in 1950 with the formation of the People's United party (PUP) and the National party. Since then, PUP has generally dominated the electoral scene, and its opposition has undergone several changes of name and identity. In the elections of November 21, 1979, PUP won thirteen of eighteen seats in the House, and the opposition party, known as the United Democratic party (UDP), took five. Subsequently, one of the opposition party representatives in the House left the UDP and formed the Christian Democratic party. PUP obtained 52 percent of the votes cast in the 1979 elections; UDP won 47 percent, and the Toledo Progressive party (TPP) took 1 percent (Adams 1984, 3). Recently, UDP has taken control of the government for the first time.

The Economy

Forestry was the only economic activity of any consequence in Belize until well into the twentieth century, when the supply of accessible timber began to dwindle. With forestry's decline, sugar has become the principal export in recent years, and efforts are being made to expand the production of citrus, rice, beef, bananas, and tropical fruit for export. Belize's major natural resource is some 809,000 hectares of arable land, only a fraction of which is under cultivation. To curb land speculation, the government enacted legislation (the Aliens Landholding Ordinance of 1973). It requires non-Belizeans to complete a development program on land which they purchase before obtaining clear title to plots of more than 4 hectares in rural areas, or about one-quarter of a hectare in urban areas.

The small-scale domestic industry is limited by the relatively high cost of labor and a small domestic market. Belize is a member of the Caribbean Community (CARICOM) and hopes that the assured access to a large market for potential grain and livestock surpluses will stimulate the growth of commercial agriculture. Belize also hopes to take advantage of its eligibility under the Caribbean Basin Initiative.

A combination of natural factors—climate, the longest barrier reef in the Western Hemisphere, miles of sandy beaches, and safe waters for boating—could support a thriving tourist industry. Unfortunately, development costs to promoters and travel costs to tourists are high compared to those in Mexico and the rest of the Caribbean. The government's policy is to encourage the tourist industry, with loan assistance from the Caribbean Development Bank (CDB) and emphasis on small, owner-operated facilities. Tourism is expected to increase slowly in the next few years.

Except for 1974, when sugar earnings tripled, Belize has consistently run a substantial trade deficit, reaching $35.1 million in 1983. The deficit is usually financed primarily by foreign aid, foreign investment, and substantial remittances from Belizeans working in the United States. Total merchandise imports in 1983 were $112.9 million. Belize's fuel bill went from $6.6 million in 1975 to $24.3 million in 1983. Exports in 1983 reached $77.8 million, the largest share of which was sugar exported to the United States and the United Kingdom, Belize's most important trading partners. Each of these countries accounts for approximately one-third of total Belizean imports.

Of the government's 1984–1985 budget, about U.S. $67.7 million (71 percent) is devoted to recurrent expenses and the remainder to capital or development spending. A national budget of $67.7 million is less than the budget of an average state university in the United States. The government raises about half of its annual operating expenses from customs duties and almost all of its capital expenses from foreign assistance. Most bilateral aid has come from the United Kingdom, but in 1982 the United States initiated a bilateral assistance program with Belize. Most multilateral aid comes from the World Bank, United Nations, and the CDB. CDB funds have financed expansion of a deepwater port near Belize City; a citrus pier in Dangriga (Stann Creek); electrification projects; an abattoir and a meat-packing plant; a hotel in Belmopan; and grain mills, storage, and drying facilities. U.S. firms can bid on such projects financed by the CDB. In 1983 the World Bank extended a $5.3 million loan for road maintenance and rehabilitation (Adams 1984, 304).

REGIONAL CULTURAL CHARACTERISTICS

Regional cultural distinctiveness may be identified along several lines. For example, occupation, religion, language, race, and ancestry are determining factors. We will discuss language first.

Belize is a bilingual country. As mentioned earlier, more than 90 percent of the population is literate, which gives Belize the highest literacy rate in the world. An overwhelming majority (85 percent) of the people speak English and its variant, Belizean Creole, but another significant proportion of the population (51 percent) is fluent in Spanish (Davidson 1983, 28). In addition, German, Garifuna, Mayan, and Kekchi are spoken in regional clusters. All in all, such differences in language in a small country make Belize a most exciting place for linguists.

Language is perhaps the prime cementing factor of enthnicity. When language changes occur, other cultural alterations are also probably taking place. In Belize, in the three areas where Spanish, English, and Mayan are the prominent languages—Corozal, Orange Walk, and Cayo Districts—the two factors do not coincide, which indicates that acculturation is underway.

When we separate the districts into rural and urban sectors, we can see that change is occurring at varying rates and in different directions. The major towns, Corozal, Orange Walk, and San Ignacio, are 60 to 70 percent Ladino (Mestizo) towns. The hinterlands surrounding these places are likewise predominantly Ladino, but at the smaller rates of 50 to 62 percent.

Perhaps because it is closest to a dynamic southeastern Mexican frontier, Corozal has been able to maintain its Spanish constituency, whereas the rural lands nearby, once Mayan, are accepting Spanish as a major language. More to the interior of the country, at Orange Walk Town, the use of English is increasing slightly. Ladino populations in the outlying areas, as well as the acculturated Mayan, maintain Spanish better. In Cayo the situation is drastically different. The Ladinos of San Ignacio are using much more English, whereas their rural compatriots use slightly less. The rural Mayan have been generally insulated from acculturation and have had relatively more difficulty learning a second language. Davidson (1983, 29) estimates that 38 percent of the population speak one language, 62 percent speak two or more languages, and 16 percent three or more languages.

Ethnic Grouping

Belize, though a small country, has several distinctive groups of people. These communities are by no means totally segregated from other communities. In Belize regional cultural distinctiveness, which is probably best termed *ethnicity*, carries the name *race* in common speech as well as in official government documents such as the 1980 census. For practical purposes, however, race refers to the physical anthropological differences and has little meaning in modern Belize. The population is simply and overwhelmingly racially heterogeneous. Still, according to the self-classification of the participants in the 1980 census, ethnic distinctions abound.

Hereafter, whenever we refer to "race," the implication is that of ethnoracial cohesiveness which distinguishes one group from another and identifies regional cultural distinctiveness. These distinguishing characteristics of regional cultural distinctiveness may include physical anthropological ancestry (i.e., race), language, religion, traditional occupations, or other ways of life (Davidson 1983, 16; Dobson 1973, 252).

The varied ethnoracial and cultural mixture in Belize may be divided into two broad cultural groupings: the Anglo-Saxon–oriented and English-speaking group, embracing the Whites, Africans, Creoles, Black Caribs (Garifunas), and East Indians; and the Spanish-Mestizo, covering the Spanish, Mestizos, and various groups of Mayan Indians.

According to the 1980 census, the nation can be divided into seven racial groups: Creole, Mestizo, Mayan, Garifuna, White, East Indian, and Chinese in decreasing percentage of population. Table 11.1 presents a summary of these results. In the table the Chinese and East Indians are combined under the category of "other," which also includes other minority groups and the nonstated category (Davidson 1983, 16–17).

Each of the traditional groups has a recognizable core, or hearth, within which its members feel "at home." Some cultures have expanded beyond their original territory (Kekchi, Mopan, Mennonite, Creole); others have contracted from acculturation (Yucatec Maya); and others (Garifuna, East Indians) have entrenched, retaining essentially the original hearths. Fortunately for the peace and well-being of Belizeans, ample space has separated the cultural core and allowed for occasional expansions.

Regional Culture Hearths (Cores)

The strong predominance of ethnoracial regional cultural hearths (or cores) in Belize is unique. Belize has a heterogeneous racial composition derived from intermittent arrivals of different peoples who were forced out of their countries by political or economic factors. These ethnoracial cultural groups have somehow retained their geographical closeness and cohesiveness within each region. In other words, this ethnoracial cultural heterogeneity has developed into regional ethnoracial cultural characteristics, and hence regional cultural differences

Table 11.1

Population of Belize by Race and Selected Geographical Divisions for 1970 and 1980

AREA	CREOLE	MAYA	WHITE	MESTIZO	GARIFUNA	OTHER	TOTAL
Nation 1970	36,767	22,368	4,445	39,271	13,669	3,414	119,934
%	30.7	18.6	3.7	32.7	11.4	2.8	100.0
Nation 1980	57,705	13,809	6,105	48,112	11,047	8,575	145,353
%	39.7	9.5	4.2	33.1	7.6	5.9	100.0
Belize District 1970 %	28,419	905	879	16,145	2,136	871	49,355
	57.6	1.8	1.8	32.7	4.3	1.8	100.0
Belize District 1980 %	38,152	407	599	6,655	1,626	3,402	50,801
	75.1	0.8	1.1	13.1	3.2	6.7	100.0
Belize City 1970 %	24,264	830	533	10,698	1,921	804	39,050
	62.1	2.1	1.4	27.4	4.9	2.1	100.0
Belize City 1980 %	30,226	159	360	4,852	1,392	2,782	39,771
	76.0	0.4	0.9	12.2	3.5	7.0	100.0
Cayo District 1970 %	1,996	5,452	1,101	6,026	962	438	15,975
	12.5	34.1	6.9	37.7	6.0	2.7	100.0
Cayo District 1980 %	7,079	1,142	1,827	11,190	434	1,165	22,837
	31.0	5.0	8.0	49.0	1.9	5.1	100.0
Belmopan 1980 %	1,667	18	114	672	273	191	2,935
	56.8	0.6	3.9	22.9	9.3	6.5	100.0

Source: Zammit (1982b, 42).

abound. According to the 1980 census data, 66 percent of Creoles live in their culture hearth. For other ethnoracial groups, the figures are 31 percent for the Mestizos (Ladinos), 72 percent for the Garifunas, 81 percent for the Mayan, 89 percent for the Mennonites, and 47 percent for East Indians. It is precisely because of such a high concentration of enthnoracial groups in their culture cores (hearths) that the characteristics of these groups translate into regional cultural distinctiveness. In this regard, Belize is a unique country for the study of regional cultural differences (Davidson 1983, 17).

According to the 1980 census, five ethnoracial regional groups (referred to as "race" in government documents) are the predominant communities. These five are the Creoles, the Garifunas, the Mestizos, the Mayan Indians, and the Whites. Each of these regional groups has specific ethnoracial cultural characteristics that translate into regional cultural characteristics because of their high concentration in their culture hearths (see table 11.1).

The Creoles

Creoles share two basic distinguishing characteristics: (1) they all have some degree of African ancestry, and (2) they all use the local English Creole dialect. Skin color runs the gamut from very dark to very light, but normally European ancestry is also evident. The term *Creole* has a somewhat specialized meaning. In the French colonies, the word is used only for those of French descent born in the colonies. The word *Criollo* in Spanish-speaking areas is used in the same sense. In Belize, however, *Creole* generally signifies those with some African blood. Creoles believe themselves to be the "true Belizeans" because most of the early settlers were supposedly their ancestors. This may not be totally true. Claims of early settlement and first occupancy have also been made by Garifunas, Mestizos, Mayans, and even East Indians. (Dobson 1973, 256–58).

The Creoles form about 40 percent of the total population and are centered around Belize City where 52 percent of them live. The Creole hearth or core is Belize District where 66 percent live and comprise 75 percent of the total population. Rural concentrations are located along the Western Highway between Belmopan and San Ignacio, and in isolated clusters in northern Belize District and a few coastal towns to the south. The number of Creoles is increasing nationwide and in all urban areas. There was a 9 percent increase in the national population in favor of the Creoles during the 1970s, and according to the latest census data (1980), they command a 57 percent majority in Belmopan (see table 11.1).

English is the main language of the Creoles, but some of the less educated Creoles speak a Creole dialect. The majority of Creoles are Protestant, but a large minority, about a third, belong to the Catholic Church. Creoles work primarily in urban occupations and heavily dominate the administration of the country and the national bureaucracy, including the police. Creoles have also provided the labor force for the forestry industry such as logging. However, only a few permanent settlements of Creole farmers exist (Davidson 1983, 20.)

The Garifunas

The Garifunas are descendants of the original Red Carib Amerindians who were the occupants of many islands of the West Indies when they were discovered by Columbus. Garifunas have long been called Caribs or Black Caribs in Belize, although today they prefer to be called Garifunas in order to denote their distinctive language and culture. Carib resistance to European domination made them known as ferocious savages, but it was precisely this determined sense of self-preservation that allowed them to survive at all. They came to Belize as early as 1802, but it was not until 1832 that their largest contingent settled along the coast to the south of Stann Creek after losing some battles to the revolutionaries of Central America. They gradually established themselves as hard-working and peaceful people in five coastal enclaves that still serve as a fragmented culture hearth where 72 percent of all Garifunas live. Outward movements from the core villages have not established new concentrations but have occurred on an individual basis (Dobson 1973, 255–56).

The Garifunas have retained their distinctive identity in spite of the fact that physically they differ very little from the Creoles. Unlike Creoles, their percentage proportion of the population has declined by almost 4 percent (from 11.4 percent in 1970 to 7.6 percent in 1980; see table 11.1).

Few of the Garifunas choose to marry outside their race or to leave the coastal enclaves where fishing and farming are the main sources of making a living. The Garifunas have retained their own language, but the majority also speak English. They are hard-working people, their most ambitious members becoming successful in professions such as the law and teaching. Many of their rural schools are staffed entirely by Garifunas, who seem to have a natural talent for acquiring languages and have thus developed useful ties with the Amerindians of the Toledo District. Nevertheless, the Garifunas have not been able to win complete societal acceptance for themselves and are regarded as different by some Creoles. The result has been a certain degree of low self-esteem among some Garifunas (Davidson 1983, 8 and 22).

The Mestizos

In Belize the Spanish-speaking people who are the descendants of Amerindians and Europeans are called Mestizos. This term is appropriate when we wish to describe the racial connotation. Culturally speaking, *Ladino* might be a more apt term in describing the mass of Mexicans and Central Americans who have immigrated into Belize.

Mestizos were once the predominant population of the country. Today they are the second most populous group coming after the Creoles (see table 11.1). They are concentrated in the so-called century-old "Mexican-Mestizo Corridor" that runs along New River between Corozol and Orange. It is from this primary hearth (or core) that acculturative forces have reached into the adjacent Mayan zone. A secondary core is located in West Central Belize around Benque Viejo and San Ignacio. Here, Mestizos from Guatemala have recently added to the earlier Spanish-speaking immigrants from Yucatan (Davidson 1983, 21). Of all Belizeans, these Mestizos are the least likely to remain settled in the hearth. Almost 5,000 currently live in Belize City (see table 11.1). At their hearth, 31 percent of the Mestizos live there (Davidson 1983, 17).

The Mayan Indians

The Mayan Indians or Amerindians are the most isolated of the various communities. In fact, the modern Mayan consists of several distinct groups, although faulty census returns and the isolation of their villages make it difficult to be precise about numbers and provenance (see table 11.1). The Maya founded most of the villages in the Cayo District and along the western frontier when they fled from the Peten seeking asylum from forced labor and heavy taxes in Guatemala.

Three modern Mayoid people can be identified in Belize. Locals generally refer to the Mopan and Yucatecans by the term *Maya* and to the Kekchi as a non-Maya group. The Kekchi are also Mayan. Together, the three comprise almost 10 percent of the total population (see table 11.1). Although some fusions have taken place among them, in their original distributions and activities some differences remain clear (Dobson 1973, 252–54). Their cores can be found in three zones: southwest Toledo, the upper Belize River Valley, and northwest Corozal-northern Orange Walk. Grossly generalized, Indian settlement in these areas proceeds from north to south: Yucatec-Mopan-Kekchi. In Toledo, Mopan live just north of the Kekchi hearth; in the Cayo borderlands the Mopan and Yucatec fuse with dominance by the Yucatec; and the north is Yucatec land.

The Yucatec, who have had the most contact with the Mestizos, have experienced the greatest number of changes. For example, at Yo Creek, Orange Walk, which was once an all-Mayan agricultural village, Spanish is the primary language, and more people work for wages outside the village farm. Today only 34 percent of the residents have Mayan surnames. Most of the Yucatec Maya live in large villages and play an important role in the social and economic life of their own communities and the country as a whole. By contrast, the Mopan Maya tend to lead more isolated lives. On the other hand, the Kekchi Maya still cling to their unsophisticated way of life. They are a self-sufficient people who grow corn and rear pigs; they continue the traditional practice of community or group work and still lead lives insulated from modern civilization. The Kekchi are a religious people who have retained some of their own traditional customs alongside Christian practices, influenced mainly by the primary schools and missions run by American Jesuits. They have kept their own language, and few have benefited sufficiently from their schooling to speak English or Spanish correctly. In fact, the Kekchi do not even understand Mopan Mayan, although as some of them are beginning to intermarry with their neighbors, this may also change in time. Perhaps because of their relative geographical isolation and conservatism, the southern Mayan (Kekchi and Mopan) seem to be virtually absent in Belmopan affairs (Davidson 1983, 23). At their hearth, the Maya have a concentration of 81 percent, which is by far the highest for any ethnoracial group in the country.

The Whites

Whites include people from European, North American, and Middle Eastern extraction. Some of the most successful businesspeople in the country are the Syrians or Lebanese who have now lived in the country for two or three generations. These people have fulfilled an important economic role (Dobson 1973, 254–55). Mennonites are the most recent group who have entered Belize on a large scale and with unusual rapidity. They are a German-speaking group originally from the Alps, and they are members of the Protestant sect that moved to northern Germany and southern Russia, and later arrived in Pennsylvania in about 1700, in Canada a century later, and finally reached northern Mexico following World War I. Because of recurring local government restrictions of their isolated, agrarian way of life, migration has become a normal occurrence (Davidson 1983, 24).

Most of the Mennonites who came to Belize entered from Mexico between 1958 and 1962. They signed a special agreement with the Belize government which guaranteed them complete freedom to practice their own distinctive form of Protestantism and to farm within their closed communities. They agreed to pay all their own expenses, and they purchased 150,000 acres of land outright at an average price of three Belize dollars per acre. The official exchange rate in 1960 was U.S. $1 = Belize $1.429. The current exchange rate is U.S. $1 = Belize $2 (Zammit 1983b, 14–15). Today this land is worth four times that amount. The Mennonites were also exempted from military service and from paying contributions to compulsory insurance and other welfare programs. They were liable for all other taxes, however. There are now separate communities at Shipyard (Orange Walk), Spanish Lookout (Cayo), and Blue Creek (Orange Walk), as well as expansions into other areas such as the Toledo District.

The Mennonites are a distinctive community within the country. They look like blond German farmers, speaking a low German and wearing traditional attire. Their children are educated only through primary school and work on their farms. The Mennonites have no interest in politics, in taking public office, or even in exercising their right to vote. Understandably, criticisms have been voiced against this exclusive community, but they have shown that they are interested in hard work and productivity. The Mennonites' knowledge of dairy farming has had a marked effect on the economy. The question now is whether the Mennonite communities will be able to retain their separate existence as their numbers expand from the current figure of 3,300, which is more than half the total white population (see table 11.1).

Belize has few Whites of British or other European extraction, but they occupy key positions in the government and are wealthy landowners. They hold the real power in Belize. It has been alleged that some of the Whites get their money from illegal drug business (Jensen 1986).

THE NEW CAPITAL

Perhaps the greatest entrepreneurial venture for any country is that of relocating its capital. Such a decision is even more momentous when the relocation is from an old traditional capital, which is also the largest city, to a location with a different regional cultural identity and to a city planned and constructed from its very beginning for the explicit purpose of a nation's capital.

Throughout Belize's long history, the most important decision will likely prove to be the one taken after the disastrous Hurricane Hattie struck in 1961. Belize City, then the capital of Belize, suffered major destruction for the second time in thirty years. This persuaded the government that the time had come to build a new capital. Belize City was built on a mangrove swamp at the tip of a narrow peninsula only 18 inches above sea level (De La Haba and Long 1972, 124). When Hattie howled inland with her 160-mile-an-hour winds, she dragged a 10-foot tide behind her. She badly mauled three-quarters of Belize City and left more than 260 Belizeans dead. Partly because of Hattie and partly because of its then 30,000 citizens, Belize City was not a pretty place. Houses are flimsy and unpainted in many areas, streets are narrow, and open canals carry sewage out to sea. Most of the structures in Belize City are made of wood, and the humidity is very high (Jensen 1986).

After detailed studies had been made, the government chose a site in 1962 near the village of Roaring Creek in the Cayo District, 50 miles inland from Belize City, at the intersection of the Western Highway and the Hemingway Highway. The movement of the capital 50 miles to the west inland must be contrasted with the maximum width of the country which is 68 miles. Another factor to be noted is the short length of time (less than one year) devoted to the planning and decision-making phase of this major enterprise. Belmopan was chosen as the name for the new capital. It is derived from the two words of Belize (a Mayan word meaning muddy water) and Mopan (a subgroup of Mayan Indians). Most of the Mopans live near Belmopan.

After the British government gave formal approval to this site and promised loans and grants amounting to over U.S. $16 million, the initial surveys were made. The new capital, situated at a pleasant site near the Belize River Valley and with views of the Mountain Pine Ridge foothills, was hacked out of the jungle and has yet to lose its raw edges. For this reason many people have shown a reluctance to leave Belize City for what they consider "backcountry" (De La Haba and Long 1972, 132–34).

A consortium of London consultants devised a scheme for the development of the new capital to be completed in several stages. It was thought that for the first few years the population would be about 5,000, but would eventually rise to 30,000 by 1990. In 1965 a commemorative stela was unveiled by Anthony Greenwood, secretary of state for the colonies, and in 1966 the task of building the new capital was begun.

The first stage of the project included all the essential services such as the water supply, generating plant, and telephone system. It also provided the first government buildings, homes for government officials, schools, a hospital, and an ecumenical center for the main religious organizations. Reinforced concrete has been used for all the buildings to enable them to withstand hurricane-force winds. At the same time, the architects have tried to provide a pleasing appearance with the maximum use of natural ventilation. The government buildings have been designed with a Mayan motif, which has been achieved by the use of plazas and pyramid-type architecture.

At the time of the 1970 census, which was conducted by the University of the West Indies, Belmopan had a population of 274, only 24 of whom were female. In August 1970 Government Ministries and their Departments were transferred to Belmopan, and on February 1, 1971, the House of Representatives assembled for the first time in its new legislative chamber on Independence Hill, bringing Belmopan to life as the center of government and the first modern capital city in Central America. In August 1971 Belmopan's population was already 2,700, and work was almost ready to begin on the second stage. This was to provide recreational areas and some facilities for small light industries. Later plans included hotels, a library, a museum, and more schools. A site has even been earmarked for a possible university. Meanwhile, the reconstruction of the Western Highway has been progressing steadily. It is unlikely that Belize City will lose it importance as the trading and mercantile center of the country, but, after nearly 300 years, it has ceased to be the administrative center (Zammit 1978, 43–44; Dobson 1973, 284).

According to a 1980 census, Belmopan's population was 2,935, including 1,452 females. This is a very negligible increase from the 2,700 in 1971 (see table 11.1). The most recent estimates put the population of Belmopan at 4,000 (Adams 1984, 1). This is a far cry from the initially projected population of 30,000 by the year 1990. Why were the government's projections so far off target?

REGIONAL CULTURAL FACTORS

There are many reasons why Belmopan did not achieve its projected population estimates and did not become a cultural, industrial, and commercial center as well as a political capital. We may never know all the elements and factors that have disrupted large-scale entrepreneurial enterprise. Regional cultural distinctiveness, however, is formed by the concentration of the ethnoracial groups in various regions (or districts) due to high-density culture hearths. This factor, with its many varied dimensions, provides the major clue to a large part of the question raised.

Table 11.1 shows the population data by race for the 1970 and 1980 census (i.e., just before the move to the new capital and ten years later). The table presents the nation's population, the population of Belize District (where Belize City, the old capital, is located), of Belize City, of Cayo District (where Belmopan, the new capital is located), and of Belmopan. A comparison of the ethnoracial composition of Cayo District, Belmopan, Belize District, Belize City, and the nation reveals the degree to which the composition of these regions differs. *The key point argued here is that the entrepreneurial creation of this new capital not only went against the grain of regional cultural characteristics, but also distorted and structurally modified these cultural characteristics in ways that were not acceptable to the core groups.* This kind of cultural intervention is not welcomed in any country where the ethnoracial groups have a high degree of cohesiveness and identity. Here, the managerial implications are that economic and business decision makers should be amply concerned with different regional identities and with regional cultural distinctions. Factors such as ethnoracial characteristics, language, educational and socioeconomic differences, as well as the typical indicators of employment preferences and standard of living all contribute to the overall sense of regional cultural distinctiveness. Managers and entrepreneurs must consider regional cultural differences whenever they make decisions that involve the movement or transfer of capital and human resources across regional cultural boundaries.

The Case of the Creoles and Mayan Indians

The Creoles, the largest group in Belize, comprised 12.5 percent of the population of Cayo District in 1979. In 1980 they comprise 56 percent of the population of Belmopan and 31.0 percent of the population of the Cayo District. Essentially, the relocation of a large group of Creoles to the Belmopan area changed the composition of Creole in the whole Cayo District (see table 11.1). In other words, as far as the Creole community is concerned, the Belmopan of 1980 is more like Belize City or Belize District than the Cayo District of 1970 into which it was injected. There must be a resistance to this kind of cultural intervention. This resistance has taken the form of resistance to move further away from Belize City (or District) and consequently has limited the growth of the new capital. People do not want to move into a region where they do not "fit" culturally and ethnoracially.

The Mayan Indians, who comprise about 10 percent of the nation's population, have had an almost negligible presence in Belize District (or Belize City). However, the 1970 census of Cayo District shows that Mayan Indians comprised 34.1 percent of the population (see table 11.1). The Belmopan of 1980 with a Mayan composition of 0.6 percent is more like Belize City of 1970 (or 1980) than the Cayo District of 1970 with a 34.1 percent Mayan population. Imagine the feelings of the early settlers of Belmopan (mostly Creole) who suddenly found themselves surrounded by so many Mayans. The 1980 census shows that the Mayan population of Cayo District has dropped to nearly 5 percent. This is a major change from the 1970 census and may in part be attributable to the injection of Belmopan into the predominantly Mayan–Mestizo District of Cayo.

In the case of Mestizos and Garifunas, table 11.1 again shows that the composition of these groups in Belmopan is more similar to that of Belize District (or Belize City) than that of Cayo District. Once more, we see that the ethnoracial composition of Belmopan does not "fit" into the District of Cayo's regional cultural characteristics. In other words, Belmopan is more like a small-size Belize City (or Belize District) implanted in the heart of Cayo District, a region with quite different regional cultural distinctiveness.

Religion and Employment Characteristics

Table 11.2, based on the 1980 census, shows the religious and employment characteristics of the nation, Belize District, and Cayo District

Table 11.2
Percentage Distribution of Population of Belize in 1980 by Religion and Employment Groups by District

Category	Classification	Nation	Belize District	Cayo District
Religion	Mennonite	3.9	0.4	7.0
	Anglican	11.8	26.3	4.9
	Methodist	6.0	12.0	1.2
	Roman Catholic	61.7	43.7	68.5
	Other	16.5	17.6	18.4
	Total	100.0	100.0	100.0
Industrial Employment Groups-Male	Agriculture (1)	44.3	14.4	45.2
	Manufacturing (2)	38.7	63.0	29.8
	Other	17.0	22.6	25.0
	Total	100.0	100.0	100.0
Occupational Employment Groups-Male	Professional (3)	20.9	35.8	20.1
	Agriculture (4)	66.8	20.5	62.5
	Other	12.3	43.7	17.4
	Total	100.0	100.0	100.0

[1]Includes forestry and fishing.
[2]Includes electricity, water and sanitary services, construction, installation, finance, insurance, real estate, commerce and community services, transport, storage and communication, and other services.
[3]Includes technical, managerial, administrative, clerical, sales and service.
[4]Includes forestry, fishery, production, and transport.
Source: Zammit (1982b, 1982c).

in percentage form. Belize City is in Belize District and Belmopan is in Cayo District. Moreover, we saw that Belmopan is more like a "small" Belize District in terms of its cultural composition. Therefore, a study of the differences of the religious and employment references of Belize and Cayo Districts will illustrate the cultural friction between Belmopan and Cayo District into which Belmopan was thrust.

With regard to religious differences, the percentage composition of Belize District (or Belmopan for that matter) and Cayo District is in startling contrast. Cayo District has a 17.5–fold concentration of Mennonites compared to Belize District (0.4 percent versus 7.0 percent), whereas Belize District has a tenfold composition of Methodists compared to Cayo District (12 percent versus 1.2 percent). The Anglican composition of Belize District is more than five times that of Cayo District (26.3 percent versus 4.9 percent). For the Roman Catholics, there is almost a 25–percentage point difference between these two districts. Hence, there are clear religious differences between Belize District (from which the Belmopan population is extracted) and Cayo District (into which Belmopan was placed).

With regard to employment, clear patterns of regional preferences and distinctiveness can be identified. Table 11.2 shows that agriculture is the predominant employment in Cayo District versus the manufacturing and service sector for Belize District. In terms of industrial employment groups, an agricultural industry composition of 45.2 percent in Cayo District versus 14.4 percent in Belize district, or a threefold factor, is observed. Although the manufacturing/service component has a 63.0 percent concentration in Belize District versus a 29.8 percent for Cayo District (and this is after the injection of Belmopan with its high service workforce into Cayo District), the difference is a factor of 2 to 1. For occupational employment groups, the results are the same—a threefold percentage composition of agricultural employment in favor of Cayo District (62.5 percent versus 20.5 percent), and an almost twofold percentage composition of professional/technical/service employment in favor of the Belize District (20.1 percent versus 35.8 percent). In essence, Belmopan with its projected and current composition of highly professional/service/technical employment is radically different as it sits in the middle of jungles and forests of Cayo District with its agricultural orientation. No wonder few have moved there.

Language and Educational Characteristics

Table 11.3, also based on the 1980 census, shows the primary languages spoken and the highest level of education attained (by adult males) for the nation as a whole as well as for the Belize and Cayo Districts, and for Belize City and Belmopan. As far as language is concerned, although Belize is a multilingual country (i.e., more than half can speak two or more languages), the difference in the primary language spoken is a major regional cultural distinction. Here again, Belmopan appears to be more like Belize District than Cayo District in terms of languages spoken. For example, 81.5 percent of the population of Belmopan speaks English, compared to 89.4 percent in Belize District

Table 11.3
Percentage Distribution of Population of Belize in 1980 by Language,
Household Dwelling Type, and Education, by District and City

Category	Classification	Nation	Belize Dist.	Belize City	Cayo Dist.	Belmopan
Language Spoken	English	50.6	89.4	91.0	47.6	81.5
	Spanish	31.6	6.3	4.4	40.2	15.1
	Maya	3.8	0.0	0.0	3.7	0.0
	Low German	3.3	0.0	0.0	6.6	0.0
	Other	10.7	4.3	4.6	1.9	3.4
	Total	100.0	100.0	100.0	100.0	100.0
Household Dwelling Type	Separate House	79.5	67.9	61.6	92.8	98.2
	Apartment	15.7	26.1	32.3	3.8	1.2
	Other	4.8	6.0	6.1	3.4	0.6
	Total	100.0	100.0	100.0	100.0	100.0
Highest Level of Education Adult-Male	Primary	73.1	68.8	65.7	73.2	36.3
	Secondary	14.5	23.4	26.3	10.8	37.8
	University	2.2	3.6	4.1	3.3	15.6
	Other	10.2	4.2	3.9	12.7	10.3
	Total	100.0	100.0	100.0	100.0	100.0

Source: Zammit (1982b, 1982c).

and a mere 47.6 percent in Cayo District (this also includes the 81.5 percent of Belmopan). The case for Spanish, Mayan, and low German is the same. In other words, Belmopan does not "fit" into the linguistic culture of the Cayo District. New settlers would not feel comfortable in the midst of this newly found regional culture where they would not be understood or understand others there.

The educational and schooling characteristics of the new settlers of Belmopan compared to those of Belize City and Cayo District (table 11.3) reveal that the Belmopan population has a much higher level of education than both Belize City (or Belize District) and Cayo District.

The numbers shown for Cayo District already include the Belmopan population. Without it, the educational level of the remainder of Cayo District would gravitate downward toward the primary school education level. Here, again, we see that the new capital resembles Belize City more closely than Cayo District in terms of the educational level of its citizens. Relocating people with a significantly higher level of education into a region with a lower level would (and did) bring resistance. Therefore, the educational and linguistic characteristics of these regions proved to be yet another barrier in this entrepreneurial transfer of a capital city across regions with radically different cultures.

Contrasting Dwelling and Shelter Regional Characteristics

Based on the 1980 census, tables 11.3 and 11.4 show the type of household dwelling, type of lighting by households, type of cooking by households, and type of toilet facilities for the nation as a whole as well as for Belize and Cayo Districts, and for Belize City and Belmopan.

As far as dwelling type is concerned, although the dwelling type characteristics of Belmopan seem to be similar to those of Cayo District, they are quite different from the type found in Belize City and Belize District where most of the new settlers are of Belmopan origin. Their adjustment would involve moving from apartment-type dwellings to separate houses where the overall responsibility for maintenance would be higher. In addition, as we will see below, table 11.4 clearly shows that, although the type of housing classification might be the same, other aspects of the household life such as lighting, cooking, and toilet facilities are quite different in Belmopan as compared to Cayo District.

In Belmopan, 4.5 percent use kerosene for lighting. This compares well with 5.4 percent in Belize City and contrasts well with 39.0 percent in Cayo District. Here, again we see that the citizens of Belmopan live much the same as those of Belize City and quite differently from those of Cayo District. The electricity figures for lighting also show the same results.

While seemingly a trite issue, it should be noted that a comparison of the type of toilet facility utilized by households shows the difference between Belmopan dwellings and those in the Cayo District dwellings. Table 11.4 shows that only 2.4 percent of dwellings in Belmopan use a pit latrine, whereas the comparable figure for Cayo District is 71.9 percent. On the other hand, 92.6 percent of dwellings in Belmopan have water closets linked to sewer, whereas only 15.2 percent have comparable facilities in Cayo District (and this 15.2 percent also includes the water closets in Belmopan, without which this 15.2 percent would have been lower).

Table 11.4

Percentage Distribution of Population of Belize in 1980 by Type of Household Lighting, Cooking, and Toilet Facility, by District and City

Category	Classification	Nation	Belize Dist.	Belize City	Cayo Dist.	Belmopan
Type of Lighting by Households	Electricity	59.3	79.6	90.3	58.6	94.4
	Kerosene	36.8	16.1	5.4	39.0	4.5
	Other	3.9	4.3	4.3	2.4	1.1
	Total	100.0	100.0	100.0	100.0	100.0
Type of Cooking by Households	Gas	32.9	42.9	46.4	33.8	72.9
	Electricity	1.1	1.8	2.1	1.3	6.3
	Wood	31.3	8.3	0.7	41.4	5.3
	Kerosene	27.4	37.7	41.0	19.7	12.8
	Other	7.3	9.3	9.8	3.8	2.7
	Total	100.0	100.0	100.0	100.0	100.0
Type of Toilet Facility	Pit Latrine	49.1	16.5	3.6	71.9	2.4
	W.C. Linked to Sewer	3.6	2.0	2.3	15.2	92.6
	W.C Not Linked to Sewer	18.1	34.1	37.9	8.8	0.3
	Other	29.1	47.3	56.2	4.3	4.7
	Total	100.0	100.0	100.0	100.0	100.0

Source: Zammit (1982c).

Regional Cultural Misfit

The people of Belmopan have far better housing facilities and a higher standard of living than their neighbors in the other villages. They also have different occupations, are more educated, speak somewhat different languages, and profess somewhat different religions than their neighbors. Moreover, their ethnoracial identity is also quite different from that of Cayo District. The whole process of relocating the capital from Belize City to Belmopan seems like a surgical transplant of a portion of "Belize City—Belize District" into the middle of Cayo District. This "transplant" was rejected by the "body" of the nation because the transplanted element (i.e., Belmopan) did not have the same "chemistry" (i.e., regional cultural distinctiveness) as the host element (i.e., Cayo District). It is no surprise that the population projections have not materialized. It might even be argued that this fledgling existence of Belmopan can be attributed to the fact that it is backed mainly—maybe only—by the government with the blessing of all the powers in the nation. These data support the assertion and major argument here that Belmopan is a regional cultural "misfit" in the Cayo District, and that all the economic powers and infusions of capital cannot, and did not, force people to leave a cohesive culture of several centuries and move to a region with different cultural characteristics. In fact, a study of all the projects in Belize (funded by a variety of sources) indicates that during the 1982–1986 period Belmopan received more than its fair share of the funds. Although Belmopan represents only about 2 percent of the nation's population, it received more than 12 percent of the funds for all the projects (Economic Report on Belize, 55–137). Thus, Belmopan is not an orphan child; in fact, it is a very well-cared-for child.

The following section compares the differences and similarities between Brazil's creation of its new capital, Brasilia, and Belmopan in the British Honduras. We will focus on the success factors that helped create Brasilia in particular.

BELMOPAN VERSUS BRASILIA

Belize was not the only country in the Western Hemisphere to move its capital from an old traditional city to a newly constructed city in the latter half of the twentieth century. Brazil moved its capital from Rio de Janeiro to Brasilia in 1960 just a decade before Belize did. Whereas Belmopan's growth has fallen far short of the initial projections, Brasilia's growth has exceeded expectations. The following discussion compares a succcessful capital move with an unsuccessful one, again emphasizing the element of regional differences.

Similarities

The Belmopan and Brasilia cases contain many similarities. Both are newly designed and constructed cities for the specific purpose of serving their nation's capital. In the case of both countries, the old capital was a port city with a relatively high population, and the new capital was inland in an area only sparsely populated. Belmopan is 50 miles away from Belize City, and Brasilia is nearly 700 miles from the old capital. When we consider the size of the countries involved, we see that these distances are comparable with each other.

In 1957 Brasilia was only a dream on an architect's drawing board; this city was to be raised in the middle of a virtual wilderness. In 1960 it was inaugurated as the newest capital in Latin America. By 1970 the city had grown so much that not only 550,000 people crowded the federal district, but also over 272,000 inhabitants lived in the as yet unfinished capital city. As the city went forward toward its completion in the 1970s, it remained one of the rare opportunities in world history for an orderly total-city design in terms of physical layout, architecture, and human habitation. In 1980 the population of Brasilia reached 1.2 million.

Brasilia has eight satellite towns that are located in the federal district of 2,245 square miles (almost one-quarter of the size of Belize). It is situated in the state of Goias on the central plateau of Brazil, which was formerly a mining and cattle-raising region. The climate is mild and dry. Thus, in many respects, quite a number of similarities exist between the "Belize City–Belmopan" move and the "Rio de Janeiro–Brasilia" move.

Differences

Unlike Belize, Brazil's new capital does not have regional cultural characteristics from nearby regions, at least not in the two states of Goias (where Brasilia is located) and Minas Gerais (where the old capital Rio is located). The population is 93 percent Roman Catholic and 98 percent Christian, unlike Belize with its regionally diverse religious preferences. Portuguese is the official language and is spoken by almost everyone, in contrast to Belize with its regionally determined language(s). Finally, although Brazil is also a multiracial, multiethnic country, most Brazilians consider themselves white, and despite class distinctions, national solidarity is strong and racial friction minimal. Except for the indigenous Indians in the Amazon region, the various ethnoracial groups are homogeneously distributed across the land, and there is no ethnoracial culture core (or hearth) such as we found in Belize. The indigenous full-blooded Indians, located mainly in the northern and western border regions and in the upper Amazon Basin, constitute less than 1 percent of the population. Their numbers are rapidly declining as contact with the outside world and commercial expansion into the interior increase. Except for this relatively small pocket of population in the northern region, the other areas of the country do not exhibit any outstanding regional clashing cultural characteristics.

Conceivably, if Brazil had tried to move its capital into the jungles of the upper Amazon Basin which has a distinctively different regional culture (and is very similar to what Belize did with Belmopan), its new capital would not have fared as well as Brasilia and we would have seen another "Belmopan." This has, to some extent, happened in the Amazon region. Recent government efforts and programs to establish reservations, to provide other forms of assistance, and to encourage an orderly move of the people to this region have been unsuccessful and the subject of a great deal of controversy.

Planning

Another factor to consider is the planning phase of such an entrepreneurial enterprise of moving capitals. In Belize, the impetus for the move was Hurricane Hattie, followed by a one-year site selection study and a four-year design and fund-raising stage. In Brazil, the idea of a capital city located in the interior had been proposed in 1789, was reiterated in 1822 when Brazil gained its independence from Portugal, and was embodied in the Constitution of 1891. The selection of Brasilia's present site in 1956 was preceded by eight years of surveying and testing the interior. Therefore, the selection of Belmopan was like a quick "knee-jerk" reaction to the disastrous Hurricane Hattie, whereas the establishment of Brasilia was deeply rooted in the Brazilian culture. When the time for it came, Brasilia stood as a symbol for Brazilians of the national will to overcome chronic economic and social problems by bringing together the resources of the country's vast untapped interior and the large coastal populations living on the boundaries of poverty.

Cultural Life

In 1962 the University of Brasilia began its academic activities. One of its main objectives was to provide scientific and cultural assistance to the city and government. The federally funded University of Brasilia is divided into a number of separate institutes and faculties with their own departments. The university is central to much of Brasilia's cultural life. The Cultural Foundation of the federal district sponsors many national meetings in the arts and letters, and several foreign information centers are available. In addition, there are large auditoriums, museums, libraries, television and radio stations, zoological parks, newspapers, magazines, theaters, cinemas, and night clubs. The city has more swimming pools than any other Brazilian city.

This is in contrast to the gloomy atmosphere of Belmopan. The author's impression of Belmopan during his stay in that city in 1976 is that of a very dull place with no social or cultural life. There is virtually no middle class in Belmopan. The majority represent a cultural clash: the relatively poor Creoles, and the rest the wealthy and powerful government officials from different regions. Not only did the city not have theaters, cinemas, and other recreational facilities, but some of the essential services such as business-class hotels and good hospitals were lacking as well. Belize City has remained the cultural, economic, and business center of Belize. All foreign legations and embassies are in Belize City, not in Belmopan. Ambassadors and other diplomatic personnel definitely prefer Belize City with its busy and full life to Belmopan in the middle of the jungle. In Brazil, however, in accordance with a government decree, all foreign embassies were to begin operations in Brasilia in September 1972.

Transportation

Transportation to and from the new capital is also a success factor in Brasilia. Highways and air routes link Brasilia with the rest of Brazil, and regular national and international air service is available. In contrast, Belmopan is not served by good roads. It took three hours to cover the 50–mile distance between Belize City and Belmopan when the author was in Belize in 1976. There is no air transportation to the capital, and anything that is manufactured in Belmopan will have to be finally brought back to Belize City for distribution or export, so why move the manufacturing facilities to Belmopan? Most of the industry, especially export products, are located near the country's airport which is close to Belize City. Hence, the possibility of commuting between Belize City and Belmopan is nil. If any laborer wishes to live in one and work in the other, he will have to stay overnight in Belmopan during weekdays and go home on the weekend. The labor workforce generally shuns such an arrangement because for Belizeans there are implications that whenever a group of men live together they may be homosexuals.

CONCLUSION

Belize is a unique country with identifiable regional cultural identities where ethnoracial groups (referred to as "race" in Belize) play an important role in the development of regional cultural distinctiveness through the strong predominance of high-density culture hearths. In the context of such regional cultural boundaries, the government of Belize decided to move its capital 50 miles inland from Belize City to Belmopan in 1970 and thereby cross the rigid regional cultural boundary between Belize District and Cayo District. Moving a nation's capital is one of the most daring entrepreneurial ventures for any a country. The differential regional cultural characteristics between Belize City and Belmopan are so great that even this government-backed enterprise fell far short of its initially projected goals. The ethnoracial cultural characteristics between these two regions were related to the ethnicity of their citizens as well as to such factors as language spoken, educational level attained, employment opportunities, religious preferences, and housing quality.

The case of Belmopan was also contrasted and compared to the case of Brasilia, the new capital of Brazil. The many similarities between the move to Belmopan and that to Brasilia demonstrated that in Brazil, unlike in Belize, the problem of crossing different regional cultural boundaries did not exist. This and conscientious, thorough planning resulted in the success of Brasilia beyond the early projections.

Regional cultural characteristics must be taken into consideration before governmental, economic, or business decision makers decide to move human and capital resources across regional cultural boundaries. The proper or improper consideration of these regional cultural factors could eventually dictate the success or failure of an otherwise ideal entrepreneurial effort.

Managers, whether working internationally or domestically, must pay attention not only to a country's national culture, but also to its regional cultural structure. The regional cultural characteristics of the garment district in New York City is quite different from those of the Amish in central Pennsylvania, although they are not far from each other geographically. If one were to try moving the garment district from New York City to the middle of Pennsylvania Dutch country, one would get a feel for what the move was like for the early (and later still) settlers of Belmopan who relocated from Belize City. The case of Belmopan provides a lesson backed by data.

The major lesson here is that managers and entrepreneurs must consider the nature of regional cultures before, not after, making critical choices, regardless of whether those choices involve markets, facilities, capital, or other material. In this case, the choice involved entire segments of regional cultural groups whose traditions and lifestyles did not fit the government's innovative but shortsighted plan.

12

Concluding Comments

Joseph W. Weiss

Nations are not monolithic cultural entities. Regions and localities within countries share the larger culture, but can and often do differ from that culture in historical experience, economic resources, social customs, and political and value preferences. The essays in this book focus on the effects regional cultural characteristics have on industrial, entrepreneurial and general management practices in eight countries.

With these readings in mind, the following set of hypotheses was derived and was aimed at identifying the roles which regional culture plays in influencing management and entrepreneurial development.

REGIONAL CULTURE AS ORGANIZATION INFLUENCER

Proposition 1: Regional culture is embodied in industrial practices and policies, and in managerial behavior and styles. Through shared values, customs, traditions, and expectations, managers reflect local and regional beliefs and attitudes. Reward systems, communication, decision making, networking, personnel policies, all these embody to some extent the values of the geographic area of the organization: "the way things are done here." Weiss and Delbecq's studies and Larsen's and Rogers's before them illustrate the differences in how high-technology computer executives in Silicon Valley and Massachusetts manage their workforces and operations. These studies and the powerful generalizations they provide serve as yet another road map for viewing and understanding managerial behavior as part of the environment of the organization. Our argument here is that regional influences are part of the "cultural mix" that influences practices and behavior in firms. National and corporate culture, as well as industrial and occupational culture, are other parts of this mix. To understand how and why managers and companies act as they do, regional culture must also be taken seriously.

Proposition 2: Regional cultures within countries vary in their value systems and histories and thus in their influences on managerial behavior and industrial practices. One need not study only the differences between Japanese and American management practices to see contrasting models. Nieves Martinez and Pedro Nueño's essay describes and distinguishes Catalonian business values from other regional business cultures in Spain. The region of Catalan has a distinctive history and set of values that reinforce austerity, individuality, and independence, all of which are reflected in the pragmatic style of that region's business managers.

Jean-Paul Larçon's essay on France also depicts contrasting regional differences that are reflected in management styles and entrepreneurial activities. The way business is done in Lyon differs from that in Paris and in the Riviera. The high-technology center of Sophia-Antipolis in southern France resembles the culture of Silicon Valley; the Lyon region more closely resembles the Route 128 culture in Massachusetts.

Max Daetwyler's essay on Switzerland presents a unique management model that embodies elements from several regions. The evolution of regional culture in Switzerland into a homogeneous mix stands in contrast to regional differences in other countries in this book. Daetwyler traced the "homogenizing" factors in Switzerland which influenced the evolution of a strong, unifying, dominant national culture. Those factors included the Swiss Army, the education system, and trade unions in the country. We include Daetwyler's example as an interesting exception to our basic proposition here and to the other regional examples.

REGIONAL CULTURE AND ENTREPRENEURSHIP

Proposition 3: Regional cultures and industrial infrastructures influence the development or impediment of entrepreneurial activities and projects. Raghu Nath's study on India provides evidence that the country's striving to locate a high-technology park in Bangalore required much effort and choice in distinguishing Bangalore from other regional locations. Bangalore's regional culture resembles Route 128 more than Silicon Valley; in addition to that culturally reinforcing environment, the resources for high-technology development are abundant. Not all regions have the same cultural and resource characteristics that promote innovative projects and entrepreneurs. Nath lists several of the success factors used in choosing that site.

Horst Albach and Hermann Tengler's study of regional economic and industrial differences in West Germany shows that closer scrutiny of regional stereotypes can open opportunities that would have been neglected. Although Bonn stands as the prototypical region of industrial success, the older region of Kassel shows the best industrial site conditions as compared with national standards. Moreover, these authors' interview studies with entrepreneurial executives reveal a number of regional cultural traits and resources believed necessary to encourage innovative activities. For example, infrastructural facilities and services; proximity to suppliers, consumers, and service companies; and highly differentiated labor markets all contribute to successful growth.

Proposition 4: Active participation of government leaders with private industrialists and university research experts is often necessary to realize and exploit entrepreneurial projects in regional locations. The basic logic that runs through several of these essays is that national governments need decentralization in order for these bodies to assist and closely work with local and regional businesses to materialize entrepreneurial ideas. A basic message from these essays is that national governments cannot rely on overly centralized policies, procedures, and bureaucracy to develop entrepreneurial projects in different regions. Decentralization is the key ingredient which governments must depend on to (1) help local university and industrialists develop projects; (2) assist in initial funding and financial promotion of such projects; and (3) share control with regional resource experts in growing and initially supporting entrepreneurial projects.

Henri Vartiainen's study of Finland's determination to use local government strategies to promote entrepreneurial activities at the regional level is an example of this logic. The author shows how local government incentives in the following areas are helping to create and promote entrepreneurship: permanent new job creation; promotion of locally based employment incentives; creation of temporary employment; and creation of employment for special target groups. Vartiainen argues that companies, local authorities, and economic organizations must be committed to the same aims to successfully develop these types of local incentives.

Jean-Paul Larçon similarly argues that France's centralizing government policies, which for centuries revolved around Paris, had to change and decentralize in order to accommodate regional industrial resources in Lyon and in the south.

Albach and Tengler's concluding message from their regional study on West Germany is that the federal government must not only decentralize its economic policies to accommodate local industrial development, but it must also work in a proactive way to promote and recruit new companies and businesses into promising regions.

Sam Hai's vivid account of the Belize government's decision to move the capital from the coast inland illustrates how overly centralized government planning can cause entrepreneurial projects to fail. The government in this case did not consider the value differences in the diverse cultural groups. The cultural values on the coast differ drastically from those inland. From the outset the inland cultural setting and infrastructure opposed such a large-scale entrepreneurial undertaking. The losses and negative consequences are described in Hai's account in this book. National governments must plan with local and regional experts to assist entrepreneurial enterprises. This is the lesson learned from Belize as well.

Taken together, these propositions focus on regional cultural characteristics as an important unit of analysis for studying organizational and management behavior, entrepreneurship, and the roles public and private sector professionals can assume in taking advantage of regional cultures for developing innovative projects. These essays have, therefore, stressed the logic of (1) recognizing the important effects of regional cultures on management behavior; (2) identifying entrepreneurial business resources and values in different regions, using a variety of methods; and (3) seeking cooperative efforts from government and business elites in promoting funding and support of entrepreneurial activities in decentralized ways. More research is needed in the search to link regional culture, management, and entrepreneurship. This book is an intended step along that path.

Bibliography

Adams, Juanta. *Belize*. U.S. Department of State Publication 8332, Background Note Series. Washington, D.C.: Government Printing Office, 1984.

Adler, Nancy. "Understanding the Ways of Understanding: Cross-Cultural Management Methodology Reviewed." Unpublished monograph, Faculty of Management, McGill University, Montreal, May 1982.

Aldrich, Howard. *Organizations and Environments*. Englewood Cliffs, N.J.: Prentice-Hall, 1979.

Alexander, J. *Research Partners Half a World Apart*. Washington, D.C.: National Science Foundation, 1986.

Ali Abbas, and Mohamed Al-Shakis. "Managerial Value Systems for Working in Saudi Arabia: An Empirical Investigation." *Group and Organization Studies* 10, no. 2 (1982): 135–51.

Arthur D. Little, Inc. "Technology Development on a State Level Focussed on National Goals." USAID Report, April 1987.

Baerwald, Thomas J. "The Nine Nations of North America." *Geographical Review* 73 (April 1983): 214–16.

Beatty, Sharon E., Lynn R. Kahle, Pamela Homer, and Shekhar Misra. "Alternative Measurement Approaches to Consumer Values: The List and the Rokeach Value Survey." *Psychology and Marketing* 2, no. 3 (1985).

Bisesi, Michael. "Strategies for Successful Leadership in Changing Times." *Sloan Management Review* 25 (Fall 1985): 61–64.

Buono, Anthony, James Bowditch, and John Lewis III. "When Cultures Collide: The Anatomy of a Merger." *Human Relations* 38, no. 5 (1985): 477–500.

Carlson, Eugene. "Southern States Increase Share of Foreign Direct Investment." *The Wall Street Journal*, October 7, 1986, p. 35.

Carney, T. F. *Content Analysis, A Technique for Systematic Influence from Communications*. Canada: University of Manitoba Press, 1972.

Castells, Manuel, ed. *High Technology, Space and Society*. Beverly Hills, Calif.: Sage, 1985.

Chopra, S. N. *India: An Area Study.* New Delhi: India Vikas Publishing House, 1977.

Collins, O., and D. G. Moore. *The Organization Makers.* New York: Appleton-Century, 1970.

Covin, J. G., and D. P. Slevin. "The Influence of Organization Structure on the Utility of an Entrepreneurial Top Management Style." *Journal of Management Studies* 1987.

Crozier, Michael. *The Bureaucratic Phenomenon.* London: Tavistock, 1964.

Davidson, William V. "Historical Cultural Geography of Belize." Unpublished Report Submitted to the United States Agency for International Development, 1983.

Deal, T., and A. Kennedy. *Corporate Cultures.* Reading, Mass.: Addison-Wesley, 1982.

De La Haba, Louis, and Michael E. Long. "Belize, the Awakening Land." *National Geographic* 155, no. 7 (1972): 124–46.

Dobson, Navda. *A History of Belize.* London: Longman Group Limited, 1973.

Dorfman, Nancy S. *Massachusetts' High Technology Boom in Perspective: An Investigation of Its Dimensions, Causes and of the Role of New Firms.* Cambridge, Mass.: Center for Policy Alternatives at the Massachusetts Institute of Technology, 1982.

Dugas, Christine, and Mark Vamos. "Marketing's New Look: Campbell Leads a Revolution in the Way Consumer Products Are Sold." *Business Week,* January 26, 1987, pp. 64–69.

Eisert, Debra C. "Values and Adaptation to Roles: Marriage and Parenting." In *Social Values and Social Change: Adaptation to Life in America,* edited by Lynn R. Kahle. New York: Praeger, 1983.

Elazer, Daniel J. *American Federalism: A View for the States.* New York: Thomas Crowell, 1972.

Farmer, R. N., and B. M. Richman. *International Business: An Operational Theory.* London: Irwin, 1966.

Fayerweather, John. *The Executive Overseas.* Syracuse, N.Y.: Syracuse University Press, 1959.

Feld, Werner J., and Cheron Brylski. "A North American Accord: Feasible or Futile?" *Western Political Quarterly* 36 (June 1983): 286–311.

Gallie, Duncan. *In Search of the New Working Class: Automation and Social Integration within the Capitalist Enterprise.* Cambridge, England: Cambridge University Press, 1978.

Garreau, Joel. *The Nine Nations of North America.* New York: Avon, 1981.

Gregory, Kathleen L. "Native-View Paradigms: Multiple Cultures and Culture Conflicts in Organizations." *Administration Science Quarterly* 28 (1983): 359–76.

Gutman, Jonathan. "A Means-End Chain Model Based on Consumer Categorization Processes." *Journal of Marketing* 46 (Spring 1982): 60–72.

Hai, Sam M., and Dorothy M. Hai. "Economy, Trade and Industrial Development in Belize: An Overview." *Proceedings of the First Congress of International Technology.* Pittsburgh: International Technology Institute, 1976.

———. "Needs Assessment for Industrialization of Belize: Problems and

Opportunities." *Proceedings of the First Congress of International Technology*. Pittsburgh: International Technology Institute, 1976.

Haire, M., E. E. Ghiselli, and L. W. Porter. *Managerial Thinking: An International Study*. New York: Wiley, 1966.

Hambrecht, William R. "Venture Capital and the Growth of Silicon Valley." *California Management Review* 26, no. 2 (1984): 74–82.

Hammond, Norman. "Unearthing the Oldest Known Maya." *National Geographic* 165, no. 1 (1982): 126–39.

Hannon, Michael, and John Freeman. "The Population Ecology of Organizations." *American Journal of Sociology* 82 (1977): 929–64.

Harbison, F., and C. A. Myers. *Management in the Industrial World*. New York: McGraw-Hill, 1959.

Hawkins, Del I., Roger J. Best, and Kenneth A. Coney. *Consumer Behavior: Implications for Marketing Strategy*, rev. ed. Plano, Tex.: Business Publications, 1983.

Henrikson, Alan K. " 'A Small, Cozy Town, Global in Scope': Washington, D.C." *Ekistics* 50 (March/April 1983): 123–45.

Hofstede, Geert. *Culture's Consequences: International Differences in Work-related Values*. Beverly Hills, Calif.: Sage, 1980.

Iglehart, Alfreda P. *Married Women and Work*. Lexington, Mass.: Lexington Books, 1979.

India Today, July 7, 1987.

Jensen, William. Personal communication, 1986.

Joint Economic Committee. *Location of High Technology Firms and Regional Economic Development*. Washington, D.C.: U.S. Government Printing Office, 1982.

Kahle, Lynn R. "Values Segmentation Debate Continues." *Marketing News* 18, no. 4 (1984a): 2.

————. "The Values of Americans: Implications for Consumer Adaptation." In *Personal Values and Consumer Psychology*, edited by Robert E. Pitts, Jr., and Arch G. Woodside. Lexington, Mass.: Lexington Books, 1984b.

————, ed. *Social Values and Social Change: Adaptation to Life in America*. New York: Praeger, 1983.

Kahle, Lynn R., and Kathleen J. Pottick. "Values and Psychological Adaptation: Psychological Symptoms and Mental Health." In *Social Values and Social Change: Adaptation to Life in America*, edited by Lynn R. Kahle. New York: Praeger, 1983.

Kahle, Lynn R., Sharon E. Beatty, and Pamela M. Homer. "Alternative Measurement Approaches to Consumer Values: The List of Values (LOV) and Values and Life Style (VALS)." Working paper, University of Oregon, 1985.

Kelkar, S. M. "Maharashtra: A Paradise for Entrepreneurs." *Indo-American Business Times* 2 (1985): 25.

Khan, H. K. "Rapid Industrial Development Gears Up Gujarat for 21st Century Leap for More Growth." *Indo-American Business Times* 3, no. 2 (1986): 27, 62.

Kish, Leslie, and Irene Hess. *The Survey Research Center's National Sample of Dwellings.* Ann Arbor: University of Michigan, Institute for Social Research, 1965.

Kotler, Philip. *Principles of Marketing.* 2nd ed. Englewood Cliffs, N.J.: Prentice-Hall, 1983.

Levetin, Teresa. "Values." In *Measures of Social Psychological Attitudes,* edited by John P. Robinson and P. R. Shaver. Ann Arbor: University of Michigan, Institute for Social Research, 1973.

Maidique, Modesto, and Robert Hayes. "The Art of High Technology Management." *Sloan Management Review* (Winter 1984): 17–31.

Major, Michel J. "Ectopia: Bellwether Region Offers Look at Future Life Styles." *Marketing News* 17 (September 6, 1983): 6.

Miller, Roger, and Marcel Cote. "Growing the Next Silicon Valley." *Harvard Business Review,* no. 4 (July–August 1985): 114–23.

"Modern India: A Profile." *Indo-American Business Times,* Special Issue, June 1985.

Naisbitt, John. *Megatrends.* New York: Warner Books, 1982.

Nath, Raghu. "Role of Culture in Cross-Cultural and Organizational Research." Paper presented at the National Meeting of the Academy of Management in San Diego, August 11–14, 1985.

————, ed. *Highlights of the Second Partnerships for Development Dialogue Conference.* New York: UNDP Study Program, 1985.

Ogilvy and Mather. "Ogilvy and Mather's Eight Nations of the United States." *Listening Post,* December 1983.

OPIC India Investment Mission, Beltsville, Md., U.S.–India Enterprises, 1983.

Peters, Thomas J., and Robert H. Waterman, Jr. *In Search of Excellence: Lessons from America's Best-Run Companies.* New York: Harper, 1982.

Piner, Kelly E. "Individual Differences Associated with Value Selection." In *Social Values and Social Change: Adaptation to Life in America,* edited by Lynn R. Kahle. New York: Praeger, 1983.

Pitts, Robert E., Jr., and Arch G. Woodside, eds. *Personal Values and Consumer Psychology.* Lexington, Mass.: Lexington Books, 1984.

Pollay, Richard W. "The Identification and Distribution of Values Manifest in Print Advertising, 1900–1980." In *Personal Values and Consumer Psychology,* edited by Robert E. Pitts, Jr., and Arch G. Woodside. Lexington, Mass.: Lexington Books, 1984.

Polsby, Nelson W. "Contemporary Transformations of American Politics: Thoughts on the Research Agendas of Political Scientists." *Politicial Science Quarterly* 96 (Winter 1981–1982): 551–70.

Pottick, Kathleen J. "Values and Adaptation to Roles: Work and Leisure." In *Social Values and Social Change: Adaptation to Life in America,* edited by Lynn R. Kahle. New York: Praeger, 1983.

Powell, Terry E., and Humberto Valencia. "An Examination of Hispanic Subcultural and Regional Value Orientations." In *Personal Values and Consumer Psychology,* edited by Robert E. Pitts, Jr., and Arch G. Woodside. Lexington, Mass.: Lexington Books, 1984.

Prakash, Ved. "Personal Values and Product Expectations." In *Personal Values and Consumer Psychology,* edited by Robert E. Pitts, Jr., and Arch G. Woodside. Lexington, Mass.: Lexington Books, 1984.

"Premier Rajiv Gandhi Makes Impressive Start; Trade, Industry Welcome Leadership of 'Clean Man'; His Policy Statements Generate Great Optimism." *Indo-American Business Times* 2, no. 2 (1985): 8–9.

Rogers, Everett M., and Judith K. Larsen. *Silicon Valley Fever: Growth of High-Technology Culture*. New York: Basic Books, 1984.

Rozen, Miriam. "Wanted: High-Tech Engineers." *Dun's Business Month* (March 1985): 35–36.

Salter, Christopher L. "The Nine Nations of North America." *Journal of Geography* 82 (March-April 1983): 80.

Saxenian, Annalee. "Silicon Valley and Route 128: Regional Prototypes or Historic Exceptions?" In *High Technology, Space and Society*, edited by Manual Castells. Vol. 28, Urban Affairs Annual Review. Beverly Hills, Calif.: Sage, 1985, pp. 81–105.

Schein, Edgar H. "Coming to a New Awareness of Organizational Culture." *Sloan Management Review* (Winter 1984): 3–16.

————. *Organizational Culture and Leadership, A Dynamic View*. San Francisco: Jossey-Bass Publishers, 1985.

Schwartz, H., and S. M. Davis. "Matching Corporate Culture and Business Strategy." *Organizational Dynamics* (Summer 1981): 30–48.

Shelly, Fred M., J. Clark Archer, and Ellen R. White. "Rednecks and Quiche Eaters: A Cartographic Analysis of Recent Third-Party Electoral Campaigns." *Journal of Geography* 83 (January-February 1984): 7–12.

Shimshoni, Daniel. "Regional Development and Science-Based Industry." In *Essay in Regional Economics*, edited by John R. Meyer and John F. Kain. Cambridge, Mass.: Harvard University Press, 1971, pp. 107–36.

Skrentny, Roger. "Spotlight on Silicon Valley's 'Laid Back' Style of Management." *Management Review* (December 1984): 10–14.

Slocum, John. "A Cooperative Study of the Satisfaction of American and Mexican Operations." *Academy of Management Journal* 14 (1971): 89–97.

Smircich, Linda. "Concepts of Culture and Organizational Analysis." *Administrative Science Quarterly* 28 (1983): 339–58.

Sommers, Montrose S., and Jerome B. Kernan. "Why Products Flourish Here, Fizzle There." *Columbia Journal of World Business* 2 (March-April 1968): 89–97.

Stafford. "The Effects of the Environmental Regulations on Industrial Location." Working Paper, University of Cincinnati, 1983.

Stevenson, H. H., and D. E. Gumpert, "The Heart of Entrepreneurship." *Harvard Business Review* 63, no. 2 (1985): 85–94.

Tamir, Lois M. *Men in Their Forties: Transition to Middle Age*. New York: Springer, 1982.

Time, July 7, 1987.

Timmer, Susan Goff, and Lynn R. Kahle. "Values and Adaptation to Society: Ascribed and Attained Demographic Correlates of Values." In *Social Values and Social Change: Adaptation to Life in America*, edited by Lynn R. Kahle. New York: Praeger, 1983a.

————. "Values and Adaptation to Society: Birthright Demographic Correlates of Values." In *Social Values and Social Change: Adaptation to Life in America*, edited by Lynn R. Kahle. New York: Praeger, 1983b.

Toffler, Alvin. *Previews and Premises*. New York: Bantam Books, 1983.

Triandis, H. D., et al. *The Analysis of Subjective Culture*. New York: Wiley-Interscience, 1972.

Vance, Rupert B. "The Regional Concept as a Tool for Social Research." In *Regionalism in America*, edited by Merrill Jensen. Madison: University of Wisconsin Press, 1952, pp. 119–40.

Van Maanen, Dabbs, and Faulkner. *Varieties of Qualitative Research*. Beverly Hills, Calif.: Sage, 1982.

Veroff, Joseph, Elizabeth Douvan, and Richard A. Kulka. *The Inner American*. New York: Basic Books, 1981.

Weiss, J. "The Dynamics of High-Technology Regional Development in Silicon Valley and Massachusetts." Working Paper, Bentley College, 1987.

Wilkins, Alan, and William Ouchi. "Efficient Cultures: Exploring the Relationship Between Culture and Organizational Performance." *Administrative Science Quality* 28 (1983): 468–81.

Williams, William J. "The Nine Nations of North America." *Annals of the American Academy of Political and Social Science* 460 (March 1982): 174–75.

Workshop on Technology Development. Finance and Human Resources in Karnataka, Bangalore, March 5–7, 1987.

Yanlkeovich, Daniel. *New Rules: Searching for Self-Fulfillment in a World Turned Upside Down*. New York: Bantam, 1981.

Young, Gerald, Frederick Steiner, Kenneth Brooks, and Kenneth Struckmeyer. "Determining the Regional Context for Landscape Planning." *Landscape Planning*, December 10, 1983, pp. 269–96.

Zammit, J. Ann. *The Belize Issue*. London: Latin American Bureau, 1978.

————. *The World of Figures*. 2nd Edition. New York: Facts on File, 1980.

————. "Brasilia." *Encyclopedia Britannica*. 15th Edition. Vol. 3 (1981a): 120–22.

————. "British Honduras (Belize)." *Encyclopedia Britannica*. 15th Edition. Vol. 3 (1981b): 307–309.

————. *Belize Economic Survey*. Belmopan: Ministry of Finance and Economic Development, 1982a.

————. *Belize—1980 Population Census Summary Tables, Bulletin 1: Population, Race, Religion, Language, Marital Status*. Belmopan: Ministry of Finance and Economic Development, 1982b.

————. *Belize—1980 Population Census Summary Tables, Bulletin 2: Employment, Industrial and Occupational Groups*. Belmopan: Ministry of Finance and Economic Development, 1982c.

————. *Economic Report on Belize, Report No. 4446–Bel*. Washington, D.C.: World Bank, 1983a.

————. *World Tables*. Baltimore: Johns Hopkins University Pres, 1983b.

Index

About the Contributors

HORST ALBACH is professor of business economics at Bonn University and the Koblenz School of Corporate Management and is general director of the Small Business Research Institute in Bonn. He is a consultant on business taxes and taxation policy as well as in antitrust cases. Dr. Albach has served on various government commissions of the Federal Republic of Germany, including the Board of Economic Advisors. His academic research has centered on questions of business investment, capital budgeting, and the theory of the growth of firms.

MAX DAETWYLER is a faculty member at the International Management Institute in Geneva. He is a respected and widely known consultant in Switzerland.

ANDRÉ DELBECQ is dean of the Leavey Graduate School of Business at Santa Clara University. His research has focused on creative problem-solving techniques, including the nominal group process, and on organizational structures that underlie innovation. In recognition of his scholarship, he was named a fellow of the Academy of Management in 1975. He has published widely and is a recognized scholar in the area of organizational innovation.

SAM M. HAI is professor of finance at the University of Wisconsin at La Crosse. He has taught at the University of Pittsburgh, Arizona State University, the Universidad Autónoma de Guadalajara, the American University of Beirut, the Medical College of Virginia, and St. Bonaventure University where he was chairman of the finance department and director of the Small Business Institute. Dr. Hai is widely published in several areas, including finance.

LYNN R. KAHLE is an associate professor of marketing at the University of Oregon. He has been a postdoctoral fellow at the University of Michigan's Survey Research Center and a faculty member in psychology at the University of Nebraska at Lincoln and the University of North Carolina at Chapel Hill. He has published research in such journals as the *Journal of Personality and Social Psychology, Journal of Consumer Research, Public Opinion Quarterly*, and *Child Development*. Among his research topics are attitudes, values, consumer behavior, and communication. His most recent books are *Attitudes and Social Adaptation: A Person–Situation Interaction Approach* and *Social Values and Social Change: Adaptation to Life in America* (Praeger, 1983).

JEAN-PAUL LARÇON is director of the Hautes Etudes Commerciales, Institute Superieur des Affaires in Jouy-En-Josas, the leading school of business management in France. He is a recognized international consultant and expert on French industry and business education. Among his many books are *Financial Strategy and Policy, Being a Business Leader, Managing Large Municipalities*, and *Structures of Power and Corporate Identity*.

NIEVES MARTINEZ is a research associate at the IESE (Instituto de Estudios Superiores de la Empresa) in Barcelona, Spain. She has published several books and articles in the fields of economics and management.

RAGHU NATH is a member of the faculty at the Graduate School of Business, University of Pittsburgh, and the president of Integrated Systems and INSOHP, which specializes in organizational system and international business development. He is the past chairman of the International and Organization Development (Eastern) Divisions of the American Academy of Management and is presently serving as vice president of the United Nations Association of Pittsburgh. He is also executive director of the World Technology Centre (WTC), which has been established by the Carnegie–Mellon University and the University of Pittsburgh in collaboration with the United Nations Development Programme. Dr. Nath is in the process of creating a network of management experts and entrepreneurs to facilitate the establishment of new joint ventures on a worldwide basis.

PEDRO NUEÑO received his industrial engineering degree at the Escuela Tecnica Superior de Ingenieros Industriales de Barcelona and his

D.B.A. at the Harvard Graduate School of Business. He has taught production management, new business ventures, international business, and industrial policy. He is widely published and is a recognized scholar and consultant in Spain and internationally. He continues to travel, consult, and teach in international business.

HERMANN TENGLER is a research assistant at the Small Business Research Institute in Bonn, where he deals with problems of regional and sectoral changes within the economy.

HENRI J. VARTIAINEN received his Ph.D. from the University of Helsinki. He has worked for the Bank of Finland Institute for Economic Research and the Confederation of Finnish Industries in Helsinki, the Secretariat of the Organization for Economic Cooperation and Development in Paris, and the Conference Board in Brussels. From 1982 to 1986 he was a senior lecturer at the Finnish Institute of Management, and he is currently a permanent lecturer at the University of Helsinki School of Economics and the Helsinki School of Business Administration. His publications in Finland include research on Finnish taxation and the functioning of the Finnish economic system. He is currently organizing post-experience training for economists at the Finnish National Fund for Research and Development.

JOSEPH W. WEISS received his M.A. from Boston College and his Ph.D. from the University of Wisconsin at Madison. Currently he is an associate professor of management at Bentley College in Waltham, Massachusetts. He has also written elsewhere on regional high-technology cultures. Dr. Weiss serves on several editorial boards and is an active consultant in both the private and public sectors.